SOJOURNS OF A PATRIOT

Richard Bender Abell

Fay Adamson Gecik

AUGUSTUS PITT ADAMSON
Wilson's Studio, 41 Bull Street, Savannah, Georgia, 1862.

SOJOURNS OF A PATRIOT

The Field and Prison Papers of An Unreconstructed Confederate.

Edited with Commentary

by

Richard Bender Abell

and

Fay Adamson Gecik

Southern Heritage Press
Murfreesboro, Tennessee

The Journal of Confederate History Series
Volume XIX
John McGlone, Series Editor

Library of Congress Cataloging-in-Publication Data:

Adamson, A _ P. (Augustus Pitt), b, 1844,
    Sojourns of a patriot: the field and prison papers of an
unreconstructed confederate / edited with commentary by Richard
Bender Abell and Fay Adamson Gecik.
    p.   on. -- (The journal of Confederate history series ; vol.
19)
    Includes bibliographical references and index.
    ISBN 1-889332-20-8 (hard)
    1. Adamson, A. P. (Augustus Pitt), b. 1844 -- Correspondence.
2. Adamson, A. P. (Augustus Pitt), b. 1844 -- Diaries. 3. Confederate
States of America, Army. Georgia Infantry Regiment, 30th.
4. Soldiers -- Georgia -- Clayton County -- Correspondence. 5. Soldiers-
-Georgia -- Clayton County -- Diaries. 6. Prisoners of war -- Illinois-
-Rock Island -- Dairies. 7. United States -- History -- Civil War,
1861-1865 -- Personal narratives, Confederate. 8. Georgia -- History -
-Civil War , 1861-1865 -- Personal narratives. 9. Rock Island Arsenal
(Ill.) 10. Clayton County (Ga.) -- Biography. I. Abell, Richard
Bender, 1943-   . II. Gecik, Fay Adamson, 1922-   . III. Title.
IV. Series.
E559.5 30th. A34 1998
973.7'82 -- dc21
(8)
                                                        97-50520
                                                          CIP

Cover art by Henry Kidd of Colonial Heights, Virginia

Printed in the United States of America

DEDICATIONS

It is with great pleasure that I dedicate this book to my former teacher, my mentor and friend, the late Edith Hanes Smith.

Fay Adamson Gecik

Past is prologue. For all my children, David Joseph, Christian Aven, and Rachel Mercedes, I remind them of their ancestors' sacrifices for their faith, native soil, hearth, family, honor, and principle. *Pro Deo et Patria.*

Richard Bender Abell

ACKNOWLEDGEMENTS

Firstly, I wish to acknowledge my cousin, Annie Adamson James, who was a grand-daughter of Augustus Pitt Adamson. It was from her that the letters came to me. For years the box containing her grandfather's letters had been stored in her attic. She allowed me to copy them, hoping that someday I would have them published for posterity. Secondly, a dear friend, Edith Hanes Smith - to whom I have dedicated this volume - had always encouraged me in my genealogical endeavors. She loaned me the A.P. Adamson Diary from her large collection of historical papers which are now in the Clayton County Historical Museum. I believe that both Annie Adamson James and Edith Hanes Smith would be pleased to see the letters and the diary finally combined and printed. I also wish to gratefully thank the Clayton County Historical Society for their permission to print those documents in their possession. After more than one hundred and thirty years since these letters were written home, some of the words have become illegible, the paper disintegrating, and some of the letters or portions thereof lost.

Fay Adamson Gecik

As in all such endeavors, this book was not simply constructed over-night. It is indeed the product of many whom in the interest of the common weal have contributed their time and energy. For his inestimable technical expertise, I wish to thank J. Bradley Horn, Esq. For his tireless research during his evening and week-end hours away from his new family, I wish to express a heartfelt gratitude to Geoffrey Guy Hemphill, Esq. His continual superb unfollowed suggestions have been of incalculable value in the composition of the final product. Also, the always dutiful librarians at the Daughters of the American Revolution Library, the National Archives, and The Library of Congress must be thanked for all their assistance. Likewise, the tendered assistance of historian Margie Riddle Bearss is recognized. Lastly, but definitely not least, I gratefully acknowledge my "A.P. Adamson widow," my wife, Lucía. She was encumbered by ticks when we hiked the battlefield of Chickamauga and will never permit me to forget her experience! *Fortiter pro patria.*

Richard Bender Abell

CONTENTS

PREFACE

This small volume is composed of some eighty letters and the prison diary of Augustus Pitt Adamson of Clayton County, Georgia. Both editors are kin descended from A.P.'s grandfather, Greenberry Adamson. For the genealogical aficionado - we are third cousins twice removed.

The reader will find that we have organized this work into three separable Parts: Part I, A Biographical Sketch of Augustus Pitt Adamson; Part II, The Letters of Augustus Pitt Adamson, further sub-divided into ten chapters; and, Part III, The Letters and Diary from his captivity at Rock Island POW Camp in Illinois. The reader will also note that three distinct typefaces have been utilized to facilitate comprehension and topical division. Italics have been used for A.P.'s actual letters and diary so that the reader will be able to identify his specific writings from the authors' prose. Roman (the actual type is Garamond) has been chosen for the editors' commentaries. And lastly, a list of "Suggested Reading" books are recommended to the enthused reader who requires more knowledge to enhance the descriptive passages we have provided.

A.P.'s grammar and spelling have been preserved as he wrote his letters, with the sole *caveat* that some misspelled personal and place names have been corrected so as not to confuse the reader. The editors had difficulty in deciphering a very few words (or they were smudged, the paper torn, etc.) and these words or portions of words are indicated by ---.

The paragraphs following many letters are in explication to what A.P. writes. Although the editors have attempted to identify all the individuals in A.P.'s writings, we regret that there were several that we could not identify. The editors herein do not present this material as the *ne plus ultra* of commentary. The purpose is not to present a footnoted learned treatise, but to convey a sense of awareness of events, individuals, conditions, or matériel to illume the topic for the reader's edification. Some of this is genealogical, which may render some readers uninterested in these explanations. We anticipate this, and can only suggest that those individuals skip over to sections that enliven more interest. Nonetheless, it is the fervent hope of the editors that all readers with an interest in The War Between the States will find some items of new knowledge for themselves.

It cannot be emphazied strongly enough that the book lists provided are not all inclusive. The editors have only listed those books with which they are familiar. No doubt many apropos works are not listed. The "Suggested Reading" sections are for those whom wish to learn more on a given topic. Further, these books do not necessarily agree one with the other in their interpretations of events or the men active in those events. The editors categorically neither concur nor demur in the these proffered perspectives. This is left to the reader's decision making process!

The colonial period set the stage for our America. The First War of Independence declared our successful revolution and separation from the homeland. Nevertheless, in many ways, the America of the Twentieth Century has been determined by the mid-Nineteenth Century cataclysm known as The War Between the States - also known as the Civil War. This war has forged both the plethora of problems and the enigmas to their solutions that still challenge us today as we peer into the Twenty-first Century. Of late, we have been subjected too much to the facile nostrums of the politically correct. Objectivity and alternatives of perspective have been anesthetized by compound errors in mis-motivated historical interpretations. In our own way, the editors trust that the reader will consider other relevant views. You may find a few in these pages.

The maelstrom of war can be viewed in microcosm through A.P. as he marches off in 1861 as an idealistic seventeen year old, and commences his sojourns in Georgia, Florida, the Carolinas, Mississippi, and finally into captivity in Illinois. He enters stage as a boy; he exits as a man. There is a timeless value in his experiences, and especially in his faith and patriotism. This work is definitely not an *apologia*. Like all of us, A.P. was not perfect - but we are proud of him. We hope that we have managed to convey some of his life travail to the reader.

PART I

A Biographical Sketch

of

Augustus Pitt Adamson

(1844-1922)

It is indeed a desirable thing
to be well descended,
but the glory belongs
to our ancestors.

Plutarch.

Sojourns of a Patriot

Headstone of Augustus Pitt Adamson, Rock Baptist Church Cemetery, Rex, Georgia. Note the flags!

Sojourns of a Patriot

A. P. Adamson (hereinafter A.P.) was born in Henry (now Clayton) County, Georgia, on 20 March 1844. His father was Nathaniel Coates Adamson, a prominent citizen of his county. His mother was Nancy Bibb McDaniel, an aunt of Gov. Henry D. McDaniel of Georgia.

On his paternal line his grandfather was Greenberry Adamson (1770-1831), born in Frederick County, Maryland, as the ninth child of Basil Adamson (1728-1785) and his wife Nancy Speirs. Basil and his eldest son, John, both served in the 1st Company, Middle Battalion, Montgomery County Militia during the first War of Independence. Basil was the son of John Baldwin Adamson (1705-1744) and his wife Lucy both of whom lived at "Adamson's Choice," sited on Captain John's Creek near Rockville, Montgomery County. This family's propositus arrived in Maryland in 1662 from Scotland.

Greenberry emigrated from Maryland with three of his sisters to Washington, Wilkes County, Georgia, in 1789. While residing in Wilkes County, he married Sarah Coates (1774-1849), daughter of Nathaniel Coates, Sr. (1747-1816) and his first wife Martha Lamar. Nathaniel Coates (for whom A.P.'s father was named) served in the War of Independence under Col. Elijiah Clark of Georgia. Thereafter he was thrice elected as High Sheriff of Wilkes County. Genealogists have concluded that Martha Lamar was the daughter of John Lamar (1713-1785) and his wife Rachel. This reknown huguenot family's progenitors also originated in Maryland, the first of the line arriving about 1659. Through them A.P. was kin to numerous participants in the American Revolution, the second President of the Republic of Texas, a U.S. Senator and Secretary of the Interior from Mississippi who became an Associate Justice of the Supreme Court, and a "chance" of Confederate officers. Greenberry moved to Morgan County in 1812 and finally to Henry County in 1822. The local histories speak of Greenberry as one of the first pioneers in Henry County. Both Greenberry and his first son, John Coates Adamson, served in the War of 1812 in Capt. Matthew Phillip's Company, 4th Regiment Georgia Detached Militia under Col. David S. Booth.

The seventh child born to Greenberry and Sarah was Nathaniel Coates Adamson who married Nancy Bibb McDaniel in 1842. Her family was related distantly to George Washington. Likewise her family was .proud to have a United States Senator and the first two Governors of the State of Alabama as kin, not to mention Gov. Henry D. McDaniel of Georgia. Their first child was Augustus Pitt Adamson.

A. P. Adamson was one of six children. His siblings were: Martha Missouri Adamson (1845-1855); Amanda Augusta Adamson (born 1846); William Felix Adamson (born 1849); Sarah Sophronia Adamson (born 1851); and, Philip Adamson, who died as an infant. Most of the correspondence in this volume is addressed to these siblings or their father, N.C. Adamson.

A. P. Adamson was brought up on a farm, with only the limited education afforded in rural mid-nineteenth century Georgia, confined to the public schools of his generation and what he learned at home. On 25 September 1861, at the age of seventeen, he enlisted in "The Clayton Invincibles." This volunteer unit was organized under Capt. Chaney A. Dollar that same month soon emerging as Company I of the 25th Georgia Volunteer Infantry Regiment. In 1862, as part of the general re-organization of the Confederate army, it became Company E of the 30th Georgia Volunteer Infantry Regiment.

Having enlisted as a private in 1861, A. P. Adamson was elected second corporal in May 1862. In August of 1863 he was elected first corporal. He served in this rank until his capture by Union troops in May 1864.

A.P. was severely wounded in the hip at the Battle of Chickamauga on 19 September 1863 which disabled him from active service for several months. While recuperating at home in Clayton County he was offered an assignment in the Medical Department under Dr. E. J. Roach of Atlanta, which assignment he declined, preferring to return to his command, which he did before fully recovering from his wound and ruefully prior to the restoration of his health.

The microfilm records at the National Archives in Washington, D.C. and other extant records reveal that A.P. was captured near Calhoun, Georgia, on 17 May 1864 by the forces under General Thomas, commanding the Department of the Cumberland. He was then transferred to the Federal Prison Camp at Louisville, Kentucky, on 24 May 1864 and re-transferred on 25 May 1864 to Rock Island Prisoner of War Camp, Illinois. He was received at Rock Island on 27 May remaining there until 25 February 1865 when he was transferred for exchange to Point Lookout POW Camp in Maryland. He was received at Boulware & Cox's Wharves, James River, Virginia, on 5 March by Lt. Col. John E. Mulford, United States Agent for Exchange of Prisoners and repatriated to his country. A.P. was part of a consignment of 602 paroled Confederate prisoners to include 97 officers. He was then admitted to Jackson

Hospital in Richmond, Virginia, on account of his debility on 7 March and given a 30 day medical furlough the next day. The war in the East was concluded by the time his furlough expired. He arrived home in Clayton County on 17 March 1865, shortly before the surrender of General Lee's Army at Appomattox on 9 April 1865. His father's property was wantonly destroyed by Sherman's army and the outlook was, indeed, foreboding, but he at once went to work on the farm. For a part of the first few years after the war he also taught school.

In November of 1866 Augustus Pitt Adamson married Martilla Ellen Cook of Clayton County, who died in 1878, leaving him with eight small children. His second wife was Martha J. Burks of Clayton County, by whom he had three children.

Three of his sons were engaged in journalism, one of whom, Robert E. Lee Adamson, was for several years engaged on *The Atlanta Constitution* and later made a name for himself in the New York newspapers and a fortune in the banking business. Another son, James Tilden Adamson, served as a lieutenant in the 3rd Georgia Regiment in The War With Spain and subsequently was City Editor of the *Brooklyn Eagle* in New York.

His son Walter Pitt Adamson also enlisted in The War With Spain and later labored as a reporter on a New York newspaper. Another son, Augustus Emory Adamson, was a prominent businessman of Jacksonville, Florida. His son, Lawrence Pendleton Adamson, was a writer and a poet. His other two sons were Linton Mallory Adamson and Christopher Columbus Adamson, who were both engaged in farming in Clayton County.

A. P. Adamson's daughters were Ada Viola Adamson Morris, Annie Ellen Adamson Cowan, Aurelia Louise Adamson Hale, and Alice Pauline Adamson Barr.

A. P. Adamson always took an active part in politics and in the public affairs of his state and county. For more than thirty years he served as a member of the Democratic Executive Committee of Clayton County. He was several times a Delegate to the convention of his party.

In 1898 he was nominated and elected to represent Clayton County in the Georgia State Legislature, serving two years and declining further re-election. He served as Justice of the Peace for his district for many years, beginning in March 1871. He served as County Registrar and also as a Jury Commissioner.

He was appointed by Governor Terrell as Trustee from Clayton County of the Fifth Congressional Agricultural School.

He was a frequent contributor to *The Atlanta Constitution* and to his county paper. He wrote a HISTORY OF CLAYTON COUNTY which was published in weekly installments in *The Jonesboro Enterprise*. He also wrote poetry thoughout his life – all to date unpublished.

A. P. Adamson took an active interest in organizing "The Reunion of the Thirtieth Georgia Regiment." He was Secretary of that organization and never missed a meeting. He was designated by his comrades to write the history of the regiment, BRIEF HISTORY OF THE THIRTIETH GEORGIA REGIMENT, published in 1912. In 1918 A. P. Adamson published PROSPECTUS GENEALOGY OF THE ADAMSON FAMILY.

He was a member of the Baptist Church from 1861 until his death in 1922. He served his church as Deacon for over thirty years. He was a Freemason and also associated with The Odd Fellows. Of interest, his father and two uncles (Augustus Young Adamson and John Coates Adamson) were also Masons, being affiliated with F& AM Jonesboro Lodge No. 87 prior to the War Between the States. Of additional interest, co-editor Mrs. Fay Adamson Gecik is descended from Greenberry Adamson through his son Augustus Young Adamson; co-editor Hon. Richard Bender Abell is descended from Greenberry through his daughter Martha Lamar Adamson Ward.

A. P. Adamson lived on his farm in Clayton County, near Rex, Georgia, on the same lot of land where he had always lived, and which land his father had purchased three-quarters of a century before his history of the Thirtieth Georgia Regiment was published in 1912. In this history he stated that he was contented and strongly attached to farm life. On 12 January 1922, Augustus Pitt Adamson died at the age of seventy-eight. He was buried at the Rock Baptist Church Cemetery, Rex, Georgia. In bas-relief upon his headstone are the flags of the two great republics - the Confederate States of America and the United States of America.

It is evident that Augustus Pitt Adamson never compromised his principles. He was proud of the blood of his ancestors that coursed in his veins. He was unquestionably patriotic and God-fearing. Moreover, Augustus Pitt Adamson was forever unreconstructed!

SUGGESTED READING

Adamson, A.P., BRIEF HISTORY OF THE 30TH GEORGIA REGIMENT, Mills Printing Company, Griffin, Georgia (1912); *reprinted*, Americana Historical Books, Fayeteville, Georgia (1993).

Adamson, A.P., PROSPECTUS GENEALOGY OF THE ADAMSON FAMILY, privately printed (1918); *reprinted*, Adamson's, Inc., Ellenwood, Georgia.

REFERENCE READING

Henderson, Lillian, ROSTER OF THE CONFEDERATE SOLDIERS OF GEORGIA 1861-1865, Volume III, Georgia Division, United Daughters of the Confederacy, Longino & Porter, Inc., Hapeville, Georgia (1994).

Daniel, Larry J., SOLDIERING IN THE ARMY OF TENNESSEE: A PORTRAIT OF LIFE IN A CONFEDERATE ARMY, The University of North Carolina Press, Chapel Hill (1991).

Sifakis, Stewart, COMPENDIUM OF THE CONFEDERATE ARMIES: SOUTH CAROLINA AND GEORGIA, Facts on File, New York (1995).

Smedlund, William S., CAMP FIRES OF GEORGIA'S TROOPS, 1861-1865, Kennesaw Mountain Press, Lithonia, Georgia (1994).

HISTORICAL FICTION READING

Davis, Maggie, THE FAR SIDE OF HOME (1963), *reprinted*, Americana Historical Books, Fayetteville, Georgia (1992).

Sojourns of a Patriot

PART II

THE LETTERS

OF

AUGUSTUS PITT ADAMSON

Sojourns of a Patriot

CHAPTER ONE

"Mustering In."

A PRAYER FOR OUR ENEMIES

O GOD, we beseech Thee, forgive and pardon our enemies, and give us that measure of Thy grace, that for their hatred we may love them; for their cursing we may bless them; for their injury we may do them good; and for their persecution we may pray for them. They have laid a net for our steps, and they have digged a pit before us; Lord, we desire not that they themselves should fall into the midst of these, but we beseech Thee keep us out of them, and deliver, establish, bless and prosper us for Thy mercy's sake in Jesus Christ our Saviour, to whom with Thee and the Holy Spirit, we desire to consecrate ourselves and our country, now and forever, imploring Thee to be our GOD, and to make us Thy people. Amen.

PRAYERS Suitable For The Times In Which We Live, Charleston, 1861. THE CONFEDERATE SOLDIER'S PRAYER BOOK.

Sojourns of a Patriot

LETTER NUMBER ONE

Campbell County, Georgia
October 20th, 1861

Dear Sister,

I avail myself of this opportunity of writing you a few lines to let you know that I am well at present. Tomorrow we will be mustered into service without a doubt. I do not expect to come home anymore. We are to be mustered in under the Confederate Government and may have to go to Kentucky or Missouri.

I had to stand guard at the commissary yesterday from twelve to one o'clock. There is very few of our company here at present. We have meeting here every night.

If Pa comes out here again I want him to bring my daguerreotype and I will send another back that I have got, without fail. Bill is sick at present.

No more. Yours,

/s/ A. P. ADAMSON

Campbell County was merged into Fulton County in 1932.

From A. P. Adamson's later work on his 30th Georgia written in later years:

The election of Abraham Lincoln to the Presidency in 1860 caused the most intensive excitement through the South, which resulted, in a few months, in the secession of several of the Southern States. In the meantime, the whole people were aroused and great enthusiasm prevailed everywhere.

After the fall of Fort Sumter in April 1861 and the call of President Lincoln for 75,000 troops, the excitement increased and many men who had opposed secession at once tendered their services to the Confederate Government, which had only been organized a few weeks before.

The volunteers were not confined to any particular class, but, on the other hand, represented every class. They came from the halls of legislation, from schools and colleges, from business houses of all kinds, and from the farms in every rural district. They embraced men and boys from sixty to fourteen or fifteen years of age. All seemed anxious to enlist early and were impatient to be hurried to the scene of military operations.

The first company to organize in Clayton County, which was A. P. Adamson's native county, was the Benjamin Infantry, named in honor of Hon. Judah P. Benjamin who served in President Davis' first cabinet as Attorney General, and thereafter as Secretary of War and ultimately as Secretary of State. This company was commanded by Capt. G. G. Crawford and formed a part of the 10th Georgia Infantry leaving Jonesboro for Virginia in May 1861.

Additionally, on that same day in May of 1861 a roll was started for the formation of another company. A. P. Adamson entered his name as the fourth volunteer on this roll and in a short while a sufficient number was obtained to organize the company. However, because of the delay in accepting troops, it was several months before A.P.'s company was mustered into service, the date of entry being 25 September 1861.

This company was commanded by Capt. C. A. Dollar and known as "The Clayton Invincibles." It left Jonesboro for Camp Bailey, near Fairburn, on 3 October 1861. It was at Camp Bailey that the 30th (at that time still the 25th) organized and trained. "A large crowd of people assembled to see the company leave. A beautiful silk banner made by the ladies was presented by Miss Ida Callaway and great enthusiasm prevailed among the boys, who appeared anxious to leave, and some feared the war would close before they had an opportunity of seeing a Yankee."

Each company had a local designation. Under the 1861 organization, Co. A was known as the "Butts' Invincibles," Co. B. as the "Bailey Volunteers," Co. C as the "Hunter Guards," Co. D as the "Hugeney Rifles," Co. E as the "Bartow Invincibles," Co. F as the "Campbell Sharpshooters," Co. G as the "Campbell

Greys," Co. H as the "Fayette Volunteers," Co. I as the "Clayton Invincibles," and Co. K as the "Chattahoochee Volunteers." Typically, there was no Co. J.

Upon reaching the camp-of-instruction, the company was placed in the regiment of Col. David J. Bailey, who had obtained leave from Governor Brown to organize a regiment of infantry for the Confederate services. This company was designated as Co. I, 25th Georgia Infantry Regiment, later redesignated Co. E, 30th Georgia Infantry Regiment, the numbers being rearranged due to the Confederate Army re-organization of April 1862.

In the early days of October 1861 ten companies of volunteers went into camp at Camp Bailey. The date of enlistment was from September 25th and for a period of twelve months.

LETTER NUMBER TWO

Camp Bailey, Campbell County, Georgia
Dec. 5th, 1861

Dear Sister,

I take this opportunity of dropping you a few lines which leaves me as well as could be expected. I went to Atlanta Sunday and got here Monday morning. There is about half of our company here. Col. Bailey and Major Tharpe came last night. We are going to leave here Sunday morning. Eight of our company are going home after the rest of our men.

Tell Ma that I want her to have something cooked and in Jonesboro Sunday at eight o'clock. I want some meat, baked, and some potato custards and some pies, but must start Saturday evening, for we will pass through soon. You cannot get there in time to start Sunday. I should like to have a light bed quilt, for we will not draw blankets.

Charlie Chriswell will take this letter and one for Mr. Sanders, which you must send to them immediately. I will write when I get to the place of our destination.

Yours in haste .....

/s/ A. P. ADAMSON

LETTER NUMBER THREE

December 16th, 1861
Miss Augusta Adamson

Dear Sister,

I take this opportunity of writing you a few lines although you neglected to answer my other letter. I said in my last that I was going to Macon, which I have done, and am well pleased with my visit. About one mile from the city, as you pass up the Central Road, presents the most magnificent scene I have ever witnessed. As far as the eye can reach nothing can be seen but immense numbers of tall buildings.

I went to Alfred Adamson's and he took us all through the town, including the graveyard, which I wish you could see. There is some of the prettiest monuments I have ever seen. In one place, in a small brick house, is a man buried on top of the ground. There is a small glass in the door which you can look through and plainly see the coffin as it sits upon two marble stones.

Macon is a larger place than Atlanta and contains more pretty buildings. The Female College and Asylum for the Blind are two splendid buildings. The ladies of Macon have more respect for a soldier than those of Atlanta. They do not pass proudly by one because they do not know them, but, on the other hand, treat them with a feeling of respect.

I went down in Twiggs [County] yesterday and was well pleased with the country. There is some talk of our receiving pay next week but I don't know how it will be. You must write to me soon. I must close as we have to go to drilling.

"Mustering In."

Yours, etc.....

/s/ A. P. ADAMSON

> *It is needless for me to say that I saw Miss Margaret Bentner when I went to Macon, for you know I did. ... APA*

Private A. P. Adamson
25th Regt.
Ga. Vol.

We have no further information on this probable romantic interest of A.P.!

The pay for a private at the beginning of the War for both sides was $11.00 per month. A corporal's pay was $13.00 per month - a salary that A.P. was to eventually achieve. A Confederate private's pay increased to $18.00 per month in 1864, but by that time severe inflation had so decimated the economy that a pair of shoes cost $125.00. Often it took up to a year for the paymaster to show up at a given unit.

A.P. writes of his drilling. The standard manual used by both belligerents was William J. Hardee's RIFLE AND INFANTRY TACTICS. This pocket sized volume detailed the proper way to drill troops, not battlefield tactics as implied in the title. Long hours, day after day, were utilized to this exercise to teach the men discipline and unit cohesion. They had much to learn about military ways before they could become a formidable battlefield force. The men not surprisingly detested the drill instruction. Withal, the ability to march as a unit (in company or by regiment), maneuver with celerity and efficiency and without the loss of organization, and quickly follow orders while in this mode, could mean the difference between success or failure in battle.

LETTER NUMBER FOUR

Camp Griswoldville, Jones County, Ga.
December 16th, 1861

Dear Father,

I take this occasion of replying to yours of the 13th inst., which I received on yesterday, and was glad to hear from your all. I have a very bad cold at present, which is very common in camps now.

We had a battalion drill for the first time on Saturday since we have been here. Col. Bailey arrived here Saturday night and Col. Tidwell has gone home today.

I got a box of provisions that you put in the train at Jonesboro. I did not know you was there till you give me the money. I understand it has not been very cold here. We sleep very well. I need nothing at present but will want a pair of shoes before very long and they cannot be got here.

The railroad track was torn up above Griffin the day we came down, by some Lincolnite, and thronged the train off the track that came down at 3 o'clock, so I understand.

I would be glad if you would come down next Monday if you can. I will close.

Yours, etc. ...

/s/ A. P. A.

This is the first mention of shoes. Hard marching soldiers could wear out several pairs of shoes a year. The Confederate quartermasters could never keep up with the demand. One constantly reads of whole units going barefoot into battle, committing long marches, and subsisting without shoes for periods of time that cause the epic of Valley Forge to pale in comparison to the Confederate soldiers deprivement. The manufacturing facility to make shoes in Atlanta began in March 1863. Leather was always at a premium due to war shortage. Often the men would send for shoes from home. They preferred brogues that seemed to wear well; shoes that had broad bottoms and big, flat heals. It was felt that boots were too heavy, twisted the ankles, and were difficult to rapidly take off and on - especially when wet. Frequently they would scour battlefields for the no longer used shoes of the dead. "All a Yankee is worth is his shoes," was a common remark of the time.

LETTER NUMBER FIVE

Griswoldville, Jones Co., Ga.
January 16th, 1862
Miss A.A. Adamson

Dear Sister,

 I take this occasion of writing you a few lines which leaves me well and enjoying myself finely I think I am getting use to this climate as all the boys are.
 There is some poor idiots here as well as at home who do not have better sense than to be constantly circulating the report that our regiment will soon be disbanded when there is no probability of it. The man who would endeaver to decoy men to desert his countrys cause is is no friend to his country. The people of Clayton Co need not believe such reports for there is not a particle of truth in them.
 I think we will be paid in a few days and that will settle the matter. Some desire that this regiment should be disbanded but it is a poor fool that would desert without even being paid for his services. Jesse Sanders talks of coming home in a few days as soon as [Capt.] Dollar gets back on duty. Will is very sick. His father is here now but will leave in a day or so. We will certainly leave here for some place in the course of two weeks probably seeing Atlanta and --neyne-ville. Bill has been down sick but is getting well again. One of Capt. Barnett's men died the other night and was sent home.
 We have no officer here but Lieut. Stewart. We drill every day with guns which is not as bad as walking so much. Tell Pa he will

have to send me a pair of shoes before long. Without fail the boys will be back tomorrow night I presume from here. Write soon. Yours.

/s/ A.P. ADAMSON

LETTER NUMBER SIX

Griswoldville, Georgia
January 19th, 1862

Dear Sister,

I tonight take the pleasure of writing you a few lines. I received your letter last night and was truly glad to hear from you. I would not have written so soon but to inform you that we expect to leave here next Wednesday for Savannah.

Col. Tidwell made an able and sensible speech here yesterday in reference to the condition of our regiment. He assured us we would shortly receive our pay and commented to a considerable length about the reports that have been circulated about our regiment and said many had busied themselves about what did not concern them and said he hoped we did not enter the service expressly for money. Give it as his opinion that we have been regularly mustered into service, but there is some that won't believe nothing. The man that would desert now in the very time of our glory is no friend to his country.

This evening at dress parade Col. Tidwell informed us that we would leave next Wednesday without fail. Jesse Sanders is gone home today and it is doubtful whether he will get back before we leave or not.

I will write to you after we get to Savannah. I am well at present except I believe that I am taking the mumps, though not certain of it. I hope to have the chance of coming home after we draw pay, if possible. I have nothing else at present. I remain your brother,

/s/ A. P. ADAMSON

The regiment remained at Camp Bailey (named for the regiment's colonel), near Fairburn, Fulton County (then Campbell County), until 16 December when it was sent to Griswoldville, Jones County, Georgia. Camp Griswold was located west of the hamlet of Griswoldville. The regiment stayed there until 22 January 1862 when it was ordered to Camp Bartow, Pembrook Plantation, Chatham County, Georgia. They arrived at Camp Bartow on 23 January 1862, going into camp some five and one-half miles below the city of Savannah on the Skidaway Road on the edge of a lake.

The reader must keep in mind A.P.'s regimental and company grade officers all of whom he continually mentions: Col. David J. Bailey was his first regimental commander until his resignation; Col. Thomas W. Mangham was his second regimental commander until made *hors de combat* at the Battle of Chickamauga; Col. James Stoddard Boynton was the third and final regimental commander; Lt. Col. M.M. Tidwell served as second in command; Maj. Cicero A. Tharp was his regimental major until 1862 when he declined re-election; Capt. Chaney A. Dollar, company commander of Co. E (previously Co. I of the Twenty-fifth) until January, 1864, when he was elected Ordinary of Clayton County; and, Lt. Joseph H. Huie who became captain of Co. E in January, 1864. Other men will be identified throughout.

Throughout his correspondence, A.P. alludes to various family members and friends. Charles Chriswell (Letter No. 2) and Jesse Sanders (Letter No. 5 *et seq.*) were friends: Chriswell was discharged from service on 21 August 1862 since he was "over age," and Sanders died in Clayton County in July 1864 after having been hospitalized at Breckinridge's Division Hospital at Marion, Mississippi. Both men served in Company E with A.P. In Letter No. 1 he mentions Bill whom presumably is the William R. Adamson mentioned below. In Letter No. 3 he talks of Alfred Adamson: Alfred was his first cousin who lived in Macon, and brother to both the James and Samuel listed below. A.P. had four known first cousins in his company on his paternal line, *viz.*:

James Rufus Adamson (1834-1865). He enlisted 25 September 1861 as a private and was captured at the Battle of Nashville, Tennessee, on 16 December 1864. He became a prisoner-of-war incarcerated at Camp Chase, Ohio, wherein he died 5 March 1865 of chronic diarrhea. He was interred there in grave No. 1556.

- Samuel T. Adamson. He enlisted as a private on 25 September 1861 and was wounded and disabled at the Battle of Atlanta on 22 July 1864. Ignoring his wounds, he persisted in his patriotic service. He was then captured-in-action at the Battle of Jonesboro on 1 September 1864. He was incarcerated as a prisoner-of-war at Camp Douglas, Illinois, being released 13 June 1865.
- William J. Adamson (1832-1863). He enlisted as a private on 1 May 1862 and died in hospital (presumably from disease) at Newton, Mississippi, on 8 July 1863. He had been married by his uncle, the father of A.P, Nathaniel Coates Adamson.
- William R. Adamson. He enlisted as a private on 25 September 1861 and subsequently was captured-in-action at the Battle of Nashville on 16 December 1864, became a prisoner-of-war interned at Camp Chase, Ohio, and was released on 12 June 1865.

A.P. had no less than 35 male first cousins on his paternal line that served in the Confederate armed forces (of some 37 of eligible military service age), almost all of whom served from Georgia and Alabama. Of these men, 12 died in service through both combat and pestilence to include two in Union POW camps, and, we know of at least an additional 9 wounded-in-action. This is a 60% casualty rate! Ruefully, these grim statistics were not untypical for the Southland during and following the War. Virtually every southern family endured inextricable suffering. One can only speculate what must have been a devastating emotional and psychological impact on family and community by such loss or disability of its manhood.

We begin to see a consistent patriotic leitmotif in A.P.'s correspondence that continues thereafter. His patriotism, Christian religious and moral principles, and family values successively exert themselves. If his later writings are any indication, these notable traits never leave him nor does he ever commit other than to be true to them.

Continually we see evinced in A.P.'s writings the quintessential Southern character traits. His letters are replete with the indicia of abiding concern for States' Rights, the principles of Jeffersonian republicanism, and a deeply felt consciousness of one's liberties, duty and honor. In the antebellum South, the fidelity to provincialism, agrarianism, and stentorian individualism, was juxtaposed, perhaps paradoxically, with a planter social structure. Nonetheless,

24

this upwardly mobile rural social system was typified by intimate personal social relationships, independence of spirit, the self-reliance of the frontier, an extended but tight-knit family structure encompassing bonds with kin of differing social levels, chivalrous romanticism, and an unremittingly personal relationship with God and the paramount importance of salvation.

At the beginning of this great civil war, A.P., like his contemporaries, is caught up in the heady euphoria of the moment. The decision to secede and form a new nation was breakneck, total and accompanied by unrestrained emotion. They were embarking on the second American Revolution - The War for Southern Independence. They were defending their state, their homes and hearth, their families, and their sacred honor. The issue from their perspective was not slavery but arrogant Washington-focused Northern coercion. In essence their desideration was not to sunder apart the Union but to protect the Constitution from a tyranny being imposed by a national government that presumptively existed only to serve the states. They, like their forefathers of 1776, were in a revolution against autocracy to preserve their inalienable rights as Americans - the paradox of a conservative revolution. They had not consciously chosen war until they were forced to choose between what they perceived as their natural right and constitutionally permissive act of secession from an increasingly incompatible union, or, submission, cowardice and disloyalty to their kindred states of the South. Their blood could not permit the latter; their heritage of constitutional government required the former. They did not merely choose secession and its presumptive corollary of armed conflict, they embraced it with consuming ardor.

Plus ça change, plus c'est le même chose!
(The more things change, the more they remain the same.)

SUGGESTED READING

Bradford, M.E., REMEMBERING WHO WE ARE, OBSERVATIONS OF A SOUTHERN CONSERVATIVE, University of Georgia Press, Athens (1985).

Cash, N.J., THE MIND OF THE SOUTH, Alfred A. Knopf, New York (1941).

Davis, William C., A GOVERNMENT OF OUR OWN: THE MAKING OF THE CONFEDERACY, The Free Press, New York (1994).

Davis, William C., JEFFERSON DAVIS, THE MAN AND HIS HOUR, Louisiana State University Press, Baton Rouge (1991).

DeRosa, Marshall L., THE CONFEDERATE CONSTITUTION OF 1861, University of Missouri Press, Columbia, Missouri (1991).

Dowdey, Clifford, THE HISTORY OF THE CONFEDERACY 1832-1865, Barnes & Noble, Inc., New York (1992).

Eaton, Clement, JEFFERSON DAVIS, The Free Press, Macmillan Publishing Co., Inc., New York (1977).

Foote, Shelby, THE CIVIL WAR: A NARRATIVE, Three Volumes, Vintage Books, Random House, New York (1986).

Johnson, Ludwell H., NORTH AGAINST SOUTH: THE AMERICAN ILLIAD 1848-1877, The Foundation for American Education, Columbia, S.C. (1993).

Thomas, Emory M., THE CONFEDERACY AS A REVOLUTIONARY EXPERIENCE, University of South Carolina Press, Columbia, S.C. (1992).

Weaver, Richard M., THE SOUTHERN TRADITION AT BAY, Arlington House, New Rochelle, N.Y. (1968).

CHAPTER TWO

"Pulaski!"

...our sole object [was] the establishment of our independence and the attainment of an honorable peace.

All that the South has ever desired was that the union, as established by our forefathers, should be preserved, and that the government as originally organized should be administered in purity and truth.

Robert Edward Lee,
General, C.S.A.

LETTER NUMBER SEVEN

Chatham County, Geo.
January 26th, 1862

Dear Father, Mother, Brother and Sisters,

I take the present opportunity of writing you a few lines from our new home. We left Camp Griswoldville last Wednesday evening at 6 o'clock and got to Savannah next morning at about 7 o'clock. We came the whole trip in the night and consequently could see very little of the country.

I had the mumps and could not go down to the river when we got to Savannah and see the boats, but I intend to go to the river in a few days. We got here in a rainy time but have fared finely.

Barton and Tom Cook and myself have been staying in a house ever since we have been here. Our camps are located six miles below Savannah and about two from the river. Wright's Legion is camped 1½ miles from here but move to Skidaway Island tomorrow and we will probably go where they now are. John Chapman was up here today. He belongs to Hanleiter's Artillery Company in Wright's Legion.

There is a great deal of difference between this and the upcountry. There is very few oak trees here. They are mostly pine and cypress. The palmetto stalk and long moss is plentiful here. The boys get as many oysters as they want to eat. The water is not very good here. I hope we will move where we can get better water.

It is thought a fight will take place somewhere about here before many days. I guess we will be armed in a few days and probably be paid. Also, I have heard that Gen. Zollicoffer has been killed in battle but hope it is not so. Two of our regiment died the week we left Griswoldville and two at the hospital there since we left.

I don't know how I will like this place after I have the chance of looking about a little. It is a beautiful country just below the Oconee River, which we crossed at the line of Wilkinson and Washington Counties. For a good ways we passed through a good

29

many counties on our way. In fact, I don't know what counties we passed through. It is thought by some that our regiment will go to South Carolina. I can see the pine and cypress trees of that gallant old state from Savannah.

I have had the mumps about a week. I will be well in a few days, I hope. You need not think that I was the author of that letter I took to Glass when I went home, for I emphatically declare I was not. Jesse Sanders got to Savannah a few minutes after we did.

I have nothing else to write. Write to me very soon. Direct your letters to Box No. 800, Savannah, Geo., in care of Capt. Dollar, D. J. Bailey's regiment. Put the Col.'s name on because it is said there is two other 25th Regiments.

Nothing more. Yours .....

/s/ A. P. ADAMSON

A.P. alludes to two other possible 25th Georgia Infantry Regiments. The editors have been able to localize only one. This 25th Infantry was organized 2 September 1861 under Col. Claudius C. Wilson and was assigned to the identical area of operations as A.P.'s regiment during the period of this correspondence (and, in fact, during most of the remainder of the War): the Department of Georgia (September-November 1861); District of Georgia, Department of South Carolina, Georgia, and Florida (November 1861-April 1862); Mercer's Brigade, Military District of Georgia, Department of South Carolina and Georgia (April-May 1862); Military District of Georgia, Department of South Carolina, Georgia, and Florida (May-October 1862); and, Wilson's Brigade, District of the Cape Fear, Department of North Carolina and Southern Virginia (December 1862-February 1863). A.P.'s regiment became associated with Wilson's command throughout the War. Brig. Gen. William H.T. Walker had been his brigade commander. When Walker was elevated to divisional command in June 1863, Wilson was elevated to brigade command. Thereafter the brigade was known as Wilson's Brigade, Walker's Division.

Our correspondent also mentions Wright's Legion. This unit was officially known as the 38th Georgia Infantry Regiment, Col. Augustus R.

Wright serving as the first commander. It was assigned to the same area of operations as the 30th through April 1862. Hanleiter's Battery was Company M of the 38th, which was separated out and formed into the Georgia Jo Thompson Artillery Battery in June 1862. Technically a Confederate legion was a combined arms unit, *i.e.*, it included units of infantry, cavalry, and artillery.

A.P. refers to Barton and Tom Cook. Ellsberry Barton Cook served in Co. E, was discharged for disability 1 December 1862, and subsequently died in 1863. Cpl. Thomas G. L. Cook was captured near Nashville on 16 December 1864, interned at Camp Chase, Ohio, and released 15 May 1865.

A.P.'s letters are now being posted from Camp Bartow, Chatham County, Georgia. Wright's Legion was at the same post during this time period. Camp Bartow was named in honor of Georgia native Francis Stebbins Bartow (1816-1861). Colonel Bartow was a Yale graduate, attorney, planter, secessionist, and Chairman of the Committee on Military Affairs in the Provisional Confederate Congress. He was serving as a militia captain when he seized Fort Pulaski subsequent to secession. Thereafter he was made the colonel of the 8th Georgia Infantry and fought valiantly at the Confederate victory of First Manassas on 21 July 1861. He was at the front of his brigade charge down Henry House Hill when he was mortally wounded. Colonel Bartow was Georgia's first martyr to the cause of nascent Southern independence. His was the first monument shaft to be placed on the battlefield at Manassas.

A.P.'s regiment was soon assigned to Mercer's Brigade. Brig. Gen. Hugh W. Mercer and his staff were headquartered on nearby Skidaway Island, Georgia. The 30th Georgia's Savannah area encampments were first at Camp Bartow, next at Camp Hardee near Thunderbolt, and finally at Camp Young. At Thunderbolt they built the extensive fortifications mounted with heavy artillery. Camp Hardee was located one-half mile below Thunderbolt, and two and one-half miles from Camp Bartow. Camp Young was located near Savannah.

LETTER NUMBER EIGHT

Camp Bartow
Chatham County, Ga.
February 2nd, 1862

Miss A. A. Adamson

Dear Sister,

 I take the present opportunity of writing you a few lines, which leaves me well at present. I have been on the sick list ever since I have been here, till today I returned to duty. Orderly Huie and Mr. Hanes and others got here day before yesterday. There is a great deal of dissatisfaction here on account of getting nothing to eat.

 The Yankees have been in two miles and a half from here. We put out pickets; one of them fired on some person which he took for a Yankee. The whole regiment was called in to line of battle directly but did not go out of the camp. It is thought that Major Tharpe instructed the picket to fire and run in to try the regt. The Yankees slipped by Fort Pulaski and came up the river and were about to hem Commodore Tatnall's fleet, but when morning came old Tatnall went by them while they poured shot fast into his fleet but he gallantly returned the fire. The firing lasted all day. We could plainly see the guns but they have left there now.

 A fight is expected every day at Skidaway, nine miles from here. Our regt. was ordered last Thursday to cook three days rations, expecting that night to be ordered to Skidaway. Some think Col. Bailey would not carry us into a battle with the guns we have, but he is brave enough to do anything, in fact, too brave.

 We get very little to eat here. The meal is half rice ground up. We have no beef but pickled beef, and some of the boys say that is mules pickled up. We are just beginning to experience the hardships of a soldier's life, but I will try and do the best I can. I wish we were back at Camp Griswold. There we fared well and we ought to have stayed there till we were armed. There is plenty of arms in

32

Savannah, it is believed, and they ought to let us have them. We are here protecting their city from the invaders with nothing but shotguns.

Our officers have done all they can to get arms, but Gen. Lawton will not supply us, but old Bailey is willing to risk them even with lightwood knots. But if he will suffer this regiment to go into battle with the guns they now have, he is not capable of commanding a regiment. But, unfortunately, Bailey is brave, too, much like the lamented Bartow, and if we are called into an action I have no doubt he will sustain most nobly.

We have received no pay yet , nor I don't know when we will. I saw Duet Mitchell the other day. He stays at Skidaway. He told me Saunders Mitchell belonged to Hanleiter's Company in Wright's Legion. I expect I will see him before long.

It is very unseasonable weather here at present. It is cold and rainy now. I have not been around about here much yet. I want to go to Thunderbolt tomorrow. It is reported here that Adjutant T. W. Mangham has resigned, but I hope it is not so. Dan Ward acted as Adjutant yesterday and today.

We drawed our knapsacks, haversacks, cartridge boxes and cap boxes the other day. I have nothing else to write. Write soon.

Your brother,

/s/ A. P. ADAMSON

Savannah, Ga. In care of Capt. Dollar
Box 800 D. J. Bailey's Regt.

The naval engagement alluded to at the beginning of this letter was most likely that of 28 January 1862. Georgia Confederate Commodore Josiah Tattnall had taken his squadron of five armed steamers to re-provision Fort Pulaski. He was surprised by a Federal reconnaisance of two squadrons that caught him in a cross fire. No casualties were reported by either belligerent.

Tattnall had seen naval service in the War of 1812, fought against Algerian pirates, chased buccaneers in the West Indies, fought in the Mexican War, and in 1858 was appointed as head of the American East Indian Squadron. It was while he was stationed in front of the Chinese Taku Forts in 1859 in support of the Anglo-French fleet that he authored the famed "blood is thicker than water" comment that has come down to us. Several months after his service at Savannah, the unwelcome duty of destroying the *CSS Virginia* fell to Commodore Tattnall so as to prevent it from falling into Yankee hands when Norfolk was abandoned by the Rebels.

The Huie clan was well represented in Co. E. Capt. Joseph H. Huie enlisted as a private in 1861, was elected third lieutenant, promoted to second lieutenant, wounded at Chickamauga, elected captain, and wounded and captured at Atlanta on 22 July 1864. 2nd Lt. Elijah Huie, presumably the Huie indicated in this letter, enlisted as orderly sergeant in 1861, was elected third lieutenant, promoted to second lieutenant, wounded in Mississippi, and surrendered at Greensboro, North Carolina, in 1865. 5th Sgt. GeorgeW. Huie, Sr., died in 1862. Albert A. Huie was captured at Nashville and died of pneumonia in POW Camp Chase on 7 March 1865. George W. Huie, Jr., survived the War. James C. Huie died at Savannah on 31 March 1862. Mathew H. Huie, captured at Calhoun and sent to POW Camp Rock Island with A.P., survived the War. Robert T.S. Huie was captured at Atlanta, sent to POW Camp Chase, exchanged on 10 March 1865, and survived the War. Robert L. Huie died in service in 1864. W.C. Huie was captured at Chickamauga and died at POW Camp Douglas.

Former sheriff Maj. Cicero A. Tharpe was first in command as a captain of Company D, then elected regimental major in October 1861, but declined re-election in 1862. A lawyer and former U.S. Congressman, Col. David J. Bailey organized the regiment during the summer of 1861, was unanimously elected colonel, and re-elected in May 1862 at Savannah. He resigned his commission at Wilmington, North Carolina, 16 January 1863 due to ill-health. He was known as an ardent supporter of "State's Rights as contended by the principles guaranteed by the Constitution."

This letter mentions A.P.'s first picket duty. Pickets were the advance guard against any enemy movement. They were the men posted outside of the unit's position for early warning. A picket detail usually consisted of a lieutenant, two sergeants, four corporals, and 40 privates. Three men were assigned to each listening post position. Therefore, pickets were the first to see the enemy should he advance, and the first to be shot or captured. This was not generally a popular assignment. Night duty meant little sleep, and there might not be time the following day for this luxury.

Perhaps an infantryman's first and foremost complaint throughout history has been his food rations. Federals subsisted on hardtack (an impenetrably hard tooth-breaking bisquit), coffee, bacon, salted meat and sugar. Meat was usually in short supply. Because salt meat was supposed to be able to be conserved for two years, it was pickled in brine. Before it could be consumed, it had to be soaked to remove the brine. It was foul-smelling. It could be too salty to eat, or tainted if not too salty! Confederates had fewer such gourmet options. Most of the South's prewar supply of meat had come from the Midwest. Now that supply was cut off. Their staple was cornbread, often mixed with water, pork grease and salt if available, and fried to make a corncake. The consistency was like "india rubber." When possible, Confederates made "cush," a mixture of bacon grease, cold beef, and water with some crumbled up corn-bread to make a form of stew or hash. Vegetables were rarely issued to Southerners. Yankees had a form of desiccated vegetables issued. Often the cornmeal issued to the troops was course and unsifted. Later in the War it included the cobs and husks. Nevertheless, all-in-all, A.P.'s issued rations seem to have been better than most.

Herein A.P. is issued some of his standard military equipment. Soldiers had to carry their own gear and weapons. They frequently discarded all but the bare essentials. Knapsacks were used for extra clothes and personal items and were worn on the back. The haversack was a foot-square canvas bag with a waterproof lining, buckled flap and a strap that was slung over the right shoulder and sat on the left hip. This became an indispensible carryall that generally held three days rations in an inner removable bag made of unpainted cotton. The cartridge box was a rectangular leather box that held 40 rifle cartridges attached to the belt. The cap boxes were generally square pouches for the percussion caps that ignited the catridge powder and fired the bullet. They were also suspended from the belt.

There is mention of Thunderbolt in this letter and those that follow. Fort Thunderbolt was a small harbor southeast of Savannah on St. Augustine's Creek. It held a heavy artillery battery that commanded the adjacent waterway.

LETTER NUMBER NINE

Chatham County, Ga.
February 17th, 1862

Dear Father and Mother,

> *I take this occasion of writing you a few lines, which leaves me well and getting along finely. The boys are all in good spirits owing to their drawing their pay yesterday, Sunday. As it was, the Privates drawed $60.20 cts., which is just <u>three months wages</u>. Pay day will come again 31st of March, I understand.*
> *There is nothing very new transpiring here at this time. We hear the firing of cannons every day but it is only the enemy firing a few random shots at some of our vessels. The enemy are above Fort Pulaski with four heavy ships of war. They have but one place of much importance to trap and that is Costins Bluff, where is stationed the 13th Geo. Regt., which was so lately commanded by the gallant and lamented Ector.*
> *If they ever succeed in passing this place they will have nothing to do but go right up to Savannah. They can take Savannah easily but is doubtful whether they try or not. They may attack the city and Skidaway Island at the same time and succeed in taking both places.*
> *The death of Walton B. Ector is deeply lamented everywhere down here, especially by his Regt., who deeply feel his loss. It is thought Major Smith will succeed him in the command, as their Lieut. Col. Douglas is not very popular among the Regt..*

I have seen the proclamation of Gov. Brown calling for twelve additional regiments to serve during the war. I think it will be a hard matter to raise them in the State without a draft.

Now is the time for the patriotic young men of Georgia who have not fully made up their minds to volunteer to rush to their country's call in this her hour of need. The soil of their own State is invaded by the vandal foe whose only aim is subjection to the tyrant's rule. Now is the time for them to respond nobly to their country's call, and, if possible, avert the danger and disgrace which would certainly fall upon them in the event they refuse to defend the Stars and Bars of the Confederate States. They should not be chagrined at the defeat of our troops at Fishing Creek, Roanoke and Fort Henry. We cannot expect to be victorious in every action, for everyone knows if Gen. Zollicoffer had sufficient force he would have gained the day at Fishing Creek, and it is useless to endeavor to hold these little islands on the coast like Roanoke. It only causes our troops to be slaughtered when, on the contrary, they would gain brilliant victories. I fear a dreadful slaughter will take place at Skidaway before long, worse than the Roanoke affair.

Yesterday and today is cold and rainy, the worse weather we have had yet, but, in general, it is very warm and reminds me of the month of April or May. Everything is earlier here than in our country. Here the people have collard plants to set out and English peas are already stuck in many places, and beets are also large enough to set out in rows. The April peach and plum trees are already blooming.

Here are some of the largest cedar trees I ever saw. The woods are thick with them. The beautiful palmetto tree flourishes here. Here is also the cypress and magnolia. In some places, indeed, this is a beautiful country in every respect. My only objection is the water, which is very bad.

I went to Savannah the other day and had a full view of the place and the Savannah River and several steam boats. Just across the river is South Carolina, which has a beautiful appearance from the city. I would have crossed the river if there had been any chance.

37

There is several of our company sick and will be taken to the Burton Hospital in Savannah shortly, I understand. Among the number is G. M. Stevens and Lieut. Stewart. We have had plenty to eat a portion of the time for the last week. Wm. Friddle and Minor Morris is here now. Tell Mr. Sanders' folks that Jess is well. I understand Mr. Huie will be down here in a few days. I will send some money to you by him. I wish you would come with him also. Captain Hurrell's and Bartlett's Co's have gone down towards Skidaway to wash.
Write soon.

/s/ A. P. ADAMSON

G. B. Stevens is presumably Green B. Stephens of Co. E. captured near Nashville 16 December 1864, interned at Camp Chase and released 12 June 1865.

A.P. was only partially correct as to his election prognostications for the 13th Georgia. After the death of Colonel Ector, Lt. Col. Marcellus Douglas was elected colonel. There were several other colonels of this regiment during the War - eventually to include James M. Smith!

Early in his letter, A.P. mentions Governor Brown. Georgia Gov. Joseph Emerson Brown, although a strong proponent of Southern independence and active early in the War in the raising of troops for the cause, was a strict State's Rights advocate regardless of the fact that his positions on many specific issues caused dissension in the war effort. He was continually opposed to many of the stances of the Confederate government and President Davis. Especially at bar was his concern with the national government's conscription policies.

With regard to the draft, the first American military conscription was enacted by the Confederate Congress in April 1862, more than a year before the Union Congress. The South was attempting a general consription, the first such experiment in American history, and it was a confusing process. The Confederacy had no alternative considering that it was being invaded, the fighting was on its territory, and the evident disparity of forces left it at a decided disadvantage (the Confederacy had a population of about 9 million, the Union about 22 million). However, predictably, the draft was unpopular. Under the Conscription Act, all healthy white males between the ages of 18 and 35 were susceptible for a three year enlistment. The Act also extended the terms of extant one year enlistments to three. In September 1862 the age limitation was raised to 45, and in February 1864 again extended to include all those men from 17 to 50 years. There were limited exemptions. Many of the governors, to include Georgia Governor Brown, were vehemently opposed to this as a usurpation of state sovereignty. To avoid the stigma of conscription, a man could volunteer and thereby also choose his unit. Many did this, and, in fact, it was encouraged.

A.P. mentions the three battles of Fishing Creek, Roanoke, and Fort Henry. Fishing Creek is also known as the Battle of Somerset, Mill Springs, Logan's Cross Roads, and Beech Grove. At this 19 January 1862 Kentucky battle between Confederate Maj. Gen. George Crittenden and Union Gen. George Henry Thomas, the near-sighted Confederate Brig. Gen. Felix K. Zollicoffer was killed when he became disoriented during a pouring rain and rode up to the Yankee troops by error and was shot at point-blank range. The death of a general officer was still an unexpected newsworthy event. At this point in the War, only three Confederate generals had been killed - to include General Zollicoffer. The loss of the Battle of Somerset made vulnerable the critical Rebel positions in the Cumberland Gap.

The Battle of Roanoke Island, North Carolina, was fought 8 February 1862 between Virginia ex-Governor Confederate Gen. Henry Wise (who happened to be married to the sister of Union Gen. George G. Meade) and Union Gen. Ambrose Everett Burnside. Wise had only a modest force of 1,900 men to fight Burnside's 13,000 men and a flotilla of 100 ships! The Confederate forces fought well from Fort Bartow but were eventually overcome in this unevenly matched engagement.

Confederate held Fort Henry, Tennessee, was assaulted on 6 February 1862 by Union Gen. Ulysses S. Grant and a flotilla of seven gun-boats led by Flag Officer Andrew H. Foote. Confederate Gen. Lloyd Tilghman realized that his position was indefensible, evacuated all but 100 artillerymen of his 3,400 man force, and with his brave gunners gamely defended their post. They were out-gunned, but kept to the fight with only four guns operating until honor permitted them to yield the fort.

Those defeats, in conjunction with the 16 February 1862 loss of Fort Donelson, boded ill for the Confederacy at the beginning of 1862. The North had secured the Carolina Outer Banks, blunted further Southern incursion into Kentucky, and threatened western and middle Tennessee by the penetration of the Tennessee and Cumberland rivers by Union gunboats. The sanguinary battle of Shiloh was to be the consequence.

LETTER NUMBER TEN

Chatham County, Georgia
March 23rd, 1862

Dear Sister,

> *I take this opportunity of writing you a few lines, which leaves me tolerable well only. I have had a very bad cold for a good while. I have nothing of importance to write to you, as nothing of interest has taken place here lately. I wrote to you some two weeks ago but have received no answer yet.*
>
> *Lieut. Mann got back yesterday evening and McConnell started home soon as he got here. We heard the other evening that the Yankees were landing in large forces at Bluffton, Carolina, and we were ordered to hold ourselves in readiness to march at a moment's warning, but ain't gone yet, nor no idea of going. Indeed, there is no chance for a fight down here and we need not hope to get good arms unless we go in for three years. On these conditions, and these only, General Mercer says we will be armed.*
>
> *I am not quite willing to try it for the war for fear we would get the same staff officers we have got now, or some equally as bad, for we was blinded before in the election of officers, but if we could get a Tidwell, a Mangham, a Hendrick, or a Dollar, I think there might be*

some danger of me re-enlisting, but under other circumstances I could not.

> *I do not want to stay down here all the summer but I believe the way we are now we will be kept here just to build bridges and breastworks for others to fight behind and we will go home without receiving any honor while in service, all being on actions by Col. D. J. Bailey and Maj. Tharpe, whose names will ever be hated by the members of this regiment.*

> *Skidaway is at last evacuated, which is a sensible move upon our part but the Yankees won't venture far. That is very certain.*

> *We drawed money the other day, twenty-two dollars each. I wish I had a good chance to send mine home.*

> *B. J. Smith, one of Captain Richards' Company, died this morning with the brain fever. He was well Friday. This is five less to the company. I wish Pa would come down. He could come very easy, and, by bringing boxes and going to Atlanta and getting a through ticket, could come at half price. I have nothing else to write at present, so nothing more. Write soon.*

Your brother,

/s/ A. P. ADAMSON

The following is quoted from BRIEF HISTORY OF THE THIRTIETH GEORGIA REGIMENT, A. P. Adamson, 1912:

For several months the men had no arms, except such as had been sent them by friends and relatives, which consisted of old-time rifles and shotguns of various kinds, mostly flint and steel locks, many of them being of little account.

The coastal defense line (laid out by Gen. Robert E. Lee who was coastal commander from 5 November 1861 to 4 March 1862) extended from above Charleston, South Carolina, to below Savannah, Georgia. The line was not immediately on the coast but several miles inland, to include Bluffton, S.C. On the Georgia side it extended from Fort Jackson on the Savannah River, to

Causten's Bluff and Fort Thunderbolt on St. Augustine Creek, Isle of Hope and Fort Wimberly on the Wilmington River, and inland to Fort McAllister on the Great Ogeechee River. Fort Pulaski was its forward position in the Savannah River entrance.

B. J. Smith of Campbell County died 2 March 1862 at Savannah. He was a member of Co. K, commanded by Captain W. B. Richards.

LETTER NUMBER ELEVEN

Camp Bartow,
30th Regt. Ga. Vols.
April 6th, 1862

Miss A. A. Adamson

Dear Sister,

    I take the present opportunity of writing you a few lines, which leaves me well and hoping these few lines may find you enjoying the same. I have nothing to write that won't interest you.
    There has been a couple of skirmishes in this vicinity lately upon Wilmington Island about one or two miles below Thunderbolt. In the first, which took place last Monday night, in which one of the enemy was killed, one wounded, 3 taken prisoners, and on Tuesday night another skirmish took place in which 3 of the enemy was killed and wounded and fourteen taken prisoners. Two of the wounded have since died at Thunderbolt and been buried.
    The prisoners are now in Savannah in jail. There are mostly Germans and belong to New York and New Jersey regiments. They all say they were compelled to enter the Federal Army so as to get something to live upon. When asked what they were fighting for they readily answered - for pay. They all expressed a willingness to enter the Confederate service and fight for the South.

They say the 46th and 97th New York Regiments is in the vicinity of Tybee Island, and also an artillery company, and are mostly Germans and half of them are opposed to the war but have to stay in the service for money. They say they were paid off in gold the first time, and the next time in paper bills with old Abe's likeness on one corner and were told this was very current in the South, and seemed astonished at hearing it was entirely worthless.

They were told that the South People were a barbarous people and one of them, when he was wounded, pleaded that our men would not cut his throat. But they say they prefer staying here rather than go back to their vessel.

These men were captured by the gallant 13th Regt. Only one of our men was hurt. His name was Brown. He was severely wounded but it is thought will recover shortly. They also took a small boat and one six pounder with the men. Wilmington Island is on St. Augustine River, which is a part of the Savannah. Causten's Bluff and Thunderbolt are also on this stream.

There is some talk of us going to Atlanta, but there is no such luck for us. Capts. Hitch and MacGouirk went to see General Brown, who promised our Regiment should have arms, if possible, in a short time. It is said Mercer is willing for us to go to Atlanta if any has to go from here but <u>old Bailey, who does everything wrong, it is thought would object on account of being too near home. This command hates Bailey and Tharpe as bad as they do an enemy. They have disgraced the regiment in the eyes of many. They have tried to do nothing for us. There is only one thing they are good for and that is to fight. They are no cowards but no sorrier officers in the Service.</u>

The next time you get a chance you can, if you wish, send me a pair of pants, some kind of summer goods, as jeans is too warm for this country and I am afraid we will have to stay here all the time. This country is good for nothing but Irish, Negroes, goats and sandflies, and rice, which we have to eat half of our time. I wish there was none here.

I got the provisions by Leut. McConnell and was not sorry to get them. Tell Sarah I haven't got time to write to her now. It is bedtime. Write to me soon.

Your brother,

/s/ A. P. ADAMSON

Editors' note: later in life, and upon more mature consideration, A.P. lined out the underlined portion of this letter.

The records divulge that on 30 March 1862, an armed boat filled with troops of the 46th New York reconnoitered the Wilmington Narrows. They encountered Capt. J. Terrell Crawford and three companies of the 13th Georgia. The Confederates reported that they inflicted upon the New Yorkers one man killed and 18 captured. One Rebel was badly wounded (apparently named Brown according to A.P.). On 1 April men of the 13th captured an additional two more Yankees on Whitemarsh Island, also affiliated with the luckless 46th.

Germans are discussed in this correspondence. The revolution of 1848 and its aftermath sparked a great wave of German immigration to the United States. They generally settled in Northern cities or the rural midwest and quickly became a significant political force. Abraham Lincoln courted this immigrant vote in 1860, and its leaders. Resultantly many German-American political leaders received high-level commissions in the Federal army. Perhaps as many as 200,000 German-Americans were therby recruited for the Union cause. New York alone provided 10 German speaking regiments. The Eleventh Corps of the Army of the Potomac, under Gen. Oliver Otis Howard, was known as the German Corps since some 15 of its 26 regiments spoke German. The South also had German units, but not as many or as pronounced as the North.

LETTER NUMBER TWELVE

Camp Bartow
30th Regt. Ga.. Vols.
April 14th, 1862

"Pulaski!"

Dear Father and Mother,

    I this morning take the opportunity of writing you a few lines. I am not very well at present. I have had a very bad cold for several days but feel considerable better today.

    There is a great deal of excitement here occasioned by the fall of Fort Pulaski, which event has cast a deep gloom over this portion of the State. The Fort surrendered last Friday evening at two o'clock. Early on Thursday morning the enemy began to bombard the Fort and continued all day. At night there was very little firing done on either side. The Garrison in the Fort fired but very little on the Fort (batteries erected by the enemy) on Thursday, but early Friday morning the bombardment was renewed and was replied to from the Fort. We could distinctly hear the report of the guns and occasionally see a shell burst over or around the Fort.

    The firing on Friday was at an average of fifteen times per minute until ten o'clock. The report of the battle we received on Friday was favorable and did not on any account prepare us for the startling intelligence of the surrender of the Fort, which reached us on Saturday. There was no one killed in the Fort and only four were wounded. The loss of the enemy is not known. It is strange that none were killed in the Fort, notwithstanding one side of the Fort was entirely demolished.

    This disaster at Pulaski can be easily accounted for. Like most of our reverses, it is the fault of the commanders and the blame should fall upon Alexander R. Lawton, who is considered by many to be an Abolitionist at heart, and, before the communication with the Fort was cut off, could have had five hundred Negroes fortifying the Fort, but, instead of doing so, he permitted the enemy to build batteries in a mile and a quarter from the Fort. The commander of the Fort, Col. Olmestead, wanted to stop them from erecting the batteries which were built there in range of the guns of the Fort is what took place. Not a gun was fired from the vessels of war which were lying off a short distance.

    In this defeat there was one hundred and thirty-five guns and five hundred men, besides a large amount of ammunition stores and provisions fell in the enemies' hands. It is a noted fact that Gen. Lawton and H. R. Jackson, who are brothers-in-law, have a brother-in-law in the Yankee fleet in this vicinity by the name of Davenport, who is a brother to Major Davenport, one of Gen. Mercer's staff, and if Mercer was only like Lawton it is the belief of many that Savannah, with all the troops here, would be taken.

As for Savannah and Forts Jackson and Boggs, they will undoubtedly fall in the course of a week or two. The citizens are all leaving. An attack on Fort Jackson is hourly expected and when they get that it would be folly to try to hold Savannah. We will move above Savannah in a few days, I expect. We have got no business here. Savannah will fall, but, if it falls, it will no doubt be laid in ashes and let old Lawton and his crew go, too, I hope.

I was gratified to hear of the brilliant victory at Corinth, especially the capture of the notorious Kentuckian, Geo. D. Prentice. I hear that Buel is killed. I hope it is so. I now believe General Johnston was a better officer than I once believed him to be and am sorry to hear of his death.

There is talk of sending the sick to Augusta or somewhere else, those who are not able for duty. We have about seventeen on the sick list in our company. There is no prospect of us getting arms. The State troops here are not allowed to go home.

I want you to write to me every chance. If we leave here I will write to you immediately. Jesse Sanders is well at this time. Write to me soon as you get this. So, nothing more.

Your affectionate son,

/s/ A. P. ADAMSON

Later in life, in re-reading this letter, A. P. Adamson made the following notation at the end of the letter: "I was wrong in my estimate of Generals Lawton and Jackson and regret that I ever wrote it. I listened too much to hearsay."

"Pulaski!"

Maryland Confederate Brig. Gen. Alexander Robert Lawton had been appointed by Gen. Robert E. Lee in November 1861 to head the Military District of Georgia with his headquarters in Savannah. Lawton eventually commanded a division in the Army of Northern Virginia replacing Gen. Richard Stoddert Ewell when Ewell was wounded at the Battle of Groveton. In turn, Lawton was replaced by Gen. Jubal Anderson Early when Lawton was wounded at the Battle of Sharpsburg. Lawton was contemporaneously considered as an accomplished field administrator but deficient in field command.

Maj. Gen. Henry Rootes Jackson was appointed to the command of the Georgia Militia on 28 December 1861. Eventually, Jackson became brigade commander of Stevens' Brigade, *vice* Wilson's Brigade, after the death of Stevens in July 1864, and the 30th Georgia was part of this brigade.

As part of its defense system, Savannah was protected by a series of forts and defense lines. Fort Pulaski is the best known, named for Revolutionary War patriot Gen. Casimir Pulaski killed at the siege of Savannah in 1779. Built on Cockspur Island at the mouth of the Savannah River between 1829 and the 1840s, then army engineer Lt. Robert E. Lee directed much of this work. Its thick brick walls were thought to be impermeable to cannon fire. On 3 January 1861 the fort was captured by the Georgia Militia commanded by Captain Bartow by *coup de main*. This was the first Federal facility seized by the South. Col. Charles H. Olmstead and some 400 troops were then installed and the artillery refurbished. Union forces under Capt. Quincy A. Gillmore assembled an impressive array of siege guns which could shoot both into and over the fortifications. These included the use of the new technological breakthrough of rifled cannon, first used in warfare at this siege utilizing a degree of accuracy and power beyond all anticipation. Batteries were set up on nearby Tybee Island. At 8:15 a.m., 10 April 1862, the barrage began. Over 5,275 shells were fired at the fort. The most penetrating being fired from the newly developed 42 pounder rifled James (which fired an 84 pound shot) and the 30 pounder rifled Parrott. By early afternoon, one of the walls had been breached, significant damage inflicted, and an opening created. Colonel Olmstead had no other recourse at this point than to surrender, which he did on 11 April at 2:00 p.m. Until this time, masonry forts were considered impregnable at the cannon

47

ranges used here, now the forts were obsolete. The new rifled guns revolutionized siege warfare, exceeding all expectations. By the successful assault on Fort Pulaski, the North effectively sealed off Savannah harbor from the blockade runners for the rest of the War. It was not necessary to attack Savannah itself.

Fort Jackson is also located on the Savannah River. This brick fortification was started as a riverine battery in 1808, garrisoned during the War of 1812, and occupied by the South during the War Between the States. Fort Boggs was on the eastern edge of Savannah. Located on the south bank of the Great Ogeechee River lies Fort McAllister. This fort was considered as an outstanding example of Confederate earthwork fortification. It was built in 1861-1862 to guard the "back door" to Savannah. It repulsed no less than seven Union attacks by armored naval craft during 1862-1863. It did not fall until 13 December 1864 when it was assaulted by General Sherman from the rear.

When A.P. refers to the victory at Corinth, it is presumed that he means Shiloh (there was a Battle of Corinth, but not until October 1862, long after this letter was written). This 6-7 April 1862 sanguinary engagement was fought by Generals Ulysses S. Grant and William Tecumseh Sherman for the North, and Generals Albert Sidney Johnston and Pierre Gustave Toutant Beauregard for the South near Shiloh Chapel not far from Pittsburg Landing on the Tennessee River. The first day surprise attack was an unqualified success for the Confederacy when 23 cannon were captured and the Union army hurled back toward the river. However, the second day's action forced their withdrawl after Union re-inforcements arrived under Gen. Don Carlos Buell and the Southerners were strongly and successfully counter-attacked. General Johnston was killed during the first day and mourned throughout the South. Although A.P. relates that General Buell was also killed, that did not occur. Federal Gen. Benjamin M. Prentiss (not George D. Prentice) surrendered his 2,200 men on the first day at what history labels the "Hornet's Nest" after the Confederates massed 62 artillery pieces at point-blank range. This was the largest concentration of artillery yet to be assembled in the War. The battle pitted 40,000 Rebels against a far greater number of Yankees. There were over 12,000 wounded on the first day alone. Shiloh was the first truly great battle of the War. The total casualties of about 23,000 men equaled more than the United

States had lost in all its previous wars combined. Romantic innocence had vanished. It was said that after Shiloh the South never smiled again. Shiloh eroded the glamour of war. Both sides now realized that this War for Southern Independence was going to be long and bloody.

LETTER NUMBER THIRTEEN

Camp Bartow
30th Regt. Ga. Vols.
April 27th, 1862

Dear Father,

> *I avail myself of this opportunity of writing you a few lines, which leaves me in good health. We have all re-enlisted for two years and five months and Lieut. Mann leaves for home this evening to get up recruits. Our company will be increased to one hundred and twenty-five if we can get them.*
> *We reorganized last Wednesday. On Thursday we elected a Colonel. D. J. Bailey was elected over Tidwell by 15 majority, he only receiving 287 votes. This shows he is not the choice of the regiment. The left wing has a large number at home. If they had been here, Tidwell would have got it by two hundred votes.*
> *This regiment has had a great many trials and has been very unfortunate, but the greatest calamity that they have had to bear will turn out to be the election of the heedless and abrupt person of David J. Bailey. It is true he has been very easy with us, but that is not the thing we want. But he knows nothing about military affairs and were he to lead us into battle we would all get cut up or taken prisoners on account of his not knowing how to command.*
> *Our company officers are Dollar, Mann, Drewry and Huie. The election of Lieut. Col. and Maj. has not yet come off. Barnett and Mangham are for Lieut. Col. Boynton and Dr. Drewry for Major.*
> *We will doubtless move from here in a day or so. We have a great many sick, and those who are well have a great deal of duty to*

do. *I have heard with regret of the fall of New Orleans, which is the worst reverse we have had yet, in my opinion.*

The troops here are falling back toward Savannah. The Yankees send out their pickets and I learn they have ventured probably some eight or ten thousand, but they will move slowly and cautiously, as they generally do, upon Savannah. I hope we can hold the place but I think it doubtful.

I understand we will get a furlough in a short time but I can't say for that. Those who are subject to the provisions of the Conscript Act had better come to our company. Our time is six months shorter than Hanes company. We have the best Captain in the regiment. Dr. Drewry will, I think, be our Major, T. W. Mangham will be Lieut. Colonel, who is one of the finest men in the world. If they come to our company they will probably remain the most of the time in our beloved State, and, if it was not for old Bailey, we would have the best regiment in the State. Try and get the Shake Rag boys to come to us at once.

The following officers were elected in the Bartow Invincibles: Captain, R. M. Hitch; 1st Lieut., R. Hightower; 2nd Lieut., O. S. Berry; 3rd Lieut., J. A. Arnold; Orderly, W. H. Smith, the son of Judge John A. Smith; 2nd Serg., John Berry; 3rd Serg., J. W. Spencer; 4th Serg., John M. Burke; 5th Serg., H. H. Hinton; Corporals: 1st, T. E. Moore; 2nd, E. J. Foster; 3rd, J. A. Dethrage; 4th, John Milam. T. A. Ward did not run and will, I hope, be Adjutant.

The following officers were elected from the several companies comprising the regiment. Butts Invincibles: Captain, Felix L. Walthall; 1st Lieut., W. D. Curry; 2nd Lieut., J. M. Ingram; 3rd Lieut., W. B. Andrews. Bailey Volunteers: Captain, H. Kendrick; 1st Lieut., A. T. Towles; 2nd Lieut., D. A. Moore; 3rd Lieut., J. G. S. Ham. Hunter Guards: R. J. Andrews, W. J. P. Phinizee, Wm. Ogletree, J. V. McElhaney. Hugeney Rifles: H. Whitaker, J. F. Barfield, L. B. Mosely, J. M. Calloway. Campbell Sharpshooters: W. N. McGouirk, C. P. Bower, J. C. Danforth, A. G. Weddington. Campbell Greys: John Edmondson, J. O. Redwine, O. Spence, W. R. Elder. Fayette Volunteers: F. M. Harrell, J. J. Martin, E. Adams, John

Smith. *Chattahoochee Volunteers:* G. F. Longino, H. D. Morris, H. H. Smith, T. J. King.

Several officers will have to take a private place, which is nothing more than they ought to do. *The following is the vote in the Clayton Invincibles for officers:*

Captain Dollar	53	2nd Sergeants	
1st Lieut.. Mann	54	G. W. Tanner	13
2nd Lt. N. B. Drewry	53	W. Q. Anthony	13
3rd Lieut. J. H. Huie	28	G. W. Gallman	9
3rd Lieut. Stewart	26	J. W. McKown	8
		J. H. Buchanan	7

3rd Serg.		4th Serg.	
R. S. Huie	9	W. A. Lawson	31
W. W. Dickson	13	R. M. Barton	14
W. A. Bray	9	J. W. Fuller	7
J. M. Smith	8		
J. G. Ansley	5		

5th Serg.	
Joel Baxley	17
John Guice	16
F. M. Johnson	10

1st Corp.		2nd Corporal	
W. B. Hurdle	16	A. P. Adamson	25
J. T. Sanders	14	W. L. Thomas	13

3rd Corp.		4th Corp.	
J. E. Lites	23	T. G. L. Cook	22

R. S. Osburn	9	*W. R. Thomas*	7
J. W. Peace	6		

There was a tie for Second Sergeant. I must close as I have no room. Write soon. I received your letter yesterday. Write again as soon as you can.

Your son,

/s/ A. P. ADAMSON

The reader must first note that A.P. was elected as second corporal by a 66% margin!

New Orleans fell on 25 April 1862 after the passage of Forts Jackson and St. Philip on the Mississippi River by Capt. David G. Farragut's powerful fleet. New Orleans was the South's largest city and port - the entrepôt for the entire Mississippi valley. Its closure was an ominous presentiment for the survival of the fledgling Confederate nation. The subsequent Northern occupation was rife with corruption and barbarism under Gen. Benjamin F. "Beast" Butler. He was also known as "Spoons" Butler for all the silverware he allegedly purloined and shipped North. Butler also had the dubious distinction of creating a Southern martyr *à la* Nathan Hale with his "judicial murder" of William Bruce Mumford, executed on 7 June 1862. Gen. Nathaniel Banks was Butler's less than sterling successor.

This and other correspondence from A.P. reveals his unbridled reliance in the democratic process. It should be noted that during this entire war for survival the Southern regiments elected both their company grade officers and non-commissioned officers. Initially field grade officers from volunteer state units were also elected, but later they were appointed by higher authority. General grade officers were always appointed by higher authority. The North utilized a similar system at the beginning but quickly foreswore such democratic allurements for the appointment system, which coincidentally enabled the political leadership the opportunity to utilize extensive promotion patronage.

LETTER NUMBER FOURTEEN

Chatham County, Georgia
May 5th, 1862

Dear Sister,

I take the present opportunity of writing you a few lines in answer to your letter that I received on Monday last. I have nothing at all important to write. I have not been well for several days but am getting better now. I think I will be all right in a few days. We are moving this evening, about 300 yards.

We had an election last Wednesday for Lt. Col. and Major. The following was the result: Lt. Col., T. W. Mangham 252, J. L. Barnett 161; Major, James S. Boynton 221, N. B. Drewry 207. Our elections are all null and void and will have to be held over. The result the next time is doubtful.

There is some talk of us being ordered to Tennessee, but there is no such good news. George Thrailkill died last week and George Gallman is lying very low. It is doubtful whether he lives or not. G. H. Buchanan and T. J. Stephens are in Savannah sick; also, several others. We will draw pay in a few days again. Some of our regiment are in Savannah at work on the latest Gunboat. We have just done moving.

I got a letter from Pa tonight and was glad to hear from home, which in the language of the poet, is Mother and Love, and is three of the sweetest words in the English language.

I will try and buy him salt if I can get it at a reasonable price as soon as we draw, but some say it cannot be got at 25 dollars, but I will try. I think Will had better come to our company. I believe this country suits me as well as any, but tell Nat, for God's sake, to stay at home. I think it best for him to stay and work. Camps would not suit him.

[The above is all that has survived of this letter.]

George W. Thirlkill of Co. E. died at Savannah 28 April 1862. George W. Gallman, also of Co. E, died at Savannah 6 May 1862. Josiah H. Buchanan of Fayette County rose to the rank of first sergeant and was wounded and permanently disabled at Chickamauga on 19 September 1863. T. J. Stephens was subsequently wounded at the Battle of Jonesboro on 31 August 1864 and survived the War. The reference to Nat probably is to one of his cousins; there were several Nathaniel Adamsons in Georgia and Alabama at this time.

Several letters have mentioned Dr. Nicholas B. Drewry. He volunteered as a private in Captain Dollar's Company, was elected second lieutenant at the May 1862 re-organization. He was ultimately commissioned as a surgeon (surgeons ranked as officers) and was transferred to several military hospitals. After A.P. was wounded at Chickamauga, Dr. Drewry was one of those who attended to him at the Medical College Hospital in Atlanta.

The concern for the availability and price of salt herein continues throughout much of A.P.'s writings. Salt was the primary means of preserving meat. It was used to pack cheese and eggs, preserve hides for leather manufacturing, and was employed in multiple chemical processes not to mention dietary supplement for man and beast. Prior to the War, the South imported much of its salt. The Confederacy had to rapidly develop this very necessary product. Most of the potential production areas were captured at the outset of the conflict. Ultimately, most of the Confederacy's salt came from the firm of Buchanan & Co. Saltworks at Saltville, Virginia. By 1864, 38 furnaces containing 2,600 kettles were producing 4 million bushels of salt a year. As is manifest in this letter, civilian shortages became common. Shortages of necessary items contributed to the rampant inflation that soon engulfed the Southland. By March 1863, flour was selling for $100 per barrel, beef was $2 per pound, apples were $25 per bushel, boots cost $50 per pair, and wood was $30 per cord. By the end of the War, inflation in the Southern republic had grown to over 6,000%! To maintain perspective, keep in mind that A.P. is garnering $11 per month, eventually to rise to the princely sum of about $18 per month!

LETTER NUMBER FIFTEEN

Chatham County, Georgia
May 12th, 1862

Miss A. A. Adamson

Dear Sister,

I avail myself of this opportunity of dropping you a few lines, which leaves me well at this time. I have nothing of any interest to write to you this time.

We expected Lieut. Mann on Saturday but learnt he did not intend to come till tomorrow. Capt. Harrell got here this evening and said he did not think Mann would be here until Thursday, but we look for him tomorrow and hope he will get in.

Fifteen Yankees were taken prisoners on yesterday, on White Marsh, by five of our men who belonged to the gallant Thirteenth Regt. We have heard the roaring of artillery all day and I understand it proceeds from fighting at Red Bluff on the Carolina side. The Yankees sent up a flag of truce from Fort Pulaski the other day to Fort Jackson in reference to the exchange of prisoners. I do not think the Yankees will make any demonstration on Savannah at all this summer.

We have heard with pleasure of the Confederate victories at Williamsburg, McDowell, and Farmington. The Yankees most always look out when Van Dorn, Price, and Stonewall Jackson gets a pull at them. I wish we could change Alex Lawton for such a one.

Our old election for officers is going to stand. Tomorrow morning we will elect a Second Sergeant owing to a tie at the previous election. Some are inclined to believe we will get to go home on furlough in a short time, but I consider it doubtful. McConnell leaves for home in a day or so, to remain.

I had as many beans today as I wanted and you may depend they took splendid. About twelve of our company are under and over age but only six or seven will go home. We don't know whether Joel

Stephens intends to come back or not, but he only likes a short time of being of the required age and will have to come, willing or not. To tell the truth, he had no business at home when, for if all of us was to go home every time we get a little sick like he was there would soon be no men here.

I fear we will have to stay here all the summer. I have nothing else to write at present. Write to me as soon as possible.

Your brother,

/s/ A. P. ADAMSON

[P.S.] I have just heard the Thirteenth Regiment brought in more prisoners.

Whitemarsh Island, across from Fort Thunderbolt on St. Augustine's Creek, was the scene of several notable skirmishes.

The Battle of Williamsburg, Virginia, was fought 5 May 1862 between Union Gen. Joseph Hooker's 40,000 men and Confederate Gen. James Longstreet's 31,000 men. After successfully accomplishing their mission to delay the Union pursuit of the Southern forces withdrawing up the peninsula toward Richmond, the Rebels withdrew westward. Both sides claimed this battle as a victory.

The 8 May 1862 Battle of McDowell was fought west of the Shenandoah Valley by Stonewall Jackson in what is viewed as the first of his outstanding Valley victories. This was seen at the time as the only Southern victory of note since the beginning of 1862, and therefore was of great morale significance with so many defeats occurring.

Mention of the inconsequential Battle of Farmington on 4 May 1862 is noted. This battle was managed by Gen. Pierre G.T. Beauregard and fought by Generals William J. Hardee and Patrick R. Cleburne against an undetermined Federal force near the small Tennessee town of Farmington along Seven Mile Creek soon after the Battle of Shiloh and prior to the evacuation of Corinth.

While General Hardee advanced toward the Federals on the Farmington Road, the corps of Confederate General Van Dorn was to attempt to find the Yankee flank. Cleburne's Brigade led Hardee's Corps on a night march engaging the enemy at 10:00 a.m. on 4 May 1862. His men drove the Northerners back several miles before halting. Van Dorn had lost his way and never appeared. Beauregard then ordered Hardee to fall back to the lines in Corinth.

Missouri Maj. Gen. Sterling Price was seen as the hero of the victories of Wilson's Creek and Lexington, Missouri. He fought well at the Confederate defeat at Elkhorn Tavern, also known as Pea Ridge. He was appalled at his casualties at Iuka and Corinth. Nonetheless, he was popular with the troops, and eventually returned to command positions in the Army of the Trans-Mississippi. He was a field commander under Gen. Theophilus Holmes at the ill-fated Battle of Helena, Arkansas in July 1863.

Mississippi Maj. Gen. Earl Van Dorn was handsome and dapper, and a Mexican War veteran. He was held responsible for the ensanguined defeat at Corinth, and transferred to the cavalry. As recompense, he led his troopers to victory at the Battles of Holly Springs and Spring Hill. Alcohol was not his only weakness. He was killed by an irate husband on 7 May 1863.

Stonewall Jackson was one of the outstanding generals of the War, and, in fact, American history. To a reader of this book, he needs no introduction.

2nd Lt. J. L. McConnell retired in May 1862 and died thereafter. Joel M. Stephens was later captured at Rough and Ready on 4 September 1864. He eventually died of typhoid fever at POW Camp Douglas, Illinois, on 1 February 1865.

LETTER NUMBER SIXTEEN

Camp Bartow, Georgia
May 12th, 1862
Miss S.S. Adamson

Dear Sister,

I take this opportunity of writing you a few lines which I hope will find you enjoying yourself finely. I have nothing to write to you that would interest you.

I don't think there is much chance for us to get into a fight although we are very eager to get into it. I hope I will get to come home in a short time but I fear it will be some time. I should like to see all the girls up there again but don't know how long it will be before I will be in Clayton [County] again.

The Thirteenth Georgia Regt. took four more prisoners this morning. It will be a long time before we can go home to stay. We are now in for three years --------.

--- Thomas W. Mangham and Liet. Pool is a young man about twenty-five years old and I heard him say on election day that he had never bought a drink of liquor and had never drank a drop in his life. He is the finest young man I have ever seen. Everybody loves him.

James S. Boynton is our major. He was elected over [Dr. Nicholas] Drewry by only one vote. He is a sober still kind of a man and I think he will make a good major. At least I am satisfied with them.

I want you to write me as soon as possible. Write all the news you can think of. Write all about the girls up there. I wish you could see this country. There is so many pretty green trees and flowers and the Savannah & St. Augustine Rivers are beautiful.

[The above is all that has survived of this letter.]

S.S. Adamson is his sister Sarah Sophronia who would be eleven years old at this time. His sister Amanda Augusta would have been sixteen years old in 1862.

Col. Thomas W. Mangham first served as regimental adjutant. Reputed for his indefatigable drilling and discipline, he was promoted.to colonel upon the resignation of Colonel Bailey in 1863. He was wounded at Chickamauga. A.P., having been wounded himself, was present when the surgeons extracted the ball from Colonel Mangham's wound. He later resigned his commission due to the lasting effects of this wound.

Lawyer James S. Boynton enlisted at first as a private in the 30th. He was elected major at the re-organization of May 1862, promoted to lieutenant colonel in December, and succeeded to colonel at the resignation of Colonel Mangham. He was seriously wounded at the Battle of Atlanta on 22 July 1864 leading his men of the 30th Georgia in a charge. Nonetheless, he remained in command until disbandment in 1865.

LETTER NUMBER SEVENTEEN

Chatham County, Georgia
May 16th, 1862

Miss A. A. Adamson

Dear Sister,

As Mr. Huie leaves today, I take the present opportunity of writing you a few lines, which leaves me well at this time and hoping these few lines may find you the same. I have nothing interesting to write to you.

We have a fine company. I guess we have about ninety men in all and should like to have a few more. The recruits have all been examined and only one was rejected, namely, W. H. Abercrombie.

I understand our company meets with strong opposition in Clayton County but presume it is mostly by its former opponents. It is said it has been circulated that this is a very sickly place, that we were badly fed, and many other things which are entirely devoid of truth.

Where there are so many men together they cannot expect to keep well. I believe we get along as well here as we would anywhere else if we would move occasionally. We are fed a great deal better than we were some time ago. I presume R. E. Morrow was very instrumental in circulating these reports, as well as others, that would impair the interest of the Clayton Invincibles.

This individual, after his return from here last Winter, I am reliably informed, heaped all the abuse he could upon Capt. Dollar and the company in reference to the manner in which he was treated while in our regiment, which every man, except two or three who would yield to him, to the last are ready to denounce all such reports as palpable and malicious falsehoods. Any person should never listen to such men. No one can do better than to come to our company.

The recruits have not drawn tents yet. I know not how we will arrange. J. T. Sanders, W. J. Adamson, H.L. Hamilton and myself are making a new mess and probably the Dickson-boys and J. M. Gilman will be with us.

In the election for 2nd Serg. W. Q. Anthony was elected. Therefore, G. W. Tanner will have to stand guard. It is reported that Lieut. Mann has been appointed quartermaster, but I cannot say as to the truth of it, but hope it is not so. Our company is going on picket today. I am not going, owing to me standing guard last night. W. R. Andrews, a newly elected Lieut. in Butts Invincibles, died last night.

I will come to a close for this time. Write to me soon.

Your brother,

/s/ A. P. ADAMSON

Joel T. Sanders died in July 1864. William J. Adamson died at Newton, Mississippi, in July 1963. Hezekiah L. Hamilton died in hospital on 11 June 1864. Sherman G. Dickson was wounded at Chickamauga and killed in 1865. Sgt. William W. Dickson was captured near Nashville, and released from POW Camp Chase. John M. Gallman survived the War. Sgt. George W. Tanner served into 1862. 3rd Lt. William R. Andrews of Co. A resigned or died in 1862. 1st Lt. John F. Mann survived the War. 2nd Sgt. William Q. Anthony was killed at the Battle of Franklin on 30 November 1864.

When A.P. refers to his "mess" and "messmates," he is referring to a grouping of four or five of his peers all of whom jointly prepare and cook their rations together. They may also tent together.

LETTER NUMBER EIGHTEEN

Chatham County, Georgia
May 24th, 1862

Miss S. S. Adamson

Dear Sister,

    I take this opportunity of writing you a few lines. I have nothing to write to you, as I have already written all I can think of to Augusta.
    Major Boynton gave us a stirring speech this evening on dress parade. We are going to draw tomorrow, so Major Boynton says. Will wants to know how his mule is getting along and whether they can plow it easy or not.
    Our company is going on picket tomorrow. I should like to see you all very well. Will is getting along very well; he is satisfied as far as I know. We have a nice company now, if they were all here. We had an election the other day of Quartermaster. W. E. Carnes was elected over W. A. Bray.
    Write me word how all the girls are getting along. I will get Pa some salt next week if I can get it at a reasonable price, and if Pa wants a hundred pounds of rice I could get it for him and send it home by Charles Chriswell, as it is very cheap here.
    I have nothing more to write, so I will close. Write soon.

Your brother,

/s/ A. P. Adamson

William E. Carnes was disabled by disease, surrendered at Tallahassee, Florida, 10 May 1865, and paroled there 18 May 1865. William A. Bray was captured at Nashville 16 December 1864, interned at Camp Chase, and released on 12 June 1865.

LETTER NUMBER NINETEEN

Camp Bartow, Georgia
June 2nd 1862

Miss A. A. Adamson

Dear Sister,

I embrace this opportunity of dropping you a few lines this evening. This leaves me well as I have been since I have been in service. I have nothing interesting to communicate to you at the present time.

We have beautiful weather now and but little sickness to what there has been. This regiment has suffered considerably, since they have been in service, with sickness. Company A has lost nine or ten men; Company B, eight; Company D, six or seven; Company E, three; Company F, six; Company G, two; Company H, three; Company I, five; Company K, seven. I do not know whether Company C, commanded by R. G. Adkins, has lost anyone or not. The health of the regiment is fast improving.

I understand we will move tomorrow, or next day, about three miles up the Shell Road. The new gunboat, Savannah, will soon be completed. It will do good fighting if it ever encounters the enemy, which it is very likely will be soon. The Yankees doubtless are preparing to attack the city. They have been going up in balloons several times for the purpose of viewing our works. Forty vessels are lying in the vicinity of Fort Pulaski, it is said.

The great battle so long looked for here is near at hand, in my opinion. But if they attack us, they will receive a hearty welcome from our forts and batteries. It is the opinion of some they will never be able to take the city, but their gunboats are so many they will be hard to repulse. I am tired of doing nothing. I would be glad if they would try it, although it may be deferred some time yet.

I have heard with pleasure of the victories of Stonewall Jackson in Virginia and they have had a tendency to rouse the desponding spirits of many who had begun to doubt of our being finally successful. I hope ere this time that indomitable warrior has entered Maryland, where I trust he will be joined by thousands of true sons of that degraded state, rendered degraded by the treachery of the notorious Hicks.

Jackson, I expect, is as good a General as we have in the field, and as he has been successful in routing the army of Milroy, ---------, and Banks, I trust he may also succeed at Baltimore in routing that of General ---------- and at once push the war into Pennsylvania and New Jersey. I heard yesterday that one force had repulsed the enemy between Richmond and Williamsburg.

Some think we will go to South Carolina before a week. We drawed money last Saturday, but instead of drawing $122 as Col. Bailey thought we would, we only got $22. $25 was held back for uniforms, the bounty was not paid, and $25 for letting.

I went to Savannah to try to buy Pa some salt but failed to do so. Mr. Stark, the man I tried, had just sold the last barrel at $50.00. It is impossible to get any in Savannah for less, and hard to get at that. I have a few clothes I should like to send home.

I will send them by express if there is no way of sending them in care of someone. General Mercer is now in Charleston, and a portion of his brigade, and if the enemy does not make a move in a short time we will go there, too.

I have nothing more to write, so I will close. Write soon.

Your brother,

/s/ A. P. ADAMSON

There were several ships christened *CSS Savannah*. The one that A.P. is discussing here is probably the ironclad steam sloop built by H.F. Willink at

Savannah and completed in 1863. On 30 June 1863 she was transferred to the Confederate States Navy under the command of Flag Officer W.W. Hunter, CSN. Under Commander R.F. Pinkney, CSN, she maintained her reputation as the most efficient vessel of the squadron. She was burned on 21 December 1864 by the Confederates so as to prevent her capture by General Sherman.

At the time of this letter, at the beginning of June, Virginia Confederate Lt. Gen. Thomas J. "Stonewall" Jackson had fought a series of brilliantly managed battles: First Kernstown with 3,000 soldiers against Union Gen. James Shields' 10,000 on 23 March (a tactical defeat, but unquestioned strategic victory); the 8 May victory at McDowell; the 23 May victory at Front Royal; and followed by the complete routing of the army of Gen. Nathaniel P. Banks at First Winchester on 25 May.

The reference to balloons is an intriguing one. Balloons were first used in the defense system around Washington on 18 June 1861. This initiated the United States "aeronaut corps." Union balloons were made of pongee silk and filled with hydrogen gas. On 24 September 1861, artillery fire was directed from a Union balloon near Falls Church, Virginia - the first time in military history that artillerists successively hit targets that they could not see being directed from an observer in a balloon. Due to the inventor's disgust with the military bureacracy, the project fell into desuetude in 1863. Confederate forces made their first ascent in the Spring of 1862 at Yorktown, Virginia. Due to shortages of required matériel, Southern balloons were manufactured of cotton coated over with an airtight material and inflated with hot air. The concept was eventually abandoned. There is little written in regard to the use of balloons at Savannah. However, there are numerous references to secesh balloons being flown at the siege of Charleston.

The "Notorious Hicks" is referenced in this correspondence. Maryland Gov. Thomas Hicks was an unabashed Unionist who refused to call the legislature into a special session until after the War had begun. No doubt he realized that if he had called the legislature into session earlier, that the probable scenario would have brought about a state convention, and a convention would probably have opted for secession. He had the state government moved to pro-Union Frederick and out of pro-Secession Annapolis when he did call the state legislature into session. On 19 April 1861, there was a bloody collision in Baltimore when a Massachusetts regiment passed through. Baltimore was pro-secessionist in its sentiments. Lincoln feared for his national capitol should Maryland decide on secession. Numerous citizens, including the Mayor of Baltimore and 19 members of the legislature, were seized by soldiers and thrown into prison. Military control was exerted, and the right under the Constitution to the writ of *habeas corpus* ignored. The opportunity to democratically vote on the issue of union or secession was forestalled from occurence.

LETTER NUMBER TWENTY

Camp Bartow
29th Regt. Georgia Vols.
June 11th 1862

Dear Sister,

I avail myself of this opportunity of addressing you a few lines, which leaves me in the enjoyment of health. Nothing of an interesting character has transpired here of late.

When I last wrote you I expected it to be the last letter that I should write from this place, but I was mistaken. It is true we received orders to move to Charleston, S. C. On Sunday night last Col. Mangham gave orders to cook four days rations, as we had orders to be ready at a moment's warning.

The regiment was in a perfect uproar at the reception of those orders. They were highly exultant at the thought of leaving. We immediately began to cook, and cooked four days rations, but on Monday we received different orders, which was a severe chagrin to some.

We are ordered to remain closer but to move to Thunderbolt. We cleaned out a camp ground yesterday and we will move tomorrow in about a quarter of a mile of Thunderbolt. I am very willing to stay here, as I believe this climate agrees with me.

The number of the several companies have been changed as follows: Company A, Capt. Henry Hendrick; Company B, Capt. R.

M. Hitch; Company C, Capt. W. N. McGouirk; Company D, Capt. Hudson Whitaker; Company E, Capt. C. A. Dollar; Company F, Capt. R. J. Andrews; Company G, Capt. F. M. Harrell; Company H, Capt. John Edmondston; Company I, Capt. Felix L. Walthall; Company K, Capt. George F. Longino.

This change makes us the center company and if we should be called into battle the center company would, as is commonly the case, bear the brunt of the battle. On Monday night a fight took place on the Savannah River below Fort Jackson. The firing lasted minutes and could be heard distinctly to this place, but the enemy were forced to retire after some time.

We hear of brilliant victories every day in Northwestern Virginia. It seems that Jackson has routed not only Banks, but has badly whipped Fremont and Shields. I regret to hear of the death of General Turner Ashby, who I considered as second to Morgan in point of courage.

J. T. Sanders, W. J. Adamson, and myself sent a box home. Started it yesterday morning. We did not pay the freight for fear it would have to be paid again. You can tell Pa that the box is Will's.

We will probably draw our bounty before many days, as some of the companies have already drawn. I have nothing else to write, so I will close. I want you to write to me soon as possible.

Nothing more at present, but remain your brother, etc.

/s/ A. P. ADAMSON

By the date of this letter, 11 June 1862, the entire South would have known of the breathtaking twin victories fought by Stonewall Jackson's troops at Cross Keys against General Frémont on 8 June, and Port Republic against General Shields on 9 June. His 17,000 man "foot cavalry" marched 400 miles in 38 days, outmaneuvered several Yankee armies that outnumbered them many times, fought and was victorious in five battles, inflicted two and a half times more casualties than they suffered, collected immense quantities of captured matériel, and chased the armies of Milroy, Frémont, Shields, and Banks out of the Valley in one of the most studied campaigns in American history.

Union Maj. Gen. Nathaniel Prentiss Banks, a prominent Massachusetts politician, was the fourth ranking officer of the Union army. Banks is best categorized as inept. He was ofttimes defeated by Stonewall Jackson. Likewise, when he was assigned as commander at New Orleans, he had one preordained victory (Port Hudson), and the chagrining defeats of Mansfield (8 April 1864) and Pleasant Hill (9 April 1864). The U.S. Congress awarded him with the offical "Thanks of Congress" for his efforts. He was one of only 14 Northern officers to be so recognized!

California's first senator and 1856 presidential aspirant, Maj. Gen. John Charles Frémont, was known as the "Pathfinder" for his Western explorations. He was defeated several times and finally resigned in high dudgeon. Frémont was execrated by many for his reprehensible and petulant conduct in shelling the ambulances, stretcher-bearers, and the wounded still remaining on the field at the conclusion of the Battle of Port Republic!

Virginia Confederate Brig. Gen. Turner Ashby was Stonewall's cavalry commander in the Valley. Independent, intrepid, and resourceful, he was killed in battle on 6 June 1862. At one point, Union Major General Banks and an army of 19,000 troops were held up at a creek crossing for six days by Ashby and 600 of his men!

Kentucky Confederate cavalry Gen. John Hunt Morgan conducted a series of successful and famous partisan raids into Union held territory. He was idolized in the South, excoriated in the North. He was killed by Union troops under questionable circumstances on 4 September 1864.

Because the Confederate military never had enough men, states were assigned recruitment quotas. If a sufficient number of men volunteered, it was unnecessary to implement conscription. In order to avoid conscription and fill the quotas with volunteers, the states and the counties in turn, would offer monetary enticements in the form of bounties to men to enlist or re-enlist when their enlistments terminated. If those with enlistments terminating chose not to re-enlist, they could become subject to conscription. Prior to the April draft legislation, the Confederate Congress, in January 1862, enacted The Bounty and

Furlough Act offering $50 and a 30-60 day leave to one-year volunteers who re-enlisted for two more years.

SUGGESTED READING

Allan, William, STONEWALL JACKSON'S VALLEY CAMPAIGN, Konecky & Konecky, New York (1995).

Casdorph, Paul D., LEE AND JACKSON: CONFEDERATE CHIEFTAINS, Dell Publishers, New York (1992).

Castel, Albert, GENERAL STERLING PRICE AND THE CIVIL WAR IN THE WEST, Louisiana State University Press, Baton Rouge (1993).

Cooling, Benjamin Franklin, FORTS HENRY AND DONELSON: THE KEY TO THE CONFEDERATE HEARTLAND, The University of Tennessee Press, Knoxville (1987).

Daniel, Larry J., SHILOH: THE BATTLE THAT CHANGED THE CIVIL WAR, Simon & Schuster, New York (1997).

Davis, William C., BATTLE AT BULL RUN: A HISTORY OF THE FIRST MAJOR CAMPAIGN OF THE CIVIL WAR, Louisana State University Press, Baton Rouge (1977).

Farwell, Byron, STONEWALL: A BIOGRAPHY OF GENERAL THOMAS J. JACKSON, W.W. Norton & Company, New York (1992).

Hearn, Chester G., THE CAPTURE OF NEW ORLEANS, Louisiana State University Press, Baton Rouge (1995).

Krick, Robert K., CONQUERING THE VALLEY: STONEWALL JACKSON AT PORT REPUBLIC, William Morrow and Company, Inc., New York (1996).

Lonn, Ella, SALT AS A FACTOR IN THE CONFEDERACY, University of Alabama Press (1965).

Martin, David G., JACKSON'S VALLEY CAMPAIGN, NOVEMBER 1861-JUNE 1862, Combined Books, Inc., Conshohocken, Pennsylvania (1994).

Martin, David G., THE SHILOH CAMPAIGN, MARCH - APRIL 1862, Combined Books, Inc., Conshohocken, Pennsylvania (1996).

McDonough, James Lee, SHILOH - IN HELL BEFORE NIGHT, The University of Tennessee Press, Knoxville (1977).

Purdue, Howell, and Elizabeth Purdue, CLEBURNE: CONFEDERATE GENERAL, Hill Jr. College Press, Hillsboro, Texas (1973).

Robertson, James I., Jr., STONEWALL JACKSON: THE MAN, THE SOLDIER, THE LEGEND, Macmillan Publishing, New York (1997).

Schiller, Herbert M., SUMTER AVENGED! THE SIEGE & REDUCTION OF FORT PULASKI, White Mane Publishing Company, Shippensburg, Pennsylvania (1995).

Symonds, Craig L., STONEWALL OF THE WEST: PATRICK CLEBURNE & THE CIVIL WAR, University Press of Kansas, Lawrence, Kansas (1997).

Tanner, Robert G., STONEWALL JACKSON IN THE VALLEY: THOMAS J. "STONEWALL" JACKSON'S SHEANANDOAH VALLEY CAMPAIGN, SPRING 1862, Doubleday & Company, New York (1976).

Thomas, Edison H., JOHN HUNT MORGAN AND HIS RAIDERS, The University Press of Kentucky, Lexington (1975).

Williams, T. Harry, P.G.T. BEAUREGARD: NAPOLEON IN GRAY, Louisiana State University Press, Baton Rouge (1955).

Sojourns of a Patriot

CHAPTER THREE

"Sparring near Savannah."

The South fought because it was invaded; indeed Virginia withdrew from the Union only because Lincoln intended invasion of the earlier seceded states. Then there were alien feet upon the soil of old Virginia - and in due course upon Georgia - and Southerners fought to defend what men hold dear, their homes and their land, not for conquest.

But the simple truth is that the South fought for freedom, the freedom to go their own way, the freedom to govern themselves. They had exercised this freedom, but the North denied it and invaded. Two societies, two ways of life, clashed: at issue was the compelled conformity of the smaller to the larger.

Sheldon Vanauken.

LETTER NUMBER TWENTY-ONE

Camp Hardee
30th Regiment, Georgia Vols.
June 22nd, 1862

Dear Sister,

I once more avail myself of an opportunity of writing you a few lines although I have nothing interesting to write. This leaves me well and enjoying myself finely and I hope this may find you the same.

There has been a great deal of excitement here occasioned mainly by the movement of troops from this portion of the country, but the excitement has subsided and everything is quiet here now. I am very glad our regiment did not go to Charleston when we were ordered to hold ourselves in readiness. I had much rather stay here. This is, I have no doubt, as healthy a location as we could find. The health of our regiment is excellent; as well as could be expected.

I would be glad if our regiment was full. We have the largest company here and I wish it was larger and I have no doubt it would have been full had it not been for the lying reports circulated in reference to the health of the troops composing this regiment, which, it is true, has been bad to a considerable extent, but not as bad was reported. But here there are some who are base enough to circulate any kind of reports that would impair our company. If those who have opposed our company from the beginning and who, if they would dare, show themselves here, they would meet with but little courtesies from our company. You are doubtless well aware to whom I allude to.

We are now stationed near Thunderbolt and have a good deal of duty to do at this time. Our regiment is now engaged in blockading the river below Thunderbolt. We also furnish pickets for Dutch Island, a small island some three miles from here. The new gunboat, or floating battery, in Savannah is nearly completed and if the Yankees attempt any unusual demonstration upon the city they will doubtless meet with a welcome reception from this battery.

Col. R. H. Anderson and Major E. C. Anderson went to Fort Pulaski the other day under a flag of true to exchange some prisoners when they were informed by General Terry, the Federal Commander, that both Charleston and Savannah would be taken in thirty days; but this is not the first time we have heard such, and I do not apprehend much danger of an attack from them.

There are not very many regiments left here now. Col. Wilson's 25th Georgia went to Charleston but have come back again. Col. Charlton H. Way's, Cols. Young's and Harrison's regiments are here yet. Col. William N. Stiles' regiment is either in Virginia or North Carolina. The 36th Tennessee Regiment, which have been here some time, left a few days ago for Knoxville. The 4th Louisiana Battalion are at Charleston.

I should not be surprised if we don't remain here some time yet, at least I hope so. We get plenty to eat now, as much as we go through with. We have excellent officers, too, except Bailey, who is absent now, which leaves Mangham in command, who is as good a commander as we could get. Capt. Dollar is absent now but we look for him back towards the last of the week.

We drawed our bounty last week and I would send mine home if I had an opportunity but know of no way to do so but to send it by express, which I may do.

I understand that Capt. Albert's company was badly cut up in the Battle of Chickahominy. I would be glad to see a list of the casualties in that company, being as that many of them are my former schoolmates and acquaintances.

I have just been reading Joseph E. Brown's letter to the President in reference to the Conscription Act and I think it is a noble document and will be endorsed by nearly every soldier in the field, as well as the friends of States Rights at home. I believe it would be a great deal better if we had Old Joe at the head of our government in the place of Jeff Davis, although I may be mistaken in thinking so.

I heard today that Capt. Huie's company had been in a fight and that James W. Adamson was badly wounded. Private Green Mitchell of Capt. Hitch's company died on Wednesday, which is the

"Sparring near Savannah."

only one of our regiment that has died lately. I have nothing more to write and my paper is out; I will close. Write soon.

Yours, etc.

/s/ A. P. ADAMSON

The reference to going to Charleston was no doubt caused by the consternation at the attack on that city's defenses by the army led by Union Gen. David Hunter. The beleaguered Confederates under Gen. John Clifford Pemberton were typically out-numbered and out-provisioned. Nevertheless, on 16 June 1862 they were victorious in the defensive Battle of Secessionville fought on James Island near Charleston. Had they been defeated, Charleston would likely have fallen to the foe. The immediate Southern commander was Gen. Nathan George "Shanks" Evans, and the on site commander was artillerist Col. Thomas Gresham Lamar, ever afterwards known as the "Hero of Secessionville." The sand fortification then known as the Tower Battery was renamed Fort Lamar. A.P. was distant kin to Colonel Lamar. The Yankee attack of some 6,500 was bloodily repulsed by less than 2,000 Confederates in hand-to-hand combat. The soldiers of the mentioned 4th Louisiana Battalion were part of the troops sent to Secessionville from the Savannah defenses.

Col. Robert H. Anderson commanded the 1st Georgia Infantry Battalion Sharpshooters, organized 20 June 1862 - only two days before this letter. Maj. Edward C. Anderson, Jr., became the second in command of the 22nd Georgia Siege Artillery Battalion when it was officially organized 26 November 1862. Connecticut Union Brig. Gen. Alfred H. Terry rose to his general's star resulting from his machinations with Connecticut politicians after the fall of Fort Pulaski. His artillery component was in part responsible for the reduction of that fortification.

Charlton H. Way was colonel of the 54th Georgia Infantry, George P. Harrison the colonel of the 32nd Georgia Infantry, William J. Young colonel of the 29th Georgia Infantry, and William H. Stiles, Jr., colonel of the 60th Georgia Infantry.

According to the National Archives records, first cousin James Wilson Adamson was wounded at the Battle of White Oak Swamp, near the Chickahominy Creek, on 30 June 1862. This battle is also known as Frayser's Farm or Glendale. He served in Co. D, 44th Georgia Infantry, as did four other family members - one received a disability discharge, one was mortally wounded at the 26 June 1862 Battle of Beaver Dam Creek, and one killed-in-action at the same battle. Beaver Dam Creek is also known as the Battle of Mechanicsville or Ellerson's Mill. The 44th Georgia participated in the repulsed charge at Beaver Dam Creek that caused it to have 335 casualties or a 65.1% loss of those engaged at this battle. As noted, two of A.P.'s cousins were part of this jarring loss. Additionally, James Wilson Adamson died in a Richmond hospital of typhoid fever on 16 October 1862. Both of these battles were part of the Seven Days Battles fought near Richmond, Virginia from 25 June through 1 July 1862 by Virginia Gen. Robert Edward Lee and Pennsylvania Gen. George Brinton McClellan. Although vastly out-numbered, Lee repulsed the Yankee invasion and brilliantly pitched it back to its supply base from which it later evacuated the peninsula altogether. The estimable Lee legend had its impetus here.

Typhoid was termed "camp fever" or "swamp fever," and was caused by ingesting contaminated water or food. Lack of proper sanitation for new volunteers not used to the discipline necessary for large groups led to typhoid being responsible for one-fourth of all disease deaths. This bacteria-borne disease's non-specific early symptoms of headache, fever and body aches appeared within two weeks of contact. The fever would rise, and within three weeks the patient would be emaciated, prostrate, and afflicted with delirium. The doctors generally treated the symptoms, and not the disease. Both armies learned the importance of sanitation during the progress of the War, so that by the end typhoid was almost eradicated.

Pvt. Green Mitchell, Sr. died in Savannah in 1862; Pvt. Green Mitchell, Jr. died in Savannah in 1863.

LETTER NUMBER TWENTY-TWO

Camp Hardee
30th Regiment, Georgia Vols.
July 4th, 1862

Dear Sister,

I avail myself of the present opportunity of writing you a few lines, which leaves me well. I have nothing to write that will interest you.

We have moved again, but only about three hundred yards nearer Thunderbolt. We had a hard rain last night accompanied by some wind and hail. It was the hardest that has fell since we have been down here. Our regiment has drawed 400 new Enfield rifles. They were brought here yesterday.

We hear glorious news from Virginia all the time. Some are inclined to believe that we will be on the way to Virginia to bag some Yankees but I put no confidence in the reports, although it is said that Col. Bailey has written to Col. Mangham to that effect.

We will get several vacancies for officers because of a reorganization of the regiment within the next ten days. They are nearly done. Our officers are being examined to test their competency to fill these places.

We will draw money again in a few days. I suppose strict military discipline is being enforced in this regiment at least, and it is the best for us that it should be.

I would be glad if Ma would send me a quilt or a blanket before long. I want nothing heavy. I am not particularly needing it as present but will in a month or so. Mr. Huie will be down before long, I suppose. If so, she can send it. If she sends a quilt, let it be a thin one because I have enough things to carry now. I have nothing else to write now, so I will close. Write soon.

Your brother,

/s/ A. P. ADAMSON

[P.S] I will send Pa sixty dollars by -------- .

From BRIEF HISTORY OF THE THIRTIETH GEORGIA REGIMENT, A. P. Adamson, 1912: "In July 1862 the regiment was armed with new Enfield Rifles and a proud body of men they were when they appeared on dress parade with their new guns."

The Enfield rifled musket was normally manufactured by the Royal Small Arms Factory in Enfield, England. Most of those sold to the South, however, were manufactured by private contractors in London or Birmingham. It fired .577 caliber ammunition, just fractionally smaller than the Union's .58 caliber Springfield rifle. and therefore close enough for Confederate ammunition to be used in captured Springfields. It weighed nine pounds, three ounces with its bayonet. It fired a bullet similar to the minié ball, was accurate at 800 yards, and relatively accurate at 1,100 yards. It was sighted in to 1,100 yards. It was generally held that its accuracy in combat was superior to the Springfield. The Model 1853 Enfield had an overall length of 55 inches and a barrel length of 39 inches. Perhaps as many as 400,000 of this popular weapon were imported into the South by blockade-runners. This rifled musket was loaded using 20 separate motions in nine steps according to the standard infantry text of the time, Hardee's RIFLE AND LIGHT INFANTRY TACTICS. The gun fired a cone-shaped 530 grain lead bullet with a hollow base which expanded upon firing into the grooves of the bore. Premade paper cartridges contained the ball and the proper amount of powder to be inserted down the barrel. A separate copper percussion cap containing half a grain of fulminate of mercury set off the powder and fired the powder and projected the ball. The cap was placed over a nipple that had a hole through it to the breech. Pulling the trigger caused the hammer to crush the cap shooting a flame through the nipple to the powder. A firing rate of three rounds per minute was considered quite good.

LETTER NUMBER TWENTY-THREE

Camp Hardee
30th Regiment, Georgia Vols.
July 13th, 1862

Dear Sister,

    I take the present opportunity of writing you a few lines, which leaves me enjoying excellent health, and hope these few lines may find you enjoying the same. I have nothing interesting to write at this time. We have heard of nothing for some time but the last battles that could interest anyone. I received yours and Pa's letters in due time and was glad to hear from you all again.

    Our regiment is partly armed with guns which are called Enfield rifles, but they are nothing extra, in my opinion. The number of our regiment has been changed to that of the 30th. That was caused by the reorganization of the regiment, I suppose.

    I regret to hear of such heavy losses as our army met with in the late battles around Richmond and I hear the victory gained was not as complete as reported. I consider it a dearly bought victory and cost our army many a valuable life. Some are inclined to believe this war will terminate in a short time but I cannot think so. I fear it will last a long time yet.

    I went to church to Mr. Smith about a mile from here this evening. There was a couple married there by Reverend A. B. Fears. They were a Mr. Tompkins and Miss Emma Johnson, the former is a member of Millen's Cavalry Battalion, the latter a Carolinian.

    You can inform Patty that she does not receive any thanks for meddling with what does not concern here, and I thought she had more respect for herself than to act so. I am not ashamed to acknowledge that I have written a few letters to Miss ---------- , but it is few and I do not think it is anyone else's business. I write very few letters except those written home, and even if I did it is my own business. But I should like to know your reasons for thinking that I had written two other girls, which you alluded to some time since, but you are mistaken sometimes.

I hope you will write to me every chance. There is no prospect of any of us going home in a long time. The old men, and boys under 18, will not get out of here before the 16th July.

Yours, etc.

/s/ A. P. ADAMSON

Lt. Col. John M. Millen commanded the 20th Georgia Cavalry Battalion, also known as the 20th Partisan Rangers Battalion. This unit was organized with seven companies in May 1862, only two months prior to this letter.

These letters are now being posted from Camp Hardee, Chatham County, Georgia. Camp Hardee was presumably named for Georgia Confederate Maj. Gen. William Joseph Hardee. The 30th was stationed here from 12 June to 4 October, 15 October to 22 October, and 24 October to 10 November 1862.

LETTER NUMBER TWENTY-FOUR

Camp Hardee
30th Regiment,
Georgia Volunteers
July 21st, 1862

Dear Father,

I take the present opportunity of sending you a few lines, which leaves me well and hoping these few lines may find you the same. I have nothing to write that will interest you.

We have had rain here in abundance for the last week. We have received four recruits the past week. Their names are William Meeks, J. W. Allen, A. J. Hutchinson, G. Strickland, and we have 99 men in our company now. I don't know what the government is keeping so many troops around for when they could be of service elsewhere and are none here. But I prefer remaining here on account of the health of our regiment.

The following is a list of the sick in our company, none of whom are abed; all can knock around: G. B. Stephens, W. Meeks, A. Betterton, M. H. Huie, and J. B. Smith. This is doing very, very well. We have got used to camp, and being exposed don't hurt them like it used to.

Col. Bailey is not going back yet and it will be better for us if he never comes back. I give you a list of my mess: J. T. Sanders, H. L. Hamilton, J. H. Buchanan, W. J. Adamson, and William Meeks.

Will wants you to get his watch and, if there is any silversmith in Jonesboro, have it repaired. If not, send it the way it is the first chance that offers. Mr. Huie probably will come down in a short while. He wrote a letter yesterday but forgot to write to his wife about it.

I will be glad to see you down here this summer. You won't have nothing to do and I think you might afford to come. I will send this, I think, by Judge Smith or B. Hightower, one or the other. I have nothing else to write, so I will close. Hoping you will write again soon, I remain your son, etc.

/s/ A. P. ADAMSON

Savannah, Georgia
Box 800
30th Regt. Ga. Vols.
Care Capt. Dollar

William W. Meeks of Co. E enlisted 1 July 1862 and died in the General Hospital at Augusta, Georgia 24 May 1863. Joseph M. Allen of Co. E enlisted in the summer of 1862, was wounded at Pine Mountain on 14 June 1864, again wounded at Jonesboro 31 August 1864, and wounded a third time with permanent disability at Franklin on 30 November 1864. G.N. Strickland enlisted in Co. C and survived the War. "Will," of course, refers to A.P's cousin and mess-mate, William J. Adamson.

Our correspondent notes that there are now 99 men in his company. This is almost maximum capacity for a company in either army. During the

War Between the States both armies had similar structure. The basic organization called for 100 men per company, 10 companies per regiment (*ergo*, about 1000 men per regiment), and 4 to 6 regiments per brigade (*ergo* 4 to 6,000 men per brigade). A Confederate division had four plus brigades. Confederate divisions were larger than there Union counterparts, which had only 3 brigades when fully manned. These were optimum unit figures. As a practical matter, companies, regiments, brigades, and divisions were invariably below strength. At the end of the War, many Southern regiments that had proudly marched off in 1861 with over a thousand men, had fewer than a dozen walk home.

Green B. Stephens enlisted 1 May 1862, was captured near Nashville on 16 December 1864, and interned at POW Camp Chase. Adolphus D. Betterton enlisted on the same date as Green, was also captured near Nashville and sent to POW Camp Chase. Mathew H. Huie likewise enlisted 1 May 1862, was captured at Calhoun with A.P., and interned at POW Rock Island. Joseph B. Smith enlisted 1 May 1862, transferred to Co. D, 1st Battalion Georgia Sharpshooters, was elected corporal, and killed by the explosion of a shell at Fort McAllister near Savannah on 12 February 1863.

LETTER NUMBER TWENTY-FIVE

Camp Hardee
30th Regt. Ga. Vols.
August 11th, 1862

Dear Brother,

I take the pleasure of writing you a few lines by C. Chriswell. I am well at this time, with the exception of a slight cold. All the old men over 35 years have been discharged and leave for home today. I hope I shall get a furlough to come home before long; in about two weeks, I think.

Our company are on picket today. I did not have to fight certain, for there is plenty of Yankees there. They also have a hospital there.

"Sparring near Savannah."

I have nothing of importance to write. I hope to hear from you soon and every chance. I will close for the present.

/s/ A. P. ADAMSON

Charles Chriswell enlisted as a private on 25 September 1861, and was discharged for being "overage" on 21 August 1862, ten days from the date of this correspondence.

LETTER NUMBER TWENTY-SIX

Camp Hardee
30th Regt. Ga. Volunteers
September 14th, 1862

Dear Sister,

I again embrace the opportunity of dropping you a few lines, which leaves me well at this time. I have nothing interesting to write at present. The health of the regiment is very good at present. There is very little sickness in camps.

I enjoyed my trip back to camp finely. We came the most of the way in the daytime, which afforded us the opportunity of having a good view of the country, which is very beautiful in many places, especially in Washington, Jefferson and Burke Counties. We got to Savannah about eleven o'clock and walked out to camp and arrived here about two o'clock.

That little sack of beans I started with was left in the care of the boys that laid over in Macon and was lost through their negligence. You can tell Ma to send me some by Jessie Sanders; also some potatoes, onions, and butter, if convenient to do so. I would have sent Pa some salt but it has risen to eight dollars per bushel and it is said to be sorry, but I will send it anyhow, if he wants it, as soon as I can.

Two men are to be baptized here today, to go to any church they desire upon a recommendation.

Our regiment has two islands to picket now, viz: Dutch Island and Whiteman's, which makes guard duty heavy upon us.

Write to me every chance that you have to do so. I will have to close for the present. Nothing more, but remain your brother, etc.

/s/ A. P. ADAMSON

P. S. We drawed our money yesterday evening. I drew $28.50 for my part, etc.

Augusta Adamson

In a number of his letters A.P. appropriately discusses religious activities. Religion played a conspicuous rôle in his regimen. In fact, it transcended the ranks. The cohesiveness of the Southern armies in general, and the Army of Tennessee in particular (organizationally, the 30th Georgia was soon to be associated with the Army of Tennessee), cannot be fully comprehended without considering its religious pilgrimage.

Both armies professed their belief in the same God, in many cases followed the identical catechism, sang the same hymns, and looked to their chaplains for succor. Withal, there was a remarkable surge of evangelism in the Confederate armies. Public prayer meetings became more frequent. Not only did preaching become more common, but the number of baptisms increased demonstrably, as this letter indicates. In the spring of 1863 revivalism began in the Army of Tennessee. During the winter and spring of 1863, more than 150,000 Southern soldiers became Christians. In the fall of 1863 meetings were reported at Missionary Ridge, Chickamauga Station, and Tyner Station. This spiritual outpouring reached a crescendo during the Dalton winter encampment of 1863-1864. On 1 May 1864 alone, more than three hundred baptisms and five hundred professions of faith were counted in the army. Sixty joined the church in Gen. States Rights Gist's Brigade. On 4 May, one of the last nights in Dalton, over a thousand men in one Georgia brigade assembled to hear preaching. This collectively became known as the "Great Revival." It was clearly inter-denominational. In the spring of 1863, the Army of Tennessee chaplains passed a strict resolution against sectarian preaching. Each regiment had a chaplain in theory; in practice all regiments did not have the requisite chaplain. And, this conversion phenomenon was not reserved for merely the enlisted men. Such notables as President Davis and Generals Bragg, Ewell, Hood, Hardee, and Joseph Johnston became members of the Church.

Lt. Gen. Leonidas Polk was an Episcopal bishop. Lee's chief of artillery, Brig. Gen. William Nelson Pendleton, was an ordained Episcopal priest. The great Stonewall preached Sunday School to the slaves before the War, and continually exercised his Presbyterianism in a sincere and pious fashion during the War, avowing that he wished not to fight on Sunday, although most of his salient victories were coincidentally achieved on Sundays! Robert E. Lee was known as a devout and Christian gentleman, and conducted himself accordingly. Religion became one of the fervent themes of the armies of Southern independence.

LETTER NUMBER TWENTY-SEVEN

Camp Hardee
30th Regt. Ga. Vols.
Sept. 23rd, 1862

Dear Sister,

I again embrace the opportunity of writing you a few lines in answer to yours, which I received on yesterday. This leaves me in very good health at this time and hope it may find you enjoying the same blessing. I have nothing interesting to write at the present time.

Will did not get off yesterday; now there is no telling when he will. I consider his chance very uncertain. Corporal John Gilmore of Company A was accidentally drowned near here on yesterday morning while going on picket to Dutch Island.

I intended to get Pa some salt but when I got back I could not get it. I hear it can be had in Savannah for $16 per bushel, but whether it is so I cannot say. Tell Miss Susan that I understand she is very much hurt at me but I cannot imagine what it can be about, but hope I was misinformed.

Israel Sanders and George Huie came to our company today as recruits. I heard Samuel Glass was coming but he did not come.

I heard a little talk yesterday that we would leave here soon but I put no confidence in the report. If we do leave here, I hope we will go where there is some fun going on.

I want you to write to me every chance you have. I have written all I can think of. Tell Felix that I ain't got time to write to him now as I am on guard today. Nothing more at present but remain your brother, etc.

/s/ A. P. ADAMSON

3rd Cpl. John Gilmore drowned near Thunderbolt on 22 September 1862. Israel Sanders presumably refers to Jesse T. Sanders who died in July 1864. George W. Huie, Jr., survived the War. Felix, of course, is A.P.'s younger brother.

LETTER NUMBER TWENTY-EIGHT

Camp Young
Near Savannah, Georgia
September 25th, 1862

Mr. W. F. Adamson

Dear Brother,

I take the opportunity of writing you a few lines which will inform you that I am well at this time. I received a letter from Augusta on Saturday last by J. C. Daniel but placed in the care of Wm. Meeks. I have nothing to write that will interest you.

The Yankee General, O. M. Mitchell, commanding the Yankees at Fort Royal and Beaufort, is dead. He died with Yellow Fever, which is raging at a considerable extent there. General Hunter, their old General, succeeds him. He is the man that made himself notorious in organizing a Negro brigade last spring. They expected to have a nice time under Mitchell but were badly disappointed.

You ought to have been down here some time ago and see old General Beauregard, but he is nothing but a Frenchman. He is dark complected and very much resembles the French, but I like his looks finely.

You can tell Ma, if she desires, she can send me a quilt or some covering if convenient to do so. If Will is yet at home sick he had better stay there and send back a certificate. Mr. Cook is here. He designs leaving today. I will send this letter by him; also, I will send Pa $15.00 by him.

Old Colonel Bailey is come back at last. We were all very glad to see the old coon again but it is thought he will resign soon. I have no time to write. They keep us continually on a stir. You must excuse this hasty written letter. Tell S. S. I will write to her soon, probably the next time I write, for I have not time now. So I will close for this time.

I remain your brother, etc.

/s/ A. P. ADAMSON

P. S. Write to me whether you have subscribed for the Countryman yet or not. The subscription rates will be raised after the first of January 1863. I am now taking the Constitutionalist. My time for the Southern Field and Fireside is out, but I shall take it again next year, it having suspended till then.

James C. Daniel enlisted 1 August 1862, was captured near Nashville on 16 December 1864, sent to POW Camp Chase, and released in June 1865.

Ohio Union Maj. Gen. Ormsby McKnight Mitchel wrote books on astronomy, practiced as a lawyer, and taught mathematics before the War. He was placed in command of the Department of the South and the X Corps on 17 September 1862. He died 30 October 1862 at Beaufort, South Carolina, of yellow fever. This dreaded summer epidemic was spread by mosquitoes. More than half of the victims died within a few days. The survivors were immunized by their experience. Ports were generally the entry mechanism from tropical areas. Many severe epidemics of Yellow Fever transpired during the War, especially in Southern port areas such as coastal North Carolina and the Mississippi River and the Gulf. A.P. states in this letter dated 25 September that Mitchel died of yellow fever. He then relates information of Mitchel's appointment in a later letter dated 3 October. His facts are correct, but his chronology is not on mark. Mitchel died of yellow fever 30 October, well after both of these letters. The editors have no explanation other than the conjectural. Putting aside Biblical prophecy and clairvoyance, A.P. could have dated a letter in the field and then actually not started to write it for several weeks; co-editor Abell experienced precisely this phenomenon in Viet-Nam. There could be present the usual rife camp rumors that often precede actual reality. Perhaps he mis-dated his own correspondence. We simply do not know.

Federal Maj. Gen. David Hunter was a friend of Pres. Abraham Lincoln. He was detested in the South for his slave emancipation in April 1862 that was promptly annulled by Lincoln, and hated for his meanspirited arson policy in the Shenandoah Valley. He was labelled as a "felon to be executed if captured." He disingenuously assumed the credit for the fall of Fort Pulaski. His field commander was defeated at Secessionville. He failed in his attempts to take Charleston, and was sent to the Shenandoah Valley from whence he was eventually shamefully evicted by Virginia Confederate Gen. Jubal Anderson Early. He later served on the military tribunal that tried the Lincoln conspriators.

The *Countryman* was a literary journal founded in 1861. It was edited and published at Turnwold, the plantation of J.A. Turner near Eatonton, Georgia, which had the hardihood to actually survive the War. Among the employees at the *Countryman* during the War was typesetter/writer Joel Chandler Harris, author of the "Uncle Remus" stories. The Augusta *Constitutionalist*, operated by James Gardner, was affiliated with the Press Association of the Confederate States of America. The *Southern Field and Fireside* was a farm and home journal published in Augusta, founded in 1859, and out of existence in 1864. Few Southern publications survived the rigors of supply shortages, severe inflation, and the destructive invasions of their homeland.

"Sparring near Savannah."

"S.S." is A.P.'s sister, Sarah Sophronia.

LETTER NUMBER TWENTY-NINE

Camp
30th Ga. Vols.
Oct. 3rd, 1862

Dear Sister,

I again take the opportunity of writing you a few lines, which leaves me well and hoping these few lines may find you enjoying the same blessing. I have nothing to write that is any ways interesting.

Time is dull here, with now and then a little excitement. The Yankees are getting some bolder than they have been heretofore. On the day before yesterday they came in about three miles from Fort Jackson with two gunboats and shelled the marsh in every direction, evidently feeling for masked batteries and to get the range of our guns, which they failed to do. Only a few shots were fired at them from Carsten's Bluff.

They have a new commander here in the person of General O. M. Mitchell, who probably thought he would make us believe the campaign would be conducted in a different manner from his predecessor, General Hunter.

The Confederate troops at Charleston and on the coast of Georgia are now under the control of General Beauregard. General Pemberton has been transferred to Virginia.

I understand that the Clayton Companies in Virginia suffered severely at Sharpsburg, Maryland. It appears that the Confederates lost a number of valuable officers in that bloody conflict, but the loss of none will be more severely felt than that of General Branch of North Carolina who had already won a brilliant reputation in the Army of Virginia.

I also notice the death of Colonel Marcellus Douglas of the 13th; G. B. Smith of the 27th; W. R. Holmes of the 2nd Georgia Regiment;

and Jeff M. and J. B. Lamar of Cobb's Legion, all of whom were excellent officers and distinguished men.

I am rejoiced to hear of the success of our army in Kentucky under Smith and Bragg, but I fear this war will continue as long as Old King Abraham is at the head of the Federal Government.

This day twelve months ago I remember well, the day we left Jonesborough for Camp Bailey, but there is a wide difference between the condition of our country at that time and the present. But no one can tell what may befall our regiment in the next twelve months and have never had to face the enemy, but I don't think we will stay here much longer without meeting them, at least I hope not.

Hot times are expected here the coming Fall and Winter. The people around Savannah feel confident of holding the place (at least, a great many of them). I wish I could feel the same but I cannot think we will be successful here, although I hope we may. But I consider the prospect a bad one.

I should like to hear from Cousin George and if he is alive I wish he would get transferred to our company. I reckon Josiah Burks will be transferred to our company. He is very anxious to do so.

There is very little sickness here now. The regiment generally is very healthy. I will send this letter by J. M. Gallman, who I will also send twenty dollars by if he goes home this evening. I don't know when Will can get off; it may be shortly. I got the coat that Ma sent by T. A. Ward; it fits me very well. I have to close. I have written all I can think of. You must write to me soon and every chance. I will close by signing myself your affectionate brother,

/s/ A. P. ADAMSON

Louisiana Confederate Gen. Pierre Gustave Toutant Beauregard was in command at the taking of Fort Sumter. He was one of the two victorious Confederate commanders at First Manassas and did not get along well with President Davis. He took command at Shiloh upon the death of Gen. A.S. Johnston, successfully commanded at Charleston, S.C., for a year and a half with a force of under 20,000, and performed with panache at the 1864 Richmond and Petersburg battles. Pennsylvanian turned Confederate Lt. Gen.

John Clifford Pemberton performed well at Secessionville, but he was mediocre at best in the campaigns leading up to the Siege of Vicksburg and the city's subsequent surrender, with the result that he became a pariah thereafter. Nonetheless, he then loyally served as a lieutenant colonel in the trenches at Richmond until the War's end.

North Carolina Confederate Brig. Gen. L. O'Brien Branch was killed by a stray bullet at the southern end of Otto's Lane just as the battle of Sharpsburg ended on 17 September 1862.

In addition, A.P. notes the death of several other Southern colonels during the 17 September battle. Col. Marcellus Douglass of the 13th Georgia Infantry received eight gunshot wounds before collapsing and expiring in the fighting in the North Woods. Col. Levi B. Smith had commanded the 27th Georgia Infantry. Lt. Col. William R. Holmes, Jr., of the 2nd Georgia Infantry was positioned with his men on the heights overlooking the Burnside Bridge when he was cut down by rifle fire from the 51st New York while he was about to assist in remunitioning his troops. He died sword-in-hand while attempting to fulfill his vow to hold the bridgehead or die trying.

Lt. Col. Jefferson Mirabeau Lamar of Cobb's Georgia Legion, was killed at Crampton's Gap, South Mountain, Maryland on 14 September 1862. His kinsman Col. John Basil Lamar was likewise killed at the same action, dying in the arms of his brother-in-law, Gen. Howell Cobb. Through his grandmother, Sarah Coates, A.P. was kin to these two colonels. Both gentlemen gave their lives in a successful heroic delaying action at the narrow top of Crampton's Gap on South Mountain while Gen. Robert E. Lee re-united his separated corps elements. The Confederates had been surprised by the uncharacteristic Union advance due to the serendipitous discovery of a copy of Lee's battle orders by Indiana troops. Lee's army could have been easily defeated in detail as they were spread out. For several valuable hours the Confederates at the three gaps on South Mountain held up the Union army, to include those at Crampton's Gap who held at bay the 12,000 troops of the Federal VI Corps with a force of eight cannon and one-tenth the number of men as the Unionists. The next day, 15 September, Stonewall Jackson accomplished the single largest Confederate capture of Union troops in the War - over 12,000. The bloodiest day in

91

American history was 17 September 1862 - the Battle of Sharpsburg, also known as Antietam - with more than 24,000 casualties. Lee fought his 40,000 soldiers against Gen. George Brinton McClellan's 75,000 to a sanguinary stand-off pitting raw Southern intrepidity against poorly managed Union hordes.

In the summer of 1862, Rebel armies in the western theatre invaded Kentucky under Generals Kirby Smith and Braxton Bragg. General Smith commenced his march from Knoxville, Tennessee, into Kentucky bypassing the Federal army at Cumberland Gap. Smith and his subordinate, Gen. Patrick Cleburne, then soundly defeated a Federal force under Gen. William Nelson at the Battle of Richmond on 30 August 1862, taking over 4,000 prisoners. He then took Lexington and captured the state capitol, Frankfurt, on 3 October. Bragg's army invaded up from Chattanooga forcing the Unionist forces to retreat to Louisville. On 4 October, Confederate troops stood by while a new secessionist governor, Richard Hawes, was installed in Frankfurt. Several days later, on 7 October, occurred the Battle of Perryville - the largest battle fought on Kentucky soil. Terribly outnumbered, the Rebels characteristically attacked the army of Gen. Don Carlos Buell. Bragg's men were victorious that day inflicting a large number of casualties on the larger army. They crushed one wing of the Union army, but the Yankees held firm on the other wing. Realizing he was outnumbered, Bragg pulled his army back and retreated.

Florida Confederate Lt. Gen. Edmund Kirby Smith served with distinction at the victory of First Manassas. He was later identified with the Army of the Tennessee and the Trans-Mississippi Army. North Carolina Lt. Gen. Braxton Bragg had been a close friend of President Davis since their Mexican War experience, and controversially commanded several Southern armies. He had the reputation of being disputatious, paralyized with indecision in a crisis, thoroughly disliked by many of his subordinates, and loosing many of his battles. He lucked out at Perryville, lost an opportunity at Murfreesboro, and did not comprehend his victory at Chickamauga. He was embarrassingly replaced after his inability to pursue the Yankees after Chickamauga and their re-grouping for the Northern onslaughts at Lookout Mountain and Missionary Ridge.

A.P. references "Cousin George." He had three known cousin Georges: George M. Adamson of the 14th Alabama Infantry; George Taylor Adamson of the 47th Alabama Infantry; and, George Robert Adamson of Cobb's Georgia Legion. The latter George was wounded and captured at Crampton's Gap, exchanged, and served on medical details until his disability retirement in July 1864. There is no evidence that Josiah Burks was ever transferred to Co. E.

1st Lt. Thomas Alexander Ward may have been kin to A.P. through A.P.'s aunt, Martha Lamar Adamson, who married Hardy Ward in Henry County in 1829. T.A. Ward enlisted in 1861, was elected first lieutenant of Co. B, later served as ordnance sergeant, and surrendered in North Carolina in 1865. He was a boyhood chum of A.P. Hardy Ward, his wife Martha Lamar Adamson and their family moved to Alabama, as did so many of the other members of the extensive Adamson clan. There were two sons by this union that saw Confederate military service: Calvin Nathaniel Ward who served in the 4th Alabama Infantry from mid-1864 through the desolation of Appomattox; and, James Adamson Ward who reportedly died in a Confederate military hospital late in the War. Both of these men were first cousins to A.P. Further, co-editor Richard B. Abell is a descendant of James Adamson Ward!

SUGGESTED READING

Bilby, Joseph, CIVIL WAR FIREARMS: THEIR HISTORICAL BACKGROUND AND TACTICAL USE, Combined Books, Inc, Conshohocken, Pennsylvania (1996).

Brennan, Patrick, SECESSIONVILLE: THE ASSAULT ON CHARLESTON, Savas Publishing Co., Campbell, California (1996).

Cannan, John, THE ANTIETAM CAMPAIGN, AUGUST-SEPTEMBER 1862, Combined Books, Inc., Conshohocken, Pennsylvania (1990).

Coggins, Jack, ARMS & EQUIPMENT OF THE CIVIL WAR, The Fairfax Press, New York (1983).

Curry, Henry Lee, III, GOD'S REBELS: CLERGY IN THE CIVIL WAR, Huntington House, Inc., Lafayette, Louisiana (1990).

Hafendorfer, Kenneth A., PERRYVILLE: BATTLE FOR KENTUCKY, K H Press, Louisville (1991).

Martin, David G., THE PENINSULA CAMPAIGN MARCH-JULY 1862, Combined Books, Inc., Conshohocken, Pennsylvania (1992).

McWhiney, Grady, BRAXTON BRAGG AND CONFEDERATE DEFEAT, The University of Alabama Press, Tuscaloosa (1991).

Parks, Joseph H., GENERAL EDMUND KIRBY SMITH, C.S.A., Louisiana State University Press, Baton Rouge (1992).

Priest, John Michael, ANTIETAM: THE SOLDIERS BATTLE, Oxford University Press, New York (1994).

Priest, John Michael, BEFORE ANTIETAM: THE BATTLE FOR SOUTH MOUNTAIN, Oxford University Press, New York (1996).

Sears, Stephen W., LANDSCAPE TURNED RED: THE BATTLE OF ANTIETAM, Ticknor and Fields, New Haven, Connecticut (1983).

Sears, Stephen W., TO THE GATES OF RICHMOND: THE PENINSULA CAMPAIGN, Ticknor and Fields, New Haven, Connecticut (1992).

CHAPTER FOUR

"Florida Interlude."

We gain successes but after every fight there comes to me an ominous paper, maked 'Casualties,' 'killed' and 'wounded.' Sad words which carry anguish to so many hearts. And we have scarcely time to bury the dead as we press on in the same deadly strife. I pray for peace. I would not give peace for all the military glory won by Bonaparte.

Wade Hampton,
Lieutenant General, C.S.A.

"Florida Interlude."

LETTER NUMBER THIRTY

Savannah, Georgia
Oct. 3rd, 1862

Dear Father,

I have written to Augusta today but an unexpected event has taken place tonight. This evening after sunset the regiment was called together and an order read by Colonel Mangham ordering us to East Florida. We leave in the morning at four o'clock for Savannah to take the cars.

Our company is on picket today with the exception of about twenty men who are going under Lt. Huie. The rest of the company will be left behind. I don't know how long we will stay in Florida. Will and Jessie are both on picket and will not go with us.

I will have to close, as we are busy fixing to start. I will write again in a few days. So, nothing more at this time.

/s/ A. P. ADAMSON

[P.S.] It is now 9 o'clock. We leave Savannah at 8 tomorrow. Don't be uneasy about me, tell Ma.

LETTER NUMBER THIRTY-ONE

Camp near Jacksonville
Duval County, Florida
Oct. 7th, 1862

Dear Sister,

I once more take the opportunity of writing you a few lines, which leaves me well-and enjoying myself finely. We left Savannah on Saturday morning for this place to relieve General Finnegan. The 29th Georgia came with us. We arrived at Groover's Station on the

97

Gulf Road about eight o'clock at night. We then took up the line of march for Monticello, a distance of 22 miles through Brooks and Thomas Counties in Georgia and Jefferson County, Florida.

At about 2 o'clock Sunday we entered Florida and arrived at Monticello at 8 o'clock, at which place we laid over till 5 PM, when we left for Lake City, Columbia County, where we arrived soon on yesterday and left at 12 Noon for this place, where we arrived last night about dusk.

We are in six miles from Jacksonville, where the Yankees are. We have no tents, nothing but the canopy of Heaven above us. We have nothing to cook in, nor have we drawn any rations yet, but will draw today. We bought potatoes this morning at a dollar per bushel, which would have sold at $7 or $8 at Savannah. The troops here, judging from what I see, fare fully as well as those at Savannah.

I don't know when we will move toward the enemy. Our pickets run them into town on Sunday, killing three of them. I hear this morning they have left since hearing of the Georgia boys, but that is all camp talk.

The crops in this state are excellent, especially in Jefferson County. There they are better than in Georgia. In Georgia in the counties of Appling, Pierce, Lowndes, Clinch, Brooks and Thomas, the crops are as fine as ever I saw.

The only place of any importance we passed on the Gulf Road was Valdosta, the county seat of Lowndes County. It is a beautiful little village and has some of the prettiest kind of women.

No tongue can speak too praiseworthy of the excellent ladies of Monticello, Florida. You know, after walking 22 miles, we felt like eating. A portion of our line got there soon in the morning; others were so fatigued they failed to reach there till Sunday, but the ladies of Monticello prepared a bountiful dinner for them, and everything that was needed was readily supplied for them. I would have been glad to have stayed there a week or so.

At Lake City we met with the same reception from the ladies of that place. But here we see none of these benevolent ladies. Alas, they have been driven from their homes by the ruthless invaders of this beautiful land of flowers, yesterday morning. At Lake City they were run from their homes the preceding night. I really felt sorry for them.

There is no such ladies around Savannah as the Florida ladies, but we hope to drive the invaders from amongst them and let them return to their homes. This is a beautiful country. I expected to find a low, sandy, barren country, but I was mistaken. In places it is low and marshy, but this is a more beautiful country than lower Georgia.

Colonel Mangham left word for Captain Dollar to come with the rest of our company. We expect them in a day or so. About twenty of our company are here, to viz: Lt. Huie, Corpl. Hurdle, Color Sergt. W. S. Allen, Privates J. T. Allen, B. Z. Allen, J. Anthony, W. A. Bray, Bradberry, Boynton, Betterton, N. Baxley, Farr, N. J. and N. R. Hanrick, Lawrence, Langston, Meeks, Ozburn, Smith, and W. N. Stephens.

I don't know how long we will stay here. I have to close, as my paper is out. I remain your brother,

/s/ A. P. ADAMSON

The 29th and 30th Georgia Infantry Regiments were ordered to reinforce the command of Florida Brig. Gen. Joseph Finegan in East Florida on 4 October 1862 by the order of General Mercer. A joint Federal army-navy expediton had been launched against Jacksonville in March, the city occupied, and the Federals then withdrawn. It was re-occupied in October after the Confederates again evacuated. General Finnegan had pulled back from Jacksonville. Meanwhile, the 30th left Savannah and arrived at Groover's Station in Brooks County at 8:00 p.m. They then marched overland to Monticello, Florida, arriving there on the 5th. They left Monticello that evening for Lake City arriving there on the morning of the 6th. On the evening of the 6th, they arrived at Baldwin, only a few miles from Jacksonville. At this point they went into camp. The enemy was expected to advance. Instead they retreated onto their gunboats which lay at anchor in the river. It was then that Capt. Chaney Dollar and about twenty-five men slipped surreptitiously into Jacksonville, remaining on the streets near the river until daybreak when they left without being discovered. At this time Jacksonville had no Confederate troops therein, and the river was full of Yankee gunboats. We are not informed as to whether A.P. was one of those 25. We are also left to speculate as to how they passed their time! Dollar was known for such daring and adventure.

The regiment remained in the Jacksonville area until 11 October when they returned to Camp Hardee, arriving there 15 October. They remained at Camp Hardee until 14 December 1862 when they were assigned to Wilmington, North Carolina, arriving there 19 December 1862.

General Finegan was born in Ireland. As an attorney he was involved with railroad construction and served as a member of the Florida secession convention. Further, he was appointed as commander of the Military District of Middle and Eastern Florida. He was capable and industrious. In February 1864, with a numerically inferior army, he soundly defeated Federal forces at the Battle of Olustee, sixty miles west of Jacksonville, causing their precipitous retreat. Later he was transferred to Virginia and, with his Florida brigade, participated with distinction at the Battle of Second Cold Harbor. He survived the War.

CHAPTER FIVE

"Infantry Boredom."

The Confederate soldier was peculiar in that he was ever ready to fight, but never ready to submit to the routine duty and discipline of the camp or the march. The soldiers were determined to be soldiers after their own notion and do their duty for the love of it, as they thought best. The officers saw the necessity for doing otherwise, and so the conflict was commenced and maintained to the end.

Carlton McCarthy.

LETTER NUMBER THIRTY-TWO

Camp Hardee
30th Regiment Georgia Vols.
October 28th, 1862

Miss Augusta Adamson

Dear Sister,

 I again take the opportunity of writing you a few lines, which leaves me well and alright. I got Pa's letter yesterday and was truly glad to hear from you all.

 Yesterday was a busy day with us all, it being the day set apart by General Beauregard for the inspection of the troops around Savannah. We took an early start in the morning to march to the city. Quite a large crowd of spectators, as well as soldiers, were out to see the Hero of Mannassas. The inspection lasted some two hours. The General spoke, it is said, in high terms of the troops in this department, especially the cavalry, which were better than any he had seen in the West.

 I reckon you already know of our trip to South Carolina. I wrote to Pa about the time we left there and give the letter to a soldier to mail at Hardeeville. I like old South Carolina some better than I expected. We did not go very far out of this state. I suppose that Beaufort District, the district we were in, is the poorest part of the state.

 We heard that they were fighting here when we started back but it was only some of the many lying reports we hear. Furloughs are stopped by the order of General Mercer; no more will be allowed to go home.

 You will find an enigma in the Field and Fireside of last week that I sent to the editor for publication. It is composed of 85 letters.

 There is a good many of our regiment sick at the present time; two died last week, to viz: Private Strickland of Company C and Private Braswell of Company D. Several of our company are sick, but not very bad. It has been very cold here for the past few days. I was very glad to hear that Pa had heard from Cousin George. I hope he will try and get a transfer to our regiment.

We are now under the command of Colonel C. C. Walton, one of the finest looking men I ever saw. We have the best regiment around Savannah, both in men and officers, and I hope we will get a few more, as I see the Secretary of War has called for more men.

I believe I will have to close, as I have written all I can think of. Write to me as soon as you get this letter. I will close. I remain your brother,

/s/ A. P. ADAMSON

Quoting from BRIEF HISTORY OF THE THIRTIETH GEORGIA REGIMENT, A. P. Adamson 1912: "During the Spring and Summer of 1862 the regiment was largely recruited, conditions as to health had improved, and the regiment in the Fall of 1862 was a large and well-disciplined body of men, presenting a fine appearance on drill and dress parade."

It is interesting to note that A.P. is engaging himself in his spare time with intellectual conundrums in composing "enigmas" for *Field and Fireside.* Obviously they had merit to be published.

Pvt. W.C. Strickland of Co. C died in 1862. The Private Braswell of Co. D could not be identified. There were two Braswells in Co. D, but both survived the War.

A.P.'s reference to being under Col. C.C. Walton is perplexing. The 30th was never known to be under such a man, nor do the records for other Georgia regiments reveal his identity. The authors proffer no explanation, unless this is a mis-trancription.

LETTER NUMBER THIRTY-THREE

Camp near Savannah
November 9th, 1862

Dear Sister,

    I once more avail myself of the opportunity of dropping you a few lines, which will inform you that I am well at this time and hoping this may find you enjoying the same blessing. I received your letter a few days ago and was truly glad to hear from you and that you were all well. I have nothing interesting to write to you.
    Our regiment is moving at this time. Three companies moved on yesterday. Ours have not moved yet but will move tomorrow. Our new camp is situated about halfway between this and Savannah. I had rather remain here than to move.
    We had considerable frost here for the last two or three mornings. The nights here are very cool but the days are pleasant. I understand that N. R. Hamrick will go home this evening on furlough. If so, I will send this letter by him. Captain Dollar has returned from Florida. He got back night before last.
    We occasionally hear the roar of the Abolitionist cannon in the direction of Beaulier and Coffee Bluff, but they never have effected anything; but sharp work is expected here soon.
    There will no doubt be a strong effort made by the enemy to capture Savannah, Charleston, and Mobile; and that, in a short time. Whether they will succeed here or not, time will alone determine; but all seem willing to meet them. But before Savannah falls there will be a great deal of bloodshed. The authorities are evidently making preparations to hold this place at all hazards. They intend to emulate the heroic example shown by Vicksburg. Already there are preparations being made to remove the non-combatants from this city and let the city be destroyed rather than share the fate of New Orleans.
    You need not believe the many reports you hear in reference to our rations being short. It is true we get scarce at times but we can

expect nothing else. We always have plenty of bread. Meat is scarce but I am very well satisfied if we can make out all the time as well as now.

I want you to send me a list of the counties of the Southern States with the exception of Georgia, South Carolina and Kentucky. I already have them. I will send you an incomplete list of several states which you can examine, and, if any are wrong, mark them out and if any are lacking, add them to my list and send the same list back after completing it.

Virginia, Louisiana, Texas and Missouri, you will have to make a full list. The balance, you will find an incomplete list with this letter. Be certain to divide Virginia into its several sections. In my list I have not divided Alabama, Tennessee and Mississippi. I did not know how but can take my list and the list of the counties which you will know how to find and designate every county in North Alabama with a capital (N) as I have marked Coosa and Jackson and those in South Alabama with a capital (S) as you will see Dale, Dallas and Mobile.

In Mississippi, which is divided like Alabama, mark the Northern counties like I have marked Attala, and the Southern like Hinds, and Tennessee is divided into East, West and Middle. Those in East Tennessee, mark with an (E) as you will see Carter and Anderson; those in West Tennessee, mark with (W) as you will find Maury, Weakley and Shelby; and those in Middle Tennessee with a capital (M) like Davidson and others you will see.

I have not made a full list but you can easily add what are left out and if I have put any that don't belong, mark them out. You can send the same back after doing so, together with those of the other states, only make them so they can be understood. Pencil and paper will do. I will have to close as my paper is out.

Yours,

/s/ A. P. ADAMSON

Pvt. Noah R. Hamrick enlisted 25 September 1861. The last muster roll on file, dated 31 December 1862, shows him ill at home. Subsequent pension records indicate that he was ill in hospital at the close of the War. This comports with A.P.'s statement.

LETTER NUMBER THIRTY-FOUR

Camp Young
Near Savannah, Ga.
November 21st, 1862

Dear Sister,

I again take the opportunity of writing you a few lines, which I will forward to Mr. Evans who expects to go home on furlough this evening. It has been some time since I have heard from you. I cannot imagine what is the matter, the reason you don't write. I have nothing new or interesting to write.

The enemy is silent at this time and have made no unusual movement except an attempt to shell out Fort McAllister at the mouth of the Ogeechee. They attacked our works there on Wednesday morning last and kept up an occasional firing for some time, and at times very brisk, till three o'clock in the evening when they hauled off after wasting three or four hundred shot and shell. Only three men were wounded in the action; none were killed on our side.

Colonel Bailey arrived here night before last after about six months absence. He was serenaded by the regiment and made a short speech returning his acknowledgments for the honor; and made a brief allusion to our present difficulties and said although we had not had an opportunity to participate in none of the battles which had been fought but that we had established our claim to a portion of the honor of these brilliant achievements signifying our willingness to do so; and felt assured we would do our duty if ever we were called into action. We were all glad to see the old Colonel again. Colonel Mangham has gone to Virginia.

Wonder what Pa thinks of our present good-for-nothing legislature. I hope he don't have as bad an opinion of them as I have. I don't think they have done anything but abase our excellent Governor, especially the House. The Senate is some better, but, if they do intend to ruin the State, maybe the sooner the better, and they are in a good way to do it.

I regret to hear of the election of that old traitor and demagogue to his party, H. V. Johnson, to the Confederate Senate; but we could not have expected any better when we are mainly guided by such men as Warren Aiken and E. J. Cabiness. I am glad to see there are some men there who still contend for States Rights and endorse the views of Governor Brown. Such a man is Linton Stephens.

I have just heard that there will be no more furloughs granted under no considerations on account of the smallpox in different places. I send, enclosed, an incomplete list of the signers of the Secession Ordinance of Georgia which I want you to compare with that list in the newspaper, which I put away, and make the list complete, correcting all errors if there be any. You will know where to find the paper, and, after completing the list, send the same back.

I have to close. Write soon.

/s/ AUGUSTUS P. ADAMSON

Pvt. John B. Evans enlisted on 11 June 1862. He was sick in a Savannah hospital on 31 December, and later furloughed from C.S.A. General Military Hospital No. 4 at Wilmington, N.C., on 30 January 1863. No later records were found.

Former Georgia Governor and Democrat Herschel Vespasian Johnson ran for Vice-President of the United States on the ticket of Illinois Senator Stephen A. Douglas in his 1860 presidential bid. Of course, Abraham Lincoln won that race. Johnson served as a Georgia Senator in the Confederate States Senate. As a strong State's Rights advocate, he proposed an amendment to the Confederate

Constitution permitting peaceful secession. He was frequently at odds with President Davis' war measures.

Warren Akin served in the Confederate Congress from Georgia. In 1861, he served as the Speaker of the Georgia House.

Linton Stephens was the brother of Confederate Vice-President Alexander H. Stephens of Georgia. During the Constitutional Convention of 1861, "Little Alec" wrote daily to his brother Linton on all that was transpiring. These letters have survived and are most valuable in understanding the constitutional deliberations leading up to that remarkable document in American consitutional history.

Our correspondent mentions the presence of smallpox. This feared contagious disease thrived in unhygenic war conditions. POW camps, as well as refugee camps for the poor, were rife with this disease. Soldiers of both sides were exposed. The medical science at the time understood to isolate the afflicted to prevent further contagion. Vaccines utilizing used human scabs as their source for inoculation were a new unperfected product. The procedure itself for the administration of the vaccination was crude at best. Each soldier would wait in line for a "doctor" to cut his arm several times with an unclean knife, and then insert a small portion of the vaccine. Sore arms and filthy conditions were not conducive to a sound and healthy army. Many soldiers would expedite the vaccination process by doing it themselves using a pocketknife and scabs from fellow troops. Infections often resulted. To comprehend the magnitude of the problem, one must realize that at the Battle of Chancellorsville, some 5,000 Confederates reportedly could not fight due to disabling infections from their self-inflicted inoculations!

Some of these letters are being posted from Camp Young, Chatham County, Georgia. The camp was near Savannah. All or part of the regiment was stationed here: 10 November to 14 December 1862; 3 January to 18 January 1863, 9 February to 9 April; 19 April to 27 April; 4 May to 8 May 1863.

LETTER NUMBER THIRTY-FIVE

November 26th, 1862

Dear Father,

I received your letter today. Was glad to hear from you. We have drawed money. I intended to have sent some money to you by Mr. Cook but he did not go home yesterday as was expected on account of not getting E. B. Cook off. If Will doesn't send a certificate he will be reported absent without leave.

The way I heard that Aunt Mander Stevens was dead was from a Mr. Robinson of our regiment who lives near them. He got a letter from his wife is how come him by the intelligence.

If Will can send back a certificate he had better stay at home till he is well, which he can easily do, I would suppose. Tell Ma to send me a pair of pants when Will comes back. She will know which to send, for she wanted me to bring them when I was at home.

We have a tight time here now, having no time to do anything for having to drill so much. But if there is anyone up there who wants to go into service, tell him this is the place. There is very little sickness here now. Mr. Cook will go home in a day or so. I will send you some money by him. I will close. Nothing more.

Your son, etc.,

/s/ A. P. ADAMSON

Pvt. Ellsberry B. Cook received his disability discharge on 1 December 1862.

Aunt Mander Stevens is presumably Mary Amanda Adamson, daughter of Greenberry and Sarah Coates Adamson, who married Thomas Stephens (both Stevens and Stephens are used interchangeably in the records). They had eight children, two of whom served in the Confederate Army, *i.e.*, Benjamin Hardy Stephens and William Lamar Stephens.

"Infantry Boredom."

LETTER NUMBER THIRTY-SIX

Camp Young
Near Savannah, Georgia
December 1st, 1862

Dear Sister,

I make choice of the present opportunity of writing you a few lines, which I will send by Mr. Huie who, I think, expects to start back tomorrow. I have nothing new or interesting to write to you. This leaves me well and I hope it may find you the same.

We have plenty of drilling to do and scarcely time for anything else. The weather is very dry and pleasant here at this time. The Abolitionists remain quiet but there is no telling how long they will stay so. There is but little sickness here at present. E. B. Cook has been discharged and will go home tomorrow. I suppose his wife got here today.

The pants I told Will I wanted are the black pair that Ma wanted me to bring when I was at home. Ma can send me a shirt before long, if convenient to do so, but I am not needing it much.

The list of counties you sent me I make out with one exception and that is the one between Hunt and Jefferson Counties in Texas. I think you left out one or two in Middle Tennessee. I think there is a Bedford County there, and more that begin with C except Cannon and Coffee.

I want to know the name of the Texas county, and also whether I am right relative to the other. I send you an incomplete list of the counties of the Northern States with the exception of Rhode Island, which I already know, which you can easily fill out; also, those of Kentucky. I will send Pa $15.00 by Mr. Huie if he goes tomorrow.

We were reviewed on last Saturday by General Mercer. He was well pleased with us. We were also presented with two beautiful banners, one a battle flag, the other a regimental banner. They were made by the daughters of Colonel Bailey and presented by Major Boynton in a short but patriotic speech.

111

I have nothing more to write at present and will close. Write soon as you can.

Your affectionate brother,

/s/ A. P. ADAMSON

A.P. discusses the new regimental flags herein. Of interest, the "Bonnie Blue Flag" was the first unoffical flag of secession and independence, perhaps in part based on the flags of South Carolina, the Republic of West Florida, and the Republic of Texas. The 1st National Flag, the "Stars and Bars," was adopted 4 March 1861 and used until superceded by the "Stainless Banner" on 1 May 1863. The "Stars and Bars" would have been the national flag at the time of this correspondence. This attractive flag was not dissimilar to the "Stars and Stripes" with its three horizontal stripes of red-white-red for the bars and a blue upper left canton or square with at first seven stars in a circle and later thirteen stars. For this reason it presented confusion in the heat and smoke of battle. The 2nd National Flag, the "Stainless Banner," was a field of pure white with the well-known Battle Flag in the upper left quadrant. This flag was in use until 4 March 1865 when it in turn was superceded by the 3rd National Flag, of a similar design but with a thick vertical red bar on the outside edge. The 2nd National created confusion, since when hanging limp on a flagpole, it could appear as a flag of surrender with the white field predominating. The famous Battle Flag - like the other banners, red, white and blue - was probably designed in concept by Congressman William Porcher Miles with variations accepted by Generals Joseph E. Johnston and P.G.T. Beauregard in the fall of 1861. It was never offically adopted by the Confederate Congress, but was accepted by the War Department in October 1862, and later by the Army of Tennessee and the Confederate States Navy in a rectangular form. This would be the "battle flag" alluded to by A.P. It probably measured a square 4 by 4 feet with its dark blue St. Andrew's Cross with thirteen white stars imposed on it on a scarlet field, the cross and field edged in white. The identical banner for artillery units would have measured 3 by 3 feet, and for the cavalry 2.5 by 2.5 feet.

Although we have no actual description of the regimental banner, we can assume that it would have been identical to the Battle Flag, but would have had written upon it the state and number of the regiment. Later, the names of the regiment's battles may have been painted or sewn on, or a pair of crossed cannon barrels with the muzzles inverted when the regiment was credited by the capture of ordnance. This was the typical pattern, and generally seen with the banners of sister Georgia regiments.

LETTER NUMBER THIRTY-SEVEN

Savannah, Georgia
December 17th, 1862

Miss A. A. Adamson

Dear Sister,

 I again, and it may be probably for the last time, avail myself of the opportunity of writing you a few lines and, ere this reaches you, I will doubtless be many miles from here. You will doubtless learn before this comes to hand of the departure of our regiment.

 We received orders on Saturday night, the 13th instant, to cook up four days rations and be ready at a moment's warning to march. On Sunday the regiment had not left. I, with several others, was sent on picket and on Sunday night they left. Had it not been for this, I would have been with them now.

 Lieut. Huie came from home today. Himself and myself and three others of our company and several of the regiment expect to start early tomorrow morning. I don't know where the regiment has gone to. The order was to Charleston, S. C., but I hear today that they are gone to Kingston or Goldsboro, N. C. I am satisfied they are at one of the three places. If they have gone to North Carolina they will hardly see Savannah again in a long time.

 J. O. Carnes got in on Sunday and brought me the box that Pa sent. Tell Pa if we come back I will try and send him some rice, but I expect it will be hard to get. J. T. Sanders is here and will stay till further orders. If the regiment don't come back in a short time I will tell him to send what things I don't carry with me home.

I went to Savannah today and saw Ira McDaniel. He stays in the commissary there. Sanders is in Bowman's Artillery and has been camped within a quarter of a mile of us for about a month. I did not know it till today. I went to see him today. They are both well.

I regret to hear of the death of T. R. R. Cobb, Maxcy Gregg and Hood, who were killed at Fredricksburg. They were all good generals and their loss will be deeply felt, especially that of General Cobb, who has many friends in Georgia.

I reckon I will have to close as it is getting late and we will have to take an early start tomorrow. I will write to you again in a few days. I still remain your affectionate brother,

/s/ AUGUSTUS P. ADAMSON

P. S. Lieut. Drew has just received a letter from Captain Dollar written from Charleston. He stated they would leave at two o'clock tonight for Wilmington, N. C. I don't know how the boys will make out. They took but few things with them. Many have sent back for things.

Yours,

/s/ A. P. ADAMSON

P. S. Colonel Bailey is not gone home yet. He went with the regiment.

/s/ A. P. A.

John O. Carnes enlisted as a private on 25 September 1861. He was furloughed for 60 days on 7 July 1863. There are no further records. In A.P.'s later writings, it is indicated that he had died since the War. Ira McDaniel is most likely a cousin on his maternal line.

Georgia Confederate Brig. Gen. Thomas Reade Rootes Cobb commanded Cobb's Legion at the Battle of Yorktown and in the James River fortifications near Richmond. His Legion took horrendous losses at Sharpsburg. He was promoted by General Lee and assumed command of the brigade recently led by his brother, Gen. Howell Cobb, who returned to Georgia. At the 13 December 1862 Battle of Fredericksburg, Cobb's Brigade was placed behind the famous stone wall. Soon after the first Federal assault was repulsed, a Yankee sharpshooter shot General Cobb in the thigh from which wound he bled to death. Today there is a marker at this site. He was an ardent secessionist, took a prominent and active role in the Constitutional Convention of 1861, and served in the Provisional Confederate Congress before pursuing his short but illustrious military career.

South Carolina Confederate Brig. Gen. Maxcy Gregg was mortally wounded when his line was attacked by the Federals under Gen. George Meade on the Confederate right at Fredericksburg. An intelligent cultured ornithologist and lawyer, Gregg was shot in the spine, lingering for two days before dying.

A.P. is in error when he includes Hood in his list of the fallen warriors. Kentucky Lt. Gen. John Bell Hood was not killed, or even wounded at Fredericksburg. He commanded the famed Texas Brigade at Gaines' Mill, Malvern Hill, Second Manassas, Sharpsburg, and Fredericksburg. He lost the use of his left arm at Gettysburg, and was again wounded while rallying his Texas Brigade at Chickamauga causing his right leg to be amputated. It is of some note that there were only ten weeks between these battles. Hood led his troops and fought with noticeable valor at these latter two engagements as he had on prior occasions. He participated in the north Georgia campaign under General Johnston, and then replaced him as army commander. His pugnaciousness was valiant but caused untold irreplaceable casualties. He abandoned Atlanta to Sherman and invaded Tennessee leading to the twin disasters of Franklin and Nashville. These battles decimated the once formidable Army of Tennessee. Both Hood and his wife died of yellow fever in 1879. Lee said of Hood, "All lion...none of the fox."

SUGGESTED READING

Cannon, Jr., Devereaux D., THE FLAGS OF THE CONFEDERACY: AN ILLUSTRATED HISTORY, St. Lukes Press and Broadfoot Publishing, Memphis, Tennessee (1988).

Cunningham, H.H., DOCTORS IN GRAY: THE CONFEDERATE MEDICAL SERVICE, Louisiana State University Press, Baton Rouge (1993).

Dyer, John P., THE GALLANT HOOD, Smithmark, New York (1994).

Hassler, William Woods, COLONEL JOHN PELHAM: LEE'S BOY ARTILLERIST, The University of North Carolina Press, Chapel Hill (1960).

Katcher, Philip, FLAGS OF THE AMERICAN CIVIL WAR 1: CONFEDERATE, *Osprey Military Men-at-Arms Series*, Osprey Publishing Ltd., London (1992).

Stackpole, Edward J., THE FREDERICKSBURG CAMPAIGN, Stackpole Books, Harrisburg, Pennsylvania (1991).

CHAPTER SIX

"Carolinas!"

Charleston

Calm as that second summer which precedes
  The first fall of the snow,
In the broad sunlight of heroic deeds
  The City bides the foe.

As yet, behind their ramparts stern and proud,
  Her bolted thunders sleep -
Dark Sumter like a battlemented cloud
  Looms o'er the solemn deep.

No Calpe frowns from lofty cliff or scar
  To guard the holy strand;
But Moultrie holds in leash her dogs of war
  Above the level sand.

And down the dunes a thousand guns lie couched
  Unseen beside the flood,
Like tigers in some Orient jungle crouched,
  That wait and watch for blood.

Meanwhile, through streets still echoing with trade,
  Walk grave and thoughtful men
Whose hands may one day wield the patriot's blade
  As lightly as the pen.

And maidens with such eyes as would grow dim
  Over a bleeding hound
Seem each one to have caught the strength of him
  Whose sword she sadly bound.

Thus girt without and garrisoned at home,
  Day patient following day,
Old Charleston looks from roof and spire and dome
  Across her tranquil bay.

Ships, through a hundred foes, from Saxon lands
  And spicy Indian ports
Bring Saxon steel and iron to her hands
  And Summer to her courts.

But still, along yon dim Atlantic line
  The only hostile smoke
Creeps like a harmless mist above the brine
  From some frail, floating oak.

Shall the Spring dawn, and she, still clad in smiles
  And with an unscathed brow,
Rest in the strong arms of her palm-crowned isles
  As fair and free as now?

We know not: in the temple of the Fates
  God has inscribed her doom;
And, all untroubled in her faith, she waits
  The triumph or the tomb.

Henry Timrod, *1862.*

LETTER NUMBER THIRTY-EIGHT

Florence
Darlington District,
South Carolina
December 19th, 1862

Dear Father,

I take the present opportunity of writing you a few lines, which will inform you that I am well. We left Savannah on Wednesday morning and reached Charleston on the same evening, and remained till next day till twelve o'clock, when we took the train on the North Eastern Rail Road but did not go but about 8 miles on account of the train being so heavy. We were left till the morning, when we left for this place, where we arrived at six o'clock tonight. We expect to leave for Wilmington at ten o'clock tonight or soon in the morning.

I have understood the regiment left this place yesterday evening. They came up the South Carolina Road to Kingsville. This place is on the Wilmington and Manchester Road. It is also the terminus of the North Eastern Road, also the Cheraw Road. Charleston is the largest city I ever saw. Atlanta is counted a large place, but Charleston is about 4 times as large and a very beautiful place.

I don't know where we will find the regiment. Some think at Goldsboro. I hear today that General Evans has whipped the Yankees at Kingston, N. C. I wrote to Augusta the night before I left. I don't know whether she has got it yet or not. I have to close, as I have a bad way of writing. I will write again soon.

Your son,

/s/ A. P. ADAMSON

There is reference to the Battle of Kinston, North Carolina. Fought on 13-14 December 1862 by Unionist Gen. John G. Foster with a force of 10,000 men and 40 cannon, against Secessionist Gen. Nathan G. "Shanks" Evans and 2,000 Carolinians. Foster's goal was to break the railroad running between Wilmington, North Carolina, and Richmond, Virginia. His specific goal was to destroy the 220 foot railroad bridge spanning the Neuse River near Goldsboro. Evans positioned his forces several miles from Kinston to the front of another bridge over the Neuse. He then capably defended that bridge area from several violent attacks holding the Yankees at bay before being turned back. After hours of further fighting the next day, he had to relinquish his position and retreat over the bridge, burning it in the process. Foster, several days later, burnt the bridge that had been his intent all along, then marched back to his base at New Bern. Undaunted, the Confederates quickly rebuilt the bridge. Rail traffic was only temporarily interupted.

LETTER NUMBER THIRTY-NINE

[This letter was written from J.T. Sanders to N.C. Adamson.]

Camp Young
December 19th, 1862
Mr. Adamson

Dear friend,

> *I suite myself this evening to whright a few lines which leaves me not well though so as to be about. As for news I have but little.*
> *They boys is all gone and I don't hardly know wher. Some ses to one plase and some to another. They left Charleston yesterday and it is sed that they went to Wilmington, North Carolina. I have no doubt but they will go to Richmon before they stop. I wood like very much to hear frome thime now.*
> *Lutenent Huie and Pitt [A.P.] left hear this morning and several others. I did not go through. I never hated to see my buddy leave so bad in my life. If I had bin able to of went, I would of bin much better satisfied. This is the lonesomest place I ever saw.*

Pitt received his box though did not git to eat much of it. Ther is more pervision now in camps then I ever saw at once. I have got about three bushells of potatoes and I expect I will hafter leave hear tomorrow. We will go about Savannah and I will hafter leave all of my pervision and I hate to do that.

I will try and send the balance of Pitt's thinges tomorrow if I can. You will find Pitt's things all at the bottom of the box and I will send Will's cane bed and a par of socks. And also I will send H.L. Hamilton's close in the same box. As I feel but little like writing, I will no more. Only remain as ever your frend,

J.T. Sanders to N.C. Adamson

[P.S] I forgot to say that W.R. Adamson has some clothes in the box.

Camp Young, Chatham County, Georgia, was located near Savannah. The regiment was there from: 10 November-14 December 1862; 3 January-18 January 1863; 9 February-9 April 1863; 19 April-27 April 1863; and, 4 May-8 May 1863, although a part of the regiment remained in North Carolina while the rest returned to Savannah.

Nathaniel Coates Adamson was the father of A.P. Jesse T. Sanders was a good friend mentioned previously in A.P.'s Company. Hezekiah L. Hamilton was also in Co. E. He was appointed a fourth corporal in 1863, admitted to the General Hospital at Savannah on 25 April 1863, and died at Atlanta on 11 June 1864. William R. Adamson, also mentioned earlier, was A.P.'s first cousin and in his company.

LETTER NUMBER FORTY

Camp Clingman near Wilmington,
New Hanover County, North Carolina
December 22nd, 1862

Dear Sister,

I embrace the present opportunity of dropping you a few lines which will let you know that I am well at this time. I got here yesterday morning and found the regiment about two miles from Wilmington. We had a very cold trip from Savannah to this place, having to ride in box cars, but we travelled but very little in the night.

We left Savannah last Wednesday morning at seven o'clock and arrived at Charleston at three in the evening and had to lay over till next day till 12 o'clock when we left for Florence on the North Eastern Road, but did not get but eight miles when we again had to lay over till next day and did not arrive at Florence till Friday night and stayed till next morning and did not get to Wilmington till about midnight but did not go to the regiment till morning.

Charleston is the largest town I ever saw. I think I may safely say it is four times as large as Atlanta and contains many more buildings. It is said that the portion of the city that was destroyed by the great fire, about one year ago, is as large as Atlanta. It must have been a great fire. I never saw such a mass of ruins before.

We did not pass any place of importance till we got to Florence. It is true King Street is a small town on the North Eastern Railroad. Florence is a small place but is an important place by it being the terminus of several railroads. Marion Court House, about twenty-five miles from Florence, is a beautiful village and the only place of any size between Florence and Wilmington.

Wilmington stands on the east side of the Cape Fear River and contains about twenty thousand inhabitants, is about as large as Atlanta, Ga., and one of the prettiest places I ever saw. A great many of the inhabitants that left the place on account of the Yellow Fever have not returned.

Our camps are about two miles from the city. We occupy the tents of the 51st North Carolina Regiment, who went to Goldsboro about a week ago. It is some cooler here than in Georgia but we will fare finely. I think I am very well satisfied but had rather stayed in Savannah.

We will go on to Virginia as soon as the railroad bridges are repaired, is the opinion of many, but I am high up, as I want to go.

There are but two regiments left at Savannah, to wit: Way's and Gordon's.

J. T. Sanders is still at Savannah. He said he would send home what things I left there. We drawed a new uniform the day before we left there but it was a sorry article. I had no use for mine, nor never expect to have. I told Jess to send them all home.

I wrote to you the night before I left. I sent $2.00 in the letter, which you and Sarah may have between you. I would advise Will and all others who are absent on sick furloughs to stay till they get well and not come here.

Please tell Ma I have as many bed quilts as I can carry. Some of the company have already drawed blankets. The rest will draw soon, I think. The shoes I got when I was at home proved to be not much account. The Quartermaster says we will draw shoes also. If not, I want Pa to have me a good pair made, let them cost what they may, I want a good pair, but let old Rad Morrow alone.

When you write to me, direct your letters to Wilmington, N. C., 30 Ga. Regt., care Captain Dollar. I want you to write soon. I will have to close. I remain your brother, etc.

/s/ A. P. ADAMSON

Camp Clingman was located two miles from the railroad station at Wilmington. It was presumably named after Thomas L. Clingman, initially North Carolina Commissioner to the Confederate government at the time of independence. At the time of this letter, Brigadier General Clingman was serving in the District of Wilmington, North Carolina. The referenced 51st North Carolina Infantry was one of the regiments in his brigade. He was to serve in the defense of Charleston harbor and Morris Island during July and August 1863.

A.P. makes note of the great conflagration that occurred in Charleston on 11 December 1861. As best as can be determined, this inferno was caused by a small cooking fire left untended by slave refugees fleeing from the areas outlying Charleston in the wake of the Yankee invasion route. The burned area covered some 540 acres.

Herein A.P. refers to Way's and Gordon's Regiments. Way's was the 54th Georgia Infantry commanded by Col. Charlton H. Way. Gordon's, commanded by Maj. George A. Gordon, was initially designated the 13th Georgia Infantry Battalion when it was first organized in April 1862. On 23 September 1862 it was increased to a regiment becoming the 63rd Infantry, commanded now by Col. George A. Gordon.

A.P. is now going in and out of the Wilmington, N.C., area. Wilmington was a small deep-water port before the War with a population of under 10,000. It had excellent rail communications. Blockade runners began to make the passages to St. George, Bermuda, and Nassau, Bahamas. One of these, the *Kate*, brought in yellow fever. From early September until 11 November 1862, Wilmington suffered 1,500 cases and 700 deaths - 15% of the town's then population. After the epidemic, city and military authorities undertook an extensive quarantine program to prevent repetition. Josiah Gorgas, the head of the Confederate Ordnance Bureau, chose Wilmington as the port of entry for his bureau's blockade runners. Private blockade runners soon joined in with the immense profits to be made in supplying the nascent Confederate nation. The July 1863 attacks on Charleston, S.C., effectively sealed off that port from the blockade runners. Wilmington became the principal port for the South until the fall of Fort Fisher on 15 January 1865.

LETTER NUMBER FORTY-ONE

Camp Young,
near Savannah, Ga.
January 4th, 1863

Dear Sister,

> *I again avail myself of the opportunity of writing you a few lines which will inform you that I am well and that the regiment has once more got back here.*
> *We left Wilmington on the evening of the 31st inst. but only crossed the river and did not leave on the train till New Year's*

morning. We arrived here last night about twelve o'clock, coming by the way of Florence and Charleston, S. C.

We have but little sickness in the regiment at this time. All that went to N. Carolina were able to get back, with one or two exceptions. Private --------of Capt. ---------- company died in the hospital at Wilmington while we were there. He was a Lieut. before the reorganization.

We drawed blankets while in North Carolina. I need nothing, without it is a shirt. I do not know how long they will let us remain here. There has been some talk of our going to Vicksburg, but I don't think we will.

I got a letter from Pa the day before we left N. Carolina but did not have a chance to write as soon as I wished. I like to stay in N. C. very well if we had been fixed up like we are here. I would have preferred that place to this. It is the sorriest looking country from here to Wilmington I have ever seen, but we, it is said, passed through the poorest section of the state. Nothing can be seen but piney woods and turpentine manufacturers. The barrels of turpentine are strengthening the railroad.

I have some hope that the war will close in a short time. The Battle of Fredricksburg I think the most complete victory we have ever ------- and the late battles in Tennessee were fully as decisive victories.

I send you some lines which I clipped from a paper in memory of T. R. R. Cobb, which I hope you will preserve. ----------- was undoubtedly the greatest we have ever ----------. Excuse this short letter. I have but little time to write.

Your brother,

/s/ A. P. ADAMSON

A.P. discusses the 13 December 1862 Battle of Fredericksburg. Union Gen. Ambose Everett Burnside's 114,000 plus army was confronted by Gen. Robert E. Lee's 72,000 troops along the Rappahannock River at and near Fredericksburg, Virginia. Fredericksburg became one of the Southland's first towns to be subjected to wholesale looting, pillage, and wanton destruction by Yankee armies. Burnside crossed over the river after the long delayed construction of several pontoon bridges and then commenced a series of 14 frontal assaults along the Confederate line. Wave after wave of brave blueclad troops charged across the fields to a stone wall at the base of Marye's Heights. They never got closer than 50 yards. Over 7,000 Federals became casualties at this point alone. Additional attacks further along the line were likewise repulsed. Total Union casualties were in excess of 12,600; Confederate casualties were about 5,300. At one point on the Rebel right, Alabama artillerist Maj. John Pelham held up an entire Yankee divison with only two cannon for a half hour until he ran out of shot! General Lee himself witnessed this event, was suitably impressed, and coined the sobriquet "The Gallant Pelham."

Reference is also made to the battles recently conducted in Tennessee. Presumably A.P. is referencing the minor Battle of Parker's Cross Roads and the major conflict of Murfreesboro. Parker's Cross Roads was fought by the "wizard of the saddle," Gen. Nathan Bedford Forrest. It occurred on 31 December 1862 resulting in the capture of numerous Federals but, nevertheless, the Rebels had to withdraw. Murfreesboro, also known as Stone's River, was fought 31 December 1862 to 2 January 1863 between Rebel Gen. Braxton Bragg's 38,000 men and Federal Gen. William S. Rosecrans' 44,000 men. The Confederates attacked and came close to overwhelming the Federals, but again Bragg's hesitation and inability to adapt to circumstances probably brought about the bloodletting, stalemate, and retreat of his army. Kentucky Confederate Gen. John Breckinridge's division made a noteworthy charge that resulted in high casualties, this against the instincts of Breckinridge who protested the order by Bragg.

LETTER NUMBER FORTY-TWO

Charleston, S. C.
January 9th, 1863

Mr. W. F. Adamson
Dear Brother,

*I take this opportunity this morning of writing you a few lines
to let you all know how I am getting along. We are again this far on
our way to North Carolina. We left Savannah Wednesday morning
and got here the same night. We lay over here yesterday but will
leave in a short time, I suppose. We are bound for Goldsboro, N. C.
-------- being expected on the Wilmington & Walden Road. I do not
know how long they will keep us there.*

*The news this morning is that General Foster is at New Bern
& Morehead City with 50,000 men, preparing to make an early
advance upon Charleston is expected there soon. We were too late to
have a hand in the battle there before, but there is a chance for us to
be soon enough the next time. We will go on the North Eastern Road
from here to Florence.*

I remain your brother,

/s/ A. P. ADAMSON

William Felix Adamson, brother of A.P., was about fourteen at this time.

Union Maj. Gen. John G. Foster with 10,000 men (not 50,000 as per
A.P.'s estimate) from the Federal strength in North Carolina was sent to
General Hunter's command for use in the coming attack on Charleston. Foster
had been a member of Fort Sumter's garrison at the time of its surrender in
April 1861 to the Southern revolutionary forces. He knew the Charleston
harbor area well, possesed a sentiment of revanchism, and composed a
thoughtful joint army/navy attack plan to reduce the fortifications and take
Charleston. Hunter was nonplussed at Foster's industry, and considered him
insubordinate. Resultantly, Foster left Hunter's command.

LETTER NUMBER FORTY-THREE

Mr. N. C. Adamson

Dear Father,

I this evening embrace the opportunity that offers of writing you a few lines which will inform you that I am well. We reached Wilmington last night but did not come out here till this morning. We have no tents with us but six to each company. Last night was a bad night but we done well. We had just crossed the river and got to the Wilmington & Welden Depot when the rain began to pour down in torrents -------- night but today is as pretty a day as I ever saw, although I --------- it does not appear so.

I do not know how long we will remain here but I do not think we will stay here long. We will go to Goldsboro in a few days, I think. General ---- says we will be into the ---- of the ---- in a few days. I understand that these of our regiment who have not got effective guns will get them soon. I myself already have an Enfield rifle.

Colonel Bailey has gone home. I understand his resignation has been accepted and there is no longer a doubt of his resignation. I expect we will draw money in a few days. We ought to have drawn some time since.

I understand the Yankees are advancing in the direction of Goldsboro with a force of 50,000. Our force there are about --------- and under the command of General G. W. Smith and the gallant Evans. General --------- brigade of N. Carolina and our brigade and the --------- are the only regiments here.

I will close for the present. I have written all I can think. I remain yours, etc.

/s/ A. P. ADAMSON

P. S. I have no postage stamp.

The reference to having six tents per company suggests that these were probably the commonly used Sibley Tents. Both antagonists used these 18 foot diameter cone shaped canvas tents supported by a single center pole. The 12 foot high tent was invented by future Confederate general, Henry H. Sibley, in 1856. He used as his paradigm the Indian teepees he had seen on the western frontier. It had a circular opening with an adjustable skirt at top and large flaps for doors. It could be erected in just a few minutes by two men. Fires and stoves could be used inside. Designed for a dozen soldiers to sleep in a circle with their feet to the center pole, it frequently held far more.

Kentucky Confederate Maj. Gen. Gustavus Woodson Smith, a Mexican War veteran and civil engineer, served in the 1862 Peninsula Campaign. He was acting as Gen. Joseph E. Johnston's second in command at the Battle of Seven Pines when Johnston was seriously wounded on the first day of this two day battle, Johnston becoming *hors de combat*. Command of the army devolved upon General Smith to complete the battle and Johnston's near success. He did not meet the challenge; his performance was wanting. By today's evaluation, he may have had a nervous breakdown. At any rate, he "lost his nerve." He froze, could not furnish the requisite orders, tactical instantaneous responses, or stategic perspectives necessary to complete the maneuvers in progress. He commanded the army from 31 May to 1 June 1862. President Davis was present and immediately replaced him with Gen. Robert E. Lee from which assignment Lee composed the Army of Northern Virginia, and the rest is history. Smith continued to serve in minor commands until his resignation. Of interest, at one time before the War, he was reputed to have been Union Gen. George McClellan's best friend.

LETTER NUMBER FORTY-FOUR

Camp near Wilmington, N. C.
January 18th, 1863

Dear Father,

     I take the present opportunity of writing you a few lines, which will inform you that I am well. I have nothing interesting to write to you. I received a letter from Augusta a few days ago by Wm. Meeks who brought it from Savannah. I also got the shirt you sent me.
     Lt. Mann is yet at Savannah, I understand. ----------- of the enemy has been expected here for several days. On Thursday we were

ordered to march. All expected a long trip but we only came about miles .

One of the enemy's war steamers ran aground opposite ----------- Sound on Wednesday night. A detachment of artillery were ordered to capture her. Our brigade was brought here to assist them, if necessary. On Friday morning our artillery opened fire upon them. After firing several shots, they hoisted a flag of truce. I understand about sixty prisoners were taken. Nineteen were brought by here, among them a Captain and Lieutenant. The prisoners were mostly foreigners. The Captain was a very good looking man. They all say the people of the North are tired of the war and desire peace. They were taken to Wilmington last night.

The cargo was valuable but owing to the marsh ---------- could not be saved. The boat and cargo was burnt yesterday evening. The name of the steamer was the Columbia.

I do not think we will stay here many days, but where we will go is very uncertain. Some think to Goldsboro, others that we will return to Savannah. I should not be surprised if we did not go back there.

The weather is very cold here now but we make out finely. The rations we draw here are better than at Savannah . We get flour, meal, bacon, pork, and beef a plenty. The only disadvantage is we have but a few cooking utensils. All we have are frying pans. I believe I had rather be at Savannah.

There is a good many soldiers around here. Our brigade is composed of the 25th, 29th and 30th Regiments. The 25th Regiment is commanded by Colonel Wilson, the Lt. Col. is Williams, Major Wynn. 29th: Colonel Young, Lt. Col. ----------, Major Lamb of Berrien County who was a delegate to the State Convention from that county. Colonel Wilson is in command of the brigade.

The 46th Georgia is also here and is one of the nicest regiments I ever saw. It is commanded by Colonel Colquitt. The 25th Regiment is here. Also the ------------. ---------- represented the state both in the Senate and Representative and of the ---------- Congress. He is said to be an excellent officer. We have not yet.

"Carolinas!"

I will have to close, for I have written all my paper.

/s/ A. P. A.

This letter is more likely than not being posted from Camp Hope, New Hanover County, North Carolina. The camp was located near Wilmington. Apparently all or part of the unit was stationed here from 20 January to 25 January 1862, and, 2 January to 29 January 1863.

William W. Meeks of Company E enlisted in July 1862 and died in General Hospital at Augusta, Georgia, on 24 May 1863. Lt. John F. Mann was an initial first lieutenant as of 25 September 1861. He went onto detached duty as an enrolling officer 31 December 1862 with no further official record. This letter indicates he was still serving in that capacity in January 1863. Later correspondence also alludes to him. Thus, A.P. has added to the blanks in the National Archives records!

The *USS Columbia*, commanded by Lt. Joseph P. Couthouy, ran aground on the coast of North Carolina. High winds and heavy seas aborted initial attempts to get her off. By 17 January, when the weather moderated, the *USS Columbia* was in Confederate hands. She was destroyed by fire and Couthouy and some 11 other crew members were taken prisoner. A.P.'s quoted figure of sixty prisoners does not square with the official U.S. government war record. His figures could therefore be misinformed camp rumor, but, likewise it would not be unknown for an embarrassed military official to alter the figures down. This was not uncommon.

The composition of Wilson's Brigade at this juncture was as follows: 25th Georgia, still technically commanded by Col. Claudius C. Wilson, Lt. Col. Andrew J. Williams, and Major soon-to-be-colonel William J. Winn; 29th Georgia, commanded by Col. William J. Young, Lt. Col. W.W. Billopp, and Maj. John C. Lamb; and, 30th Georgia - A.P.'s regiment. The mentioned 46th Georgia was commanded by Col. Peyton H. Colquitt. The 46th was to see action at Jackson, Chickamauga, Dalton, and Calhoun with A.P.

SUGGESTED READING

Cozzens, Peter, NO BETTER PLACE TO DIE: THE BATTLE OF STONE'S RIVER, University of Illinois Press, Chicago (1991).

Cozzens, Peter, THE DARKEST DAYS OF THE WAR: THE BATTLES OF IUKA & CORINTH, The University of North Carolina Press, Chapel Hill (1997).

Krick, Robert K., STONEWALL JACKSON AT CEDAR MOUNTAIN, The University of North Carolina Press, Chapel Hill (1990).

Stackpole, Edward J., FROM CEDAR MOUNTAIN TO ANTIETAM, Stackpole Books, Harrisburg, Pennsylvania (1993).

Stackpole, Edward J., THE FREDERICKSBURG CAMPAIGN: DRAMA ON THE RAPPAHANNOCK, Stackpole Books, Harrisburg, Pennsylvania (1991).

CHAPTER SEVEN

"Hurry Up and Wait."

God has been our shield, and to his name be all the glory.... How I do wish for peace, but only upon the condition of our national independence.

Thomas J. "Stonewall" Jackson,
Lieutenant General, C.S.A.

Sojourns of a Patriot

"Hurry Up and Wait."

LETTER NUMBER FORTY-FIVE

Camp Young
Near Savannah, Ga.
February 9th, 1863

Miss A. A. Adamson

Dear Sister,

    I again avail myself of the opportunity of writing you a few lines, which leaves me well at present and hoping these few lines may find you enjoying the same blessing.
    We have once more returned to our old camp. We left Wilmington on the 6th inst. and arrived here last night at ------ o'clock and I hope we will never have to go to Wilmington again while we are in service. I am actually tried of North Carolina, especially the portion we were in. If we have to leave here again, I hope it will be somewhere else. I had much rather stay in Georgia.
    I suppose you have heard of the repulse of the Abolitionists at Fort McAllister. Their attack upon that place led many to believe they will soon attack Savannah. All the troops that were at Beaufort, N. C. that were expected to make the attack upon Wilmington, it is said, are at Fort Royal, S. C. It is thought they will soon attack Savannah or Charleston, but, owing to this being the weakest place, it is believed will be the first to be attacked. But we will be prepared to give it a bloody reception here, no doubt.
    The health of our regiment is good, and our company. W. Conine was left at Wilmington, sick. We have no Major yet. ------------ is trying to get promoted but it is hoped will fail. If left to the regiment he could not command 100 votes. Lt. ------------ has resigned, which will cause us to have to elect a new Lt. soon. I will close. Write to me soon.

    Your brother,

    /s/ A. P. ADAMSON

135

LETTER NUMBER FORTY-SIX

Camp Young
Near Savannah, Georgia
February 12th, 1863

Miss A. A. Adamson

Dear Sister,

    With pleasure I avail myself of the present opportunity of writing you a few lines which will inform you that I am well at this time. I received your letter yesterday that was addressed to Wilmington, N. C. I also received one from Sarah and ----------yesterday by Will, who got in yesterday.
    I wrote to you a few days ago to let you know that we had come back to old Georgia. We stayed in the old North State as long as I wanted to stay. I was very glad when we received orders to return. North Carolina is, indeed, a poor country, and, as Major Jones says in his writings, is noted for tar and turpentine. The railroads are strung all along with barrels of turpentine and I will assure you he said nothing ---------- in regard to the old North State. I do not know how the people manage to live in such a poor country.
    The weather while we was there was very cold a good portion of the time. We had a severe storm there one morning before day which left but four tents standing. We also had a slight snow the same morning but not enough to lie.
    We got plenty to eat there and I believe our rations were better there than we get here, but all were anxious to return and when we received orders the men were indeed gratified. Nothing could have pleased them better than to have brought them back to their native state.
    I suppose General Mercer is expecting an attack upon Savannah from the recent order he has issued to troops of this department appealing to them to illustrate the valor of Georgia's noble sons who have been victorious on many a hard fought battlefield.

We are still without a Major. Our officers, I fear, are trying to deprive us of our right to elect one. Captain ---------- has made verbal efforts to be promoted to the place. He has taken undermining ways which few officers would be so low to take to receive the appointment. Captain Hendricks is the senior Captain and Captain Dollar second senior, and if the place is filled by promotion one of them ought to have it. If we have an election, Captain Dollar will carry everything. ---------- would stand no chance at all, but as it is I fear he will succeed.

This paper that I am writing upon is Yankee paper. It was taken off the U. S. Steamer Columbia on the coast of North Carolina.

What makes you think I am popular with the girls around Tanner's Church, and who are they? I cannot imagine but should like to know, but you must be joking I am inclined to believe. We drew money day before yesterday after so long a time. I do not think Pa ought to have sold his and it would have been better if he had kept it.

Drewry, I reckon, has resigned. Orderly ---------- will no doubt be elected in his stead. Write to me soon and write a long letter. Tell Sarah & ---------- I have not got time to write to them now but will do so as soon as I can. I will close. I remain

Your brother,

/s/ A. P. ADAMSON

[P.S.] We have made up a club of eleven and sent for the Southern Field and I like it much better since it has been enlarged.

LETTER NUMBER FORTY-SEVEN

Camp Young
Near Savannah, Georgia
February 23rd, 1863

Miss A. A. Adamson

Dear Sister,

    With pleasure I avail myself of the present opportunity of writing you a few lines which will inform you that I am well at present. I have nothing important to write. I received your letter by Mr. Huie but have neglected to write to you since for the very fact that I have had nothing to write. I wrote Pa a few lines by Captain Dollar, which I suppose he got. I want Pa to send me a pair of shoes as soon as convenient. I am not needing any clothing at all.

    I do not believe there is much danger of a fight down here soon, although the waters are alive around here with Yankee gunboats. We all went to Savannah last Friday to be reviewed by General Beauregard. He was much pleased with the performance of the troops. He is still in Savannah.

    I got a letter today from Griffin Masters. He was well when he wrote. Will is still on the sick list. I have had excellent health this Winter. I have not been on the sick list in ten months, not since last May.

    I sent a pair of pants by Mr. McKown. Also, some paper and envelopes. They were marked to Mr. Sanders and rolled up with Will's things. I want you to send me that Speller and Definer that I sent home last year. I am getting so tired of doing nothing. I want something to study.

    You must excuse this badly written letter. No paper. Pen and ink are all so bad I can't hardly write at all. I am ashamed of such a letter as this and if I can't do better next time I won't write at all.

    I have been taking the -------- ever since last September. How do you like the Prize Story? I want you to continue taking the paper. I will close. Write soon as possible.

Your brother,

/s/ A. P. ADAMSON

Mr. McKown had three sons and/or family members in Co. E: E.H. McKown, captured at Atlanta in July 1864; James G. McKown, enlisted 1 May

1862, extant records last mention him 31 December 1862, and then apparently he obtained a substitute in Green B. Holbrook; and, Joseph W. McKown, enlisted 1 May 1862, captured at Nashville on 16 December 1864, died of pneumonia at POW Camp Chase on 20 March 1865, and subsequently interred in grave No. 1713.

LETTER NUMBER FORTY-EIGHT

Camp near Savannah, Ga.
February 25th, 1863
Dear Brother,

I avail myself of the present opportunity of dropping you a few lines which leaves me well. I wrote to Augusta a day or so ago but have concluded to write to you, as I have an opportunity of doing so. I have nothing to write that will interest you.

We have plenty of drilling to do and that's all we have to do. Heavy firing was heard this evening in the direction of Genesis Point. It may be the Yankees are going to make another attack upon Fort McAllister. We were reviewed last week by General Beauregard. He was well pleased with the performance of the troops. I wish you could see General Beauregard. I believe him to be one of the best Generals in the service.

Well, old fellow, how long has it been since you saw Suzy and do you ever see ---------- ? I would be glad to see them myself, but it is not in my favor to do so, and what has become of ---------- and all the other girls that I am acquainted with? Write to me all about them, especially the two first named. I understand that the little boys has parties like five hundred these times. I know they are great parties.

Tell Pa that he need not send me any shoes, for I drew a pair of very good shoes this evening and I don't want more here. If he has had any made, tell him to keep them, for I will need them if this little war don't end some time.

You must write to me every chance you have. Write a long letter. I will have to close. I remain your brother, etc.

/s/ A. P. ADAMSON

LETTER NUMBER FORTY-NINE

Savannah, Georgia
March 1st, 1863

Miss A. A. Adamson

Dear Sister,

I avail myself of the present opportunity of writing you a few lines, which leaves me well at the present, and hoping these few lines may reach and find you all enjoying the same blessing. I have nothing interesting to write to you, nor do I feel much like writing.

Last night we were marched to Causten's Bluff. It was thought by the military authorities that an attack would be made last night, which accounts for our trip there. The authorities here are expecting an attack hourly, and, owing to the movement of the enemy recently, it appears that they are making preparations for some kind of movement but it is uncertain whether the blow will be struck here or at Charleston. But ample preparations have been made here to resist any attack that may be made by the Abolitionists.

Heavy firing was heard yesterday in the direction of Genesis Point. It is very probable that the enemy wished to make another attempt to take that place. We expect orders to march at a moment's warning.

Last night we had a bad trip through the rain. It rained nearly all night. It is very likely, in the opinion of the officers, that we will have to march again before twenty-four hours.

I have drawed a pair of shoes. You can tell Pa not to send me none. I have been taking the Southern Field and Fireside ever since last September and am well pleased with it. I want you to continue taking it, cost what it may.

I have not heard from you in some time. I do not know why you do not write oftener. I sent a book home by William Meeks. I suppose you will receive it ere this reaches you. I will close for the present time. Write soon and often.

I remain your brother, as ever.

/s/ A. P. ADAMSON

LETTER NUMBER FIFTY

Savannah, Georgia
March 11th, 1863

Miss A. A. Adamson

Dear Sister,

I again avail myself of the opportunity of writing you a few lines. I have nothing at all to write and therefore my epistle will be a dry and uninteresting one. I received a letter from Pa by Captain Dollar on Monday last. With that exception, I have received none since Mr. Huie was down here.

We are attached to the brigade of General William H. T. Walker, who has recently been appointed a Brigadier General. General Walker is a Georgian and distinguished himself in the War With Mexico. It is said he has been wounded ten times. I have seen him a time or two. He is quite an ordinary looking old fellow. His brigade consists of the 25th, 29th, 30th and 1st sharpshooters and Gordon's Regiment.

With the Second Georgia State Troops and several batteries of light artillery the Yankee fleet have left the Ogeechee River after their unsuccessful effort to take Fort McAllister. Everything is quiet here now. General ----------'s brigade of North Carolinians, which have

141

been here for several days, have returned. There is no prospect of a fight here now.

I got a letter from Cousin George last week. I believe I sent it home. He was well. I wish Pa would write to him to try and get a transfer to our company. He could easily do so now. Under the late Act of Congress the Secretary of War is authorized to transfer men serving in regiments from other states to regiments from their own state.

Will is getting along tolerably well. I don't think he has had but one chill since he got back here. I think he had better stayed at home longer.

[The above is all that remains of this letter.]

Maj. Gen. William Henry Talbot "Hell-Fighting Billie" Walker of Augusta, Georgia, was courageous, experienced, patriotic, of passionate convictions, a man concerned with his personal honor, a family man, and a Christian. He was killed in action at the Battle of Atlanta on 22 July 1864. As an officer during the War with Mexico 1846-1848, he fought with distinction at the Battle of Churubusco. There he was mentioned in dispatches and promoted from captain to brevet major. At the Battle of Molino del Rey he was critically wounded while heroically leading his men. He was then promoted to brevet lieutenant colonel. Prior to his Mexican adventure, he campaigned in the Second Seminole War in Florida in 1837-1838 with his indomitable courage noted. He was seriously wounded in one fight with the Indians and expected to die. A.P.'s regiment tracks first with Walker's Brigade and then Walker's Division for the remainder of A.P.'s service. Walker commanded this brigade from March to May 1863, which included : 25th Georgia, 29th Georgia, 30th Georgia, 1st Georgia Sharpshooter Battalion, and the 4th Louisiana Battalion. After he was promoted to major general, his division from May to September 1863 was composed of: Wilson's Brigade (Walker's old brigade, *ergo* the 30th Georgia); Gist's Brigade; Gregg's Brigade; Ector's Brigade; McNair's Brigade; Adam's Cavalry Brigade; several sharpshooter battalions; and, the Louisiana Siege Battery and Bledsoe's Missouri Battery. From September 1863 to January 1864, to include the Battle of Chickamauga, his division was composed of: Wilson's Brigade; Gist's Brigade; Gregg's Brigade; Maney's Brigade; Baldwin's

Brigade; and, divisional artillery to include Howell's Georgia Battery, Beauregard's South Carolina Battery, and Bledsoe's Missouri Battery. From February to July 1864, Walker's Division was composed of: Steven's Brigade (who replaced Wilson, killed 27 November 1863, and, *ergo*, the 30th Georgia); Gist's Brigade; Jackson's Brigade; Mercer's Brigade; and artillery support units.

LETTER NUMBER FIFTY-ONE

[The following is a letter from G. M. Adamson to N. C. Adamson]

March 11th, 1863
Camp near Fredricksburg, VA

Mr. N. C. Adamson

Dear Uncle,

> *I suit myself this morning to drop you a few lines which leaves me well at present hoping to hear from you soon. I have not heard from you in so long that it seems like I am lost from all my Clayton friends. I have writen to you and several others around you and get no letters. I recon you write but the letters are misplaced. We are at Fredricksburg but direct your letters to Richmond, Va, 14th Ala. in cear of Capt. Milane, Co. F.*
> *I recieved a letter from Pitt a few days ago. He was well. I have writen to him. I heard from Green and Seale a few days ago. They was not well and sayed they got nothing to eat hardly at all. They are at Vicksburg, Miss. I learned that brother John Adamson is coming to my company in a few days. He will be 18 years old the 24th of May.*
> *The car will soon leave. I must close and start my letter. So give my best love and respects to family and connection friends. There is som cannon a firing today up the river some 15 or 20 miles from hear. We are expecting it hear every hour. I must close. Write soon.*

> */s/ G. M. Adamson*

George M. Adamson enlisted in Co. F, 14th Alabama Infantry on 31 July
1861. His unit fought at Williamsburg, Seven Pines, Gaine's Mill, and, Frayser's
Farm where George was captured on 30 June 1862. He was sent to POW Camp
Fort Columbus, New York, from whence he was exchanged on 5 August 1862.
He then participated in the fighting at Second Manassas, and Sharpsburg where
he was wounded in action on 27 September 1862, and sent to Chimborazo
Hospital in Richmond. Upon release, he rejoined his regiment and was
wounded again at the Battle of Salem Church near Chancellorsville on 3 May
1863. He died from his wounds on 9 May 1863. The National Archives records
do not disclose that any other Adamsons ever served in Co. F. However, two
of his first cousins - and, therefore first cousins to A.P. - did serve in Co. K:
Nathaniel Thomas Adamson who was killed in action 5 May 1862 at the Battle
of Williamsburg; and, Cpl. Samuel M. Adamson, who received a disability
discharge for dyspepsia on 19 December 1861, and yet is subsequently found
being issued a bounty in April 1864 in this same unit as a sergeant. At some
point he was apparently commissioned as a captain in Co. F, 3rd Regiment,
Alabama Reserves. He saw service in the Army of Mobile, and surrendered 4
May 1865. Nathaniel and Samuel were brothers.

George M. Adamson mentions "Green and Seale" as being at Vicksburg.
They were both brothers to George. "Seale" is Seaborn Henry Adamson who
enlisted in Co. I, 41st Georgia Infantry. He was wounded at Perryville, fought
at Baker's Creek (also known as Champion Hill), and at the Vicksburg siege.
He later fought at Chattanooga, Rocky Face Ridge, was seriously wounded
again 14 May 1864 at Resaca, and finally captured 17 February 1865 at
Columbia, S.C. He was briefly interned at POW Camp Hart's Island, New
York. "Green" would be either his brother Joseph Greenberry Adamson, or his
brother Cpl. James Greenberry Adamson, both of whom served in Co. K, 56th
Georgia Infantry and were present for the siege of Vicksburg. There is no extant
record on a John Adamson serving in the 14th Alabama, presumably he was
never transferred.

LETTER NUMBER FIFTY-TWO

Camp Young
Near Savannah, Geo.
April 4th, 1863

Dear Brother,

I again avail myself of the opportunity of writing you a few lines, which leaves me well at present. I have nothing important to write.

We have been under marching orders for two or three days but the time will be out tonight. We will not have to go. An attack was expected upon Charleston the 2nd of this month and we have been in readiness to go there at a moment's warning. There are no indications of an attack here now.

We elected a Lieutenant last Wednesday to fill the vacancy of Dr. Drewry. Orderly Huie was elected without opposition, receiving 38 votes. J.H. Buchanan was elected Orderly Sergeant. The vote ------- - Buchanan ------- W. Q. Anthony 22. I am well satisfied with the result. W.J. Adamson has been received. Also Brown and Crow. Jack Parker was rejected. I have not heard from Cousin George recently. I will hear in a day or so.

Old fellow, I will give you a list of my mess-mates: J. T. Sanders, W. R. Adamson, T. G. L. Cook, W. L. Hamilton, and E. C. Campbell. We have all drawed a new uniform. Also, shirts and drawers, a pair to the man. The health of our regiment is excellent. I saw William Mitchell yesterday. He has had the measles but is getting about again.

Who is Pa in favor of for the next Governor? I guess he is in favor of Gartrell, Iverson, Thomas, or Linton Stephens, or some other States Rights man like ----------, who I think is the best of all.

I will have to close. Write soon. I received your letter day before yesterday, but write again.

Your brother,

/s/ A. P. A.

A.P.'s cousin, James Rufus Adamson, was "received." He died in POW Camp Chase, Ohio, of chronic diarrhea in 1865. Brown must refer to George W. Brown who enlisted 16 March 1863, and died at Canton, Mississippi, 3 June 1863. Crow can only refer to Meredith Crow who was enlisted in August 1862, captured at Rough-and-Ready, Georgia, on 7 September 1864, sent to POW Camp Douglas, Illinois, and released 17 June 1865.

Measles is mentioned here. This was the first of the communicable diseases to generally hit a unit. The first death in Co. E was that of Henry M. Sanders who died 10 November 1861 of measles. Rural raised soldiers were the worst affected inasmuch as few of them had ever been exposed and developed an immunity to the measles virus. Sometimes whole units were infected by this virus. An epidemic generally would run its course in three to four weeks. Pneumonia was the feared sequela. It was reported that in one Confederate camp of 10,000 men, 4,000 were stricken.

LETTER NUMBER FIFTY-THREE

Camp Walker
Near Charleston, S. C.
April 19th, 1863

W. F. Adamson

Dear Brother,

> *I take the opportunity of writing you a few lines. I have but a short time to write, as we are expecting to start to Georgia today. Some of the regiments are already gone. I am very glad to -----------. I have had a very bad cold ever since we have been here but haven't been on the sick list.*

I suppose you heard about the repulse of the Yankees in Charleston harbor and the sinking of the iron mailed Keokuk which was thought to be predicted, but have been driven away with the ------- -- of their best -----------. They have all left here now. General Beauregard says our brigade will go to Tennessee in two or three weeks if there are no hostile movements by the enemy on -----------.

We drawed money the day before yesterday. Will draw again about the first of next month. I got a letter from Cousin George a few days ago. He thinks it doubtful about him getting a transfer. I also got a letter from Sarah and Augusta at the same time. I will close. Write soon to Savannah.

Your brother,

/s/ A. P. ADAMSON

The 7 April 1863 attack on Fort Sumter in Charleston Harbor was an unmitigated disaster for the Union Navy. In an act of defiance toward the impending Union naval attack, the band inside the fort struck up "Dixie" and the garrison raised the flags and fired a thirteen gun salute to the Confederacy. Union Rear Admiral Samuel F. Du Pont commanded the flotilla of nine ironclad ships (to include seven monitors) that carried some of the heaviest ordnance yet to be used in naval warfare. They steamed in to the attack at 3:00 p.m. The plan was to repeat the success enjoyed at Fort Pulaski. However, the Southerners had learned from that experience, and it was not to be repeated. The fort was left largely intact, but the Federal fleet was badly damaged. The *USS Keokuk* received over 90 direct hits and sank the next morning. In fact, the Confederates quietly salvaged the two eight-ton 11 inch guns and added them to the Charleston defenses. Du Pont's flagship, the *USS New Ironsides*, was hit 50 times, the *USS Weehawken* received 53 hits, the *USS Passaic* 35, the *USS Montauk* 47, the *USS Nantucket* 51, and the *USS Patapsco* 47. A chagrined Du Pont withdrew his fleet. Shortly afterward Du Pont was replaced.

The year 1863 witnessed four major campaigns - Vicksburg, Gettysburg, Chickamauga and Charleston. The first a Southern loss, the second a resounding stand-off bringing about a retreat, the third a hard-fought resolute

Rebel victory, and the fourth an unmitigated triumph. The action at Charleston continued through September, and saw new technologies perfected previously unknown to mid-nineteenth century warfare - a changing local front, and joint naval and land exercises. New innovations in ironclads, field fortifications, engineering, siege artillery usage, etc. were unique. After the humiliating rebuff of Admiral Du Pont, the Yankees initiated frontal assaults on Morris Island and Battery Wagner (incorrectly referred to on occasion as Fort Wagner). They launched several more naval attacks and a siege of Battery Wagner, replete with siege lines, parallels, gabions, etc. In addition, the Federals maintained an artillery siege of Fort Sumter and the city of Charleston with concomitant civilian terror. They also attempted a daring but futile amphibious assault on Fort Sumter itself. All these operations were to no avail. In the end, a stubborn Confederate defense permitted a needed morale boosting strategic victory. In 1863 hope still remained in the Pandora's box of the Confederacy!

Of interest, A.P. had a first cousin (William Lamar Stephens) serving in the 12th Georgia Artillery Battalion at Battery Wagner during the Union infantry assault of 11 July 1863.

LETTER NUMBER FIFTY-FOUR

Camp Young
Near Savannah, Ga.
April 21st, 1863

Miss A. A. Adamson

Dear Sister,

    I take the present opportunity of writing you a few lines in reply to yours of the 10th inst., which I received last night upon arriving at camp. I am very glad we have got back to our old camp but there is but little likelihood of our remaining here long.
    When we were in South Carolina Colonel Mangham, together with Colonel Colquit of the 46th Georgia, did all they could to get our regiment detailed for a permanent City Guard in Charleston but

General Beauregard said he did not need any more men at Charleston and if there were no movements made by the enemy indicating a ---------- one brigade would go to Tennessee in two or three weeks.

I see by the papers that the enemy are concentrating a large force in Tennessee preparatory to a final struggle. They are taking Grant's army away from Mississippi and Franklin's Division away from the Rappahannock. If this be so, we will likely go there in ten or twelve days.

The enemy had all left Charleston Har. before we left. They got a severe drubbing on the ---------- and lost their best, which seemed to dishearten them very much, but still they claim to have made a successful reconnaissance, but it was like a great many other --------- of theirs that had ----------.

I want you to send me that Grammar which was sent home. I will try and do without the Bible by getting a Testament, but don't forget to send the Grammar the first chance you have.

Joe Brown is my first choice for Governor, but I don't think he will run. Therefore, my next will lie between Linton Stephens and Judge Thomas. I don't know whether Iverson is sound enough on the Joe Brown doctrine of States Rights, but he once was, but if old Joe runs he will get the vote of nearly every soldier in the Service.

I got a letter from Cousin George last week. He says it will be a hard matter for him to get a transfer but he intends to get one if there is any possible chance. I need no clothing at this time except a pair of cotton socks but I expect I could get them as cheap in Savannah as anywhere else. I suppose I have written enough this time. This leaves me well except a slight cold. Write to me soon as you can.

I remain your brother.

/s/ A. P. ADAMSON
Co. C 30th Ga. Regt.

P. S. I have been taking The Companion three weeks

LETTER NUMBER FIFTY-FIVE

Camp near Pocotaligo
Beaufort Dist., S. C.
April 27, 1863

Miss A. A. Adamson

Dear Sister,

    I avail myself of the present opportunity of writing you a few lines, which leave me well and getting along finely.
    We left Savannah last Wednesday night for Coosawhatchie where we arrived the next morning, but were ordered immediately to this place. We are in camp about two and one-half miles from Pocotaligo Station. I don't know how long we will remain here nor what we were sent here for, but suppose it was to relieve some North Carolina troops who were going back to Wilmington. My opinion is that we will go back in a short time. I am better satisfied with this place than any other we have yet been at. It looks more like our own country than any we have been in before.
    I want you to send me those pants and that Grammar which was sent home when you have a sure chance. I am not needing the pants at the present time but you can send them when you have a chance.
    If we stay on the coast this Summer we will probably get furlough. But it is very doubtful. A soldier's chance is so uncertain.
    I am in favor of Lucius P. Gartrell for Governor of Georgia. I think he is the very man for the place, an able defender of States Rights, the earnest advocate of the soldiers, is the man who is most popular with the soldiers; all know that Gartrell is this. He has always defended States Rights and has looked more to the interest of the soldier than any other man in Congress. He has all along been in favor of increasing their pay, which is very necessary. .
    Joe Brown is very popular among the soldiers, but I think he had better give way, although I believe him to be the greatest man in

150

Georgia, and if we give him up let us try Gartrell, and I truly hope the people of the Seventh Cong. Dist. will send such a man as Colonel Bailey or Bigham of Troup [County] to the next Congress. Let us have no more Tripps, Kenans, Holts and Clarks. I see that Judge Cabiness was spoken of for Governor but God forbid that he shall ever control the destiny of Georgia.

Tell Pa if he wants a cheap and good paper to take The Atlanta Commonwealth, the cheapest paper in the State. I will close.

I remain your brother,

/s/ A. P. ADAMSON

No doubt this letter is being posted from Camp Mangham, Jasper County, South Carolina. The camp was located near Pocataligo. The 30th was stationed here from 27 April to 4 May 1863.

Lucius Jeremiah Gartrell of Wilkes County, Georgia, was twice elected to the Georgia House of Representatives as a Whig of the state's rights faction of his party. He became a Democrat by 1849. He was considered pro-Southern pro-secession, and pro-slavery. He was elected to the U.S. Congress in 1857, and in 1861 to the Confederate House. He was counted as a supporter of President Davis. He was pressed to run for governor in 1863, but declined the proffer. He served until 1864, declining to seek re-election. B.H. Bigham represented Troup County in the Georgia legislature.

Georgia Congressman Robert Pleasant Trippe was an opponent to secession, and was associated with John Bell's Constitutional Union Party in 1860. He served as a Unionist at Georgia's secession convention, but then loyally entered its army as a private post-secession. He served only until he was elected over his commanding officer, Judge E.G. Cabaniss, to represent Georgia's Seventh District in the First Confederate Congress. Judge Cabaniss of Monroe County was considered one of the leaders in the Georgia House. He, also, was pressed to run for governor in 1863, but declined.

Congressman Augustus Holmes Kenan of Milledgeville, was an ardent Unionist and opposed to secession and slavery. He then loyally supported secession and served in both the Provisional and First Confederate Congresses. He supported President Davis, but had tensions with Governor Brown. He lost his bid for re-election in 1863. Congressman Hines Holt was at first a member of the Whig Party, later the Know-Nothing Party, and then the Unionist Party. He served in the Confederate Congress, pushed for peace negotiations with the North, and resigned his seat in 1862.

Georgia Congressman William W. Clark served in the First Confederate Congress, supported President Davis, and was critical of Governor Brown. He lost his 1863 re-election bid to a more aggressive States' Rightist.

Ultimately the Georgia gubernatorial contest of 1863 was between incumbent Gov. Joseph Brown and Joshua Hill. Brown received 36,558 votes to Hill's 18,222. A third candidate, Timothy Furlow, received 10,024 votes. The military vote was over-whelmingly for Brown.

LETTER NUMBER FIFTY-SIX

Camp Young
Near Savannah, Geo.
May 5th 1863

Miss A. A. Adamson

Dear Sister,

I again avail myself of the opportunity of writing you a few lines. I have but little to write, as we are busy preparing to leave for Jackson, Mississippi. We will either leave tonight or in the morning. We got here from Pocotaligo yesterday at 12 o'clock. They wanted us to start on then but the officers had it postponed till we could prepare.
I am very willing to go if I was well. I am not very well, nor have not been for several days, but, considering all things, I am doing finely although if I can I will go to the hospital for a few days. I

presume that most of the sick will be left. We will not go by Atlanta, I do not reckon. I understand we will go from Macon to Columbus and on to Montgomery, Ala.

I expect to send a box home today if I can get it to Savannah. If I send it, tel Pa that there is a bed quilt for J. H. Buchanan, a Geography and a Dictionary for R. N. Barton. The remainder of the things is Jesse Sanders', W. J. Adamson's and mine. He will know which is mine.

I am taking The Southern Field and Fireside, The Constitutionalist, and The Literary Companion, all of which I will have changed to Jonesborough.

T. F. Cowan will go home this evening, having procured a substitute. I will send this letter by him. Joe Tanner's substitute has deserted. We have heard nothing from him since he left. A good many officers in our regiment have resigned. Five Captains have tendered their resignations. Captain Dollar, I think, will be Major, he being Senior Captain.

I do not know how many and which regiments will go to Mississippi, but several will go. I will close. You will hear from me again in a day or so.

I remain your brother, etc.

/s/ A. P. ADAMSON

P. S. There is also an overcoat in that box for G. B. Holbrooks. Tell Pa to send it to his wife.

The *Southern Literary Companion* of Newnan, Georgia ,was founded in 1859. It did not survive the rigors of the War. The other publications have heretofore been commented upon.

Pvt. Thomas F. Cowan enlisted 1 May 1862, was on detached duty in Atlanta from 4 June to 31 December 1862, and, as we understand from this letter, found a substitute for his service so that he could return home. Both sides permitted this practice. Substitutes were usually paid by the party they were replacing. However, if the substitute died, deserted, or left military service for some other reason, the original party could be conscripted. Pvt. Green B. Holbrook enlisted 1 May 1862 as a subsitute for James G. McKown. He was admitted to 1st Mississippi C.S.A. Hospital at Jackson, Mississippi, on 27 August 1863. He returned to duty 7 October 1863.

LETTER NUMBER FIFTY-SEVEN

Camp Young
Near Savannah, Geo.
May 7th, 1863

Mr. N. C. Adamson

Dear Father,

 I hasten to drop you a few lines this morning which I will send by Dr. Cowan. The regiment has not yet left but will leave, in all probability, this evening at 3 o'clock. The 25th Regiment left yesterday evening, the 4th Battalion and the 1st Battalion. Georgia Sharpshooters have also left. They are now moving the baggage to Savannah. Everything is in a bustle.
 I do not suppose I will go with the regiment. All those who are on the sick list are going to be left behind. I am doing very well. Captain Dollar is also going to stay behind, he being left in charge of the camps. We will carry but little baggage to Mississippi.
 I wrote to Augusta on the 5th inst. and sent the letter by T. F. Cowan. All we know is that we were ordered to Jackson, Mississippi. I don't know how long I will remain here before I will follow after the regiment. I think it will not be more than three or four days.
 The boys are all in fine spirits and appear to be very willing to go. There is not much sickness among the men now. All are doing very well. Orderly J. W. Sellman has been elected 3rd Lt. in Company C to fill the vacancy of Lt. J. C. Danforth, deceased. I suppose I have written enough, so I will close. I remain .

"Hurry Up and Wait."

Your son, etc.

/s/ A. P. ADAMSON

Orderly 3rd Lt. James W. Selman was elected second lieutenant in 1863. Second Lt. John C. Danforth died at Savannah in 1863.

SUGGESTED READING

Brown, Russell K., To The Manner Born: The Life of General William H.T. Walker, The University of Georgia Press, Athens (1994).

Burton, E. Milby, The Siege of Charleston, 1861-1865, University of South Carolina Press, Columbia, S.C. (1970).

Rosen, Robert N., Confederate Charleston: An Illustrated History of the City and the People During the Civil War, University of South Carolina Press, Columbia, S.C. (1994).

Wise, Stephen R., Gate of Hell: Campaign for Charleston Harbor, 1863, University of south Carolina Press, Columbia, S.C. (1994).

CHAPTER EIGHT

"Blooded at Jackson."

War may be glorious at a distance, and its fruits may sometimes be the only nutrient of Liberty, but a sight of the harvest which it gathers upon the battlefield is anything but inspiring.

Evander McIver Law,
Brigadier General, C.S.A.

"Blooded at Jackson."

For over a year the Union objective had been to sever the Confederacy in two by wresting control of the Mississippi River. Vicksburg, the "Gibraltar of the West," was the key to the Mississippi. The guns and fortifications at Vicksburg overlooked the river and prevented Federal free access of its length. Gen. Ulysses S. Grant capably commanded the Federal forces, Lt. Gen. John C. Pemberton commanded the besieged army, and Gen. Joseph E. Johnston commanded the relief force. Johnston was informed by telegram of his assignment on 9 May 1863.

The first Union attempts to move on Vicksburg in December 1862 led to the twin Confederate victories at Holly Springs, Mississippi, and at Chickasaw Bayou over Union General Sherman just north of Vicksburg. After a series of delays, setbacks, riverine defeats, miscues, and infertile engineering blunders, in April 1863, General Grant at last succeeded in getting his army on the eastern bank of the Mississippi just south of Vicksburg. This led to the Federal successes at Grand Gulf, Port Gibson, Raymond, and Baker's Creek. His goal was to neutralize the Confederate forces at the rail hub of Jackson, then complete his sealing off of Vicksburg and starve it into submission if he could not take it by assault.

The 30th Regiment was in camp in Savannah when the brigade received orders to report to Gen. Joseph E. Johnston at Jackson, Mississippi, for the relief of the besieged army at Vicksburg. Johnston himself arrived at Jackson on 13 May 1863. The 30th was the last regiment in the brigade to receive rail transportation. Due to congestion and connection difficulties, the 30th took a train from Georgia to Montgomery, Alabama, then entrained on the Alabama & Florida Railroad to Mobile, retrained onto the Mobile & Ohio Railroad to Meridian, Mississippi, and the final stride to Jackson.

Grant's corps commanders, Generals Sherman and McPherson, had taken Jackson the first time as part of the Vicksburg campaign on 14 May when Johnston evacuated north. Grant's corps commander Maj. Gen. James B. McPherson had just concluded the Battle of Raymond on 12 May. At this time Union corps commander General McClernand was preparing to fight at Baker's Creek. After General Sherman had evacuated Jackson this first time, General Johnston directed Brig. Gen. States Rights Gist to retake the sacked and vandalized city, which included the incineration of two hospitals and the Catholic Church.

159

The 30th detrained in the Jackson area late on 14 May 1863. On the 15th the regiment came under fire seeing its first hostile action to the west of Jackson. They were hastily formed into line, skirmished with the enemy for an hour or two, and retrograded. They then marched in a heavy downpour, with the mud going over the tops of the men's shoes and inside. They continued their movement through Canton, and eventually to Yazoo City on the Yazoo River far to the north of Vicksburg. They arrived at Yazoo City from 31 May to 1 June, remaining there until 11 June. During this campaign, T.W. Mangham was colonel of the 30th Georgia. This was part of Johnston's general order conveyed by General Gist to General Walker to advance across the Big Black River and re-inforce and secure strategic Yazoo City - of value because of its naval yards and stores. The weather, lack of potable water, and reduced rations caused a great deal of illness and discomfort.

On 16 May 1863 General Pemberton marched 17,500 troops out of Vicksburg to join forces with Johnston. Grant's forces under the command of Maj. Gen. John A. McClernand blocked Pemberton's passage at Champion Hill near Baker's Creek, preventing the planned union with Johnston. After a sanguinary rebuff, Pemberton's army withdrew back towards Vicksburg. The next day, 17 May, the armies again engaged at the Battle of the Big Black River. The Confederate forces again withdrew, and re-entered the entrenchments at Vicksburg. The Federals attacked the entrenchments on the 19th and the 22nd, both times being bloodily repulsed. The Yankees then began to dig their own trenches to circumvallate the Confederate entrenchments. The siege of Vicksburg had now begun. For 47 days the the Unionists would remorselessly maintain this historic siege which would not terminate until 4 July 1863. Union troop strength would eventually reach over 77,000 men; the city and garrison had perhaps 29,000 troops and civilians. During the famous siege, the civilians were reduced to living in hillside caves while the massive Union artillery batteries on land and water pounded the environs. The land batteries alone included over 220 heavy artillery pieces.

Through the month of June, Johnston kept his undermanned relief force hovering in Grant's rear waiting for the opportunity to pounce on the much larger Federal army. Walker's wing of Johnston's army marched from Yazoo City to Vernon 11-15 June where they remained until their advance to Porter's Creek on 1-2 July. At last after much pressure from Richmond, Johnston began an extensive reconnaissance of the Union positions along the Big Black River on 29 June. On 1 July, although vastly outnumbered, Johnston advanced. Walker's Division, including the 30th Georgia, was then marched to a point east of the Big Black River. According to at least one source, this point was at Birdsong's Ferry, but according to A.P.'s regimental history it was near where the Jackson-Vicksburg Railroad crosses the river - which would be several miles south of Birdsong's Ferry. It was at this moment that the Vicksburg garrison capitulated. The 30th Georgia had been anticipating engaging the Federal forces on 4 July to aid the beleaguered garrison when they received word of the surrender of General Pemberton. Of Pemberton's army, only 11,000 were healthy enough to participate in the surrender. This permitted Grant to now send his forces towards Johnston's army and the fortifications at Jackson.

The consequence of the succumbing of the Vicksburg garrison was an immediate retreat enacted by the troops outside of the Jackson fortifications. During this immediate 4 July retrograde movement, the 30th regiment was ordered to march in the rear of the column keeping up stragglers, and furnish aid to the sick and disabled. After passing through Clinton, the 30th marched to the west of Jackson. At this point on 7 July they came under hostile artillery fire. The men formed along a nearby dry creekbed, threw up breastworks, and remained there several days exposed to enemy fire. Several men were wounded while the 30th held this position. General Sherman arrived outside of Jackson with 50,000 troops on 10 July. He was reluctant to attack Johnston's formidably appearing lines, so he waited for his siege guns to arrive. Numerous skirmishes, assaults, and probes occurred. On 15 July 1863, Companies A, E and H of the 30th Georgia were placed on picket duty. On the 16th they were charged by a Yankee force which had a limited degree of success in taking their position. This was part of the general advance by Sherman's forces.

Jackson was under siege 10-17 July 1863. During this period Walker's Division occupied the trenches to the north of Jackson in the general vicinity of the Deaf and Dumb Asylum, with his area of defense fortification bisected by the New Orleans, Jackson & Great Northern Railroad line.

On the night of 16 July, after a week of intense fighting against overwhelming odds, Johnston felt constrained to evacuate Jackson. Preparatory to crossing the Pearl River on the eastern edge of Jackson, Walker's Division assembled on the low level ground east of the capitol, and crossed the upper bridge at Carson's Ferry on the road to Brandon. On the 18th, Walker marched his division eastward on the Wire Road south of the railroad line towards Morton.

Sherman's troops entered for the second occasion into Jackson and remained for sufficient time to more thoroughly than the first time burn, loot, and devastate the capitol city and the surrounding countryside in a precursor to the malevolent cataclysm he would wreak later on his expeditions to Meridian, Mississippi, and the March to the Sea in Georgia and South Carolina. Jackson was reduced to ashes. The blackened chimneys, "Sherman's sentinels," were all that remained of many residences. The countryside for a radius of 30 miles around Jackson was in ruination.

That evening of the 16 July, the 30th Georgia was ordered to re-take their picket position as part of the delaying action to hold the Bluebacks in place while Johnston evacuated Jackson. The regiment went over their breastworks, formed a line of battle in plain view of the Yankee sharpshooters, and attacked in line preceded by Co. E deployed as skirmishers. A.P. would have been part of this advancing skirmish line. They received heavy Union volley fire, returned same, raised the Rebel yell and charged. They took the position re-establishing the line they had previously lost. Gen. W.H.T. Walker witnessed this action and complimented them for their dauntless élan.

On 17 July, Sherman, after following the retrograding Confederate forces for about 12 miles, decided to withdraw his own army back first to Jackson and then on the 23rd to the security of Vicksburg. Having accomplished their desideratum of opening the Mississippi River, the Federals opted not to push their luck. This is recounted in A.P.'s letters of 20 July 1863. The 30th remained at Morton, suffering outbreaks of typhoid, until 24 August 1863. The regiment then proceeded by rail to join General Bragg's army near Chattanooga.

LETTER NUMBER FIFTY-EIGHT

Camp near Morton
Rankin County, Miss.
July 20, 1863

Mr. W. F. Adamson

Dear Brother,

I take pleasure this evening in dropping you a few lines, which leaves me well and doing finely. We have had a hard time for some time. We had to lie in the ditches around Jackson for seven days, all the time exposed to the fire of the enemy, and I had as soon been somewhere else.

We was in no drawn battle but had to charge a brigade of Yankees and had the satisfaction to make them skedaddle. I came out safe, not receiving a scratch. Although the bullets whizzed around us, our men went through without a single man flinching.

We had to leave Jackson on Thursday night, as they had got heavy reinforcements and would have surrounded us. They charged our breastworks three times but had to skedaddle. We had rather a hard time of it on our retreat on Saturday evening. It rained all the time and the mud ----------. If I could see you I could tell you a great deal about our campaign.

W. T. Adams of our company died at Yazoo City some time ago. The Stephens boys, I hear, have been sent to Meridian. I expect we will fall back to Alabama but we never know one day what we will do the next. I could not carry my knapsack but cut it up and made a sack out of the oil cloth to carry my things in. Tell Ma to rest easy about me, for I will make out the best I can. I will close.

/s/ A. P. ADAMSON

Pvt. William T. Adams enlisted 25 September 1861. He died at Yazoo City, Mississippi on 2 July 1863.

LETTER NUMBER FIFTY-NINE

Rankin County, Mississippi
July 20th, 1863

Miss A. A. Adamson

Dear Sister,

I am once more favored with the opportunity of writing you a few lines to let you know how I am getting along. I would have written sooner but have not had an opportunity of doing so.

We have had a very bad time of it for the last ten or twelve days. On the 8th inst. we were carried out and placed in readiness to meet the enemy, who was near at hand. Breckenridge Division was placed on the left, Loring's upon the right, Reneke and Walker in the center. The most of the troops were placed in the entrenchments. Our brigade was posted in a ravine to be held as reserves.

On Thursday evening we could distinctly hear the firing of the enemy's artillery and, late at night, that of musketry. All felt confident that the next day would be the day of trial. The skirmishing was very heavy Thursday night. The gallant Colonel Wirt Adams of Jackson's Cavalry was killed the next morning. The enemy thronged out skirmishers within 3/4 of a mile of our entrenchments, who kept advancing. About 9 o'clock a shell from the enemy's battery passed directly through our lines, which killed one and mortally wounded another of the 4th Lou. Batt. and killed one of the 8th Ga. Battalion. About twenty shells passed over us during the morning on consequence of our exposed position.

We were moved farther to the right, where we were perfectly secure, on Saturday morning. We were posted in an old creek run near the entrenchments in range of the enemy's skirmishers. On Sunday the enemy shelled our lines for an hour and a half and I assure you I had as soon been somewhere else. The canister shot fell thick around us, the larger balls passing over. They also, at the same time, charged the lines of General Breckenridge but were quickly repulsed, with a loss of about 500 killed, wounded and prisoners, and three stand of colors which were brought around and exhibited to all the troops. The colors were taken by the 47th Georgia and 4th Florida Regiments and were the colors of some Illinois Regiments. They also charged Loring's lines on Saturday but driven back with considerable loss.

They again shelled us on Monday and Tuesday. On Tuesday evening they began to shell the town. Major John C. Lamb of the

29th Georgia was killed on Tuesday evening. He was from Berrien County and a Delegate to the State Convention in 1861 and was much beloved by his regiment. The enemy kept up heavy skirmishing the whole time but done but little injury.

Our company and Captains Towles' and Redwine's was sent out as skirmishers on Wednesday and occupied the front line within a few hundred yards of them till morning, when we were relieved and went to the rear lines about twelve o'clock.

The Yankee line of skirmishers charged our front line and run them back to the rear of where we were posted. This compelled us to skedaddle to the entrenchments. The firing of the enemy was very rapid. Thus the enemy gained the whole slope of woods, which was considered an important position.

On Thursday evening Colonel Mangham received orders to charge their line and regain our former position. About 3 o'clock we were formed in line, with the 14th Texas on our right. We had to charge across an open field for about 300 yards. Our company was deployed as skirmishers in front of the regiment and were very much exposed when we got within about 150 yards of the woods.

The regiment, which was in the rear of the skirmishers, raised a yell and moved forward at double quick in excellent order. Our company were in front and had only to lie down to let the regiment pass over us. When we formed and took our place in line with the regiment after they had been halted the firing was indeed terrific. The Yankees, of course, fled. It was too hot for them.

At night we were sent back after having gained the woods. Our loss was slight. Sergt. Lawson was wounded by my side within two paces of me. His wound is slight in the wrist. J. F. Daily severely wounded in the head. P. J. Daily severely in the leg. Sergt. A. W. Ballentine of Company C, and William Walker, Company H was all that were killed in the charge. Several were wounded before. Our company had none killed, seven wounded. A. C. Smith was wounded on skirmish. J. H. Buchanan, W. P. Conine and John Guice were struck with spent balls but remained with the Company A. Captain A. T. Towles severely. Lieut. J. G. S. Hamm, thigh

165

broken, since amputated. James Brady, severely. A. L. Lewis, Isaac Hammill and Wilkerson slightly.

Company B was not in the fight. Company C, killed Sergt. Ballentine. Wounded Sergt. S.M. McCarty, Perry Bullington, and J. Henderson. Company D, wounded, William Draugham and Elbert Millirous. Company F, Dumas, slightly. Company G, killed Uriah Mann, wounded, W. J. Cox, Geo. Spratlin, Peter Spraggings and L.B. McElroy. Company H, killed, William Walker, several wounded. Company I had several wounded.

General Walker was well pleased with the action of the regiment. The enemy loss is not known. Two dead officers were found just on our left, where the most of them were concentrated. The 11th Illinois was the regiment which we charged, and a whole brigade was further back in the woods.

On Thursday night, much to our surprise, we began to evacuate the place, as the enemy was endeavoring to surround the place. We have been marching ever since. We are now about thirty miles from Jackson, near the railroad in Rankin County, near the line of Scott and Rankin.

Saturday we had a bad time, having to march through the rain. The roads were very bad. Some think we will remain here several days. Our brigade and Gist's are here. The remainder of the army are about four miles back.

There is talk of sending these two brigades to Charleston but the news is too good to be true. I see no chance for the Army to make a stand in this state. No one knows where we are going. We have been going East and I don't care if we keep going that way.

Some say Grant's army is following us. If he gets too far from his supplies we can whip him. If he has got six men to our two. But I have seen as much fighting as I want to see and am perfectly satisfied without being in any other.

Our regiment has been spoken of in complimentary terms by nearly all the officers for the unflinching courage shown by them in charging the Yankee force. Joe Johnson is, indeed, a great general and knows what is best. So far he has conducted matters so as to win the favor of all his men.

I have stood the march very well so far, although I am nearly worn out, but I am getting used to it. I am well at present. Will was not in the fight. He is somewhere, sick. Jesse Sanders came out safe and is doing very well. Sergt. Baxley of our company was taken prisoner on the retreat from Big Black [River] and has been paroled.
   I will close this letter for fear I may weary your patience. I will write again soon as I can. Til then, rest easy. So I will close.

Your brother,

/s/ A. P. ADAMSON

At the time of this letter, William Wirt Adams was still a colonel of cavalry. He was not killed at Jackson as indicated by A.P., or even during the War. A Kentucky born Mississippi planter, he rendered service to the Republic of Texas. Later he served as a Mississippi state legislator and secessionist. He fought well at Shiloh and Iuka. From May to June 1863, he served in Maj. Gen. William H.T. Walker's Cavalry Brigade, at first under Brig. Gen. John Adams, and then under William Henry "Red Fox" Jackson. A.P. alludes to this last commander in his correspondence. At the time of Federal General Sherman's Meridian raid, he was such the "proverbial thorn" in Sherman's side, that Sherman feared him almost as much as he did Forrest. He was promoted to brigadier general because of his actions against Sherman. He then served under Lt. Gen. Nathan Bedford Forrest until the end of the War.

There is mention here of Kentucky Confederate Maj. Gen. John Cabell Breckinridge. He was a lawyer by profession, Mexican War veteran, U.S. Congressman, Vice-President of the United States under Pres. James Buchanan, U.S. Senator, and candidate for President in 1860 representing the Southern Democrats. He came in second in the electoral college. Although initially adverse to secession, he strained to maintain Kentucky as a neutral in the coming conflict between the states. Nevertheless, an order was issued for his arrest for being a suspected Confederate sympathizer, although he had committed no treasonous act. He fled South before being taken into custody, and was appointed brigadier general in charge of the famed "Orphan Brigade."

167

His war record was enviable. He fought well at Murfreesboro, leading a savage but futile charge on the Yankee left on 2 January 1863, and at Chickamauga. His victory over Federal Gen. Franz Sigel at the Battle of New Market in 1864 was the last complete victory the Confederacy was to have in the Shenandoah Valley. In February 1865, he was appointed Secretary of War in the Davis Cabinet. He fled to Cuba, then Europe and Canada after the War before returning to Kentucky in 1868.

North Carolina Gen. William W. "Old Blizzards" Loring was a one-armed Mexican and Indian Wars veteran. Early in the War, he served in Western Virginia where he had a "run-in" with Stonewall Jackson. This did not prevent him from becoming a corps commander. He incurred the wrath of General Pemberton when he retreated the wrong way after the Battle of Baker's Creek, also known as Champion Hill, but, by doing so, paradoxically saved his command from later surrendering at Vicksburg. He was Johnston's senior division commander at Jackson. Later he served as a corps commander in the Army of Tennessee, and lastly served at Atlanta and in the Carolinas.

In the second letter dated 20 July, we have our first reference to canister. A canister artillery round was a thin-walled metal cylinder packed with musket balls, or larger lead, lead coated porcelain, or iron balls and sawdust. Actually, any small metal objects that were available would do. The shot would spray out of the mouth of the artillery piece with murderous effect decimating anyone downrange. This was a most lethal weapon when applied on infantry at close quarters. It was only effective at ranges of 600 yards or less. Its effect was likened to a huge shotgun. Some writers will refer to "grapeshot." This is technically an error. Grapeshot is correctly defined as a naval round not used by ground forces.

4th Sgt. William A. Lawson was wounded at Jackson on 16 July 1863, and admitted to French's Division Hospital at Lauderdale, Mississippi. He was again wounded and disabled at the Battle of Franklin on 30 November 1864, but survived the War. Philip J. Dailey was wounded in the left hand and arm at Jackson on 16 July, leaving him permanently disabled. John F. Dailey was wounded on 16 July in the head from which wound he subsequently died. Sgt. A.W. Ballentine and William L. Walker were both killed 16 July 1863. Allen

C. Smith was wounded the same day, was disabled and sent home. Sgt. Josiah H. Buchanan was wounded for his second time at Chickamauga, becoming permanently disabled, and pronounced unfit for further duty. Both William P. Conine and John Guice received minor wounds. Capt. A.T. Towles of Co. A died of his severe wounds. 3rd Lt. J.G.S. Ham of Co. A also subsequently died of his wounds. William Brady of Co. A died in Mississippi in 1863. Augustus L. Lewis, Isaac Hammill, and Tip Wilkerson all survived their slight wounds.

2nd Sgt. S.M. McCarty died in 1863. R. Perry Bullington survived, as did Jackson Henderson. William M. Draughan and Elbert Millirous were wounded slightly. Uriah Mann died of his wounds. W.J. Cox, GeorgeW. Spratlin, and Peter Spraggins all survived. William Walker was wounded.

Virginia Gen. Joseph Eggleston Johnston was the fourth highest ranking general in the Confederacy. He had served well in Indian campaigns and the Mexican War. Johnston was known as a good organizer, administrator, planner, and strategist. He was known to be sensitive to the conditions effecting his troops and thereby earned their affection. Unfortunately he had a continuing feud over his initial army ranking with President Davis which tended to negatively color their mutual interaction. He skillfully co-operated with General Beauregard at First Manassas, and commanded at the Battle of Seven Pines until he was wounded and made *hors de combat* for several months. He was replaced by Gen. Robert E. Lee. He was in command of the relief army for Pemberton at Vicksburg that sparred with the forces of Grant and Sherman near Jackson, but could not relieve the besieged forces. Later he conducted a masterful Fabian campaign in northern Georgia against his larger Yankee assailant Gen. William Tecumseh Sherman. He was maneuvered ever southward toward Atlanta where he was replaced by the more overtly bellicose Gen. John Bell Hood. After Hood's mismanaged leadership virtually ruined the Army of Tennessee at the Battles of Franklin and Nashville, Johnston was again placed in command until the conclusion of hostilities. In the waning days of the War he fought the Battle of Bentonville, North Carolina, giving Sherman a surprise attack and drubbing. His army was successful during the first day of that battle, but retreated during the second day outnumbered and outprovisioned by the Northern leviathan. He served two terms in the U.S.

House after the War. He was one of the pallbearers at the funeral of General Sherman in 1891 from which he caught a cold and died the next month!

5th Sgt. Joel Baxley of Co. E was in fact captured and paroled in June 1863 in Mississippi. He was later admitted into the 1st Mississippi C.S.A. Hospital at Jackson for chronic diarrhea on 25 August 1863. He deserted from the hospital on 3 September 1863.

LETTER NUMBER SIXTY

Camp, 30th Ga. Reg.
Scott County, Miss.
July 24, 1863

Miss S. S. Adamson

Dear Sister,

I this evening take the opportunity of writing you a few lines, although I have nothing to write that will interest you. We were in hot places at Jackson. I am out alright, although the balls and shells made a very unpleasant music very near me.

We have now been laying over for four or five days. I don't know how long it will be until we again resume our march, but I hope it will not be long. Nearly half the company are absent, sick. Taking all things into consideration, we make out very well. You may tell Ma not to be uneasy about me. Also, that my neck has got well.

Serg. Lawson, P. J. and J. F. Daily, A. C. Smith, J. H. Buchanan, John Guice, and W. P. Conine were wounded during the siege of Jackson, the three last with spent balls, which did not stop them from duty. I will write again soon.

I remain your brother,

/s/ A. P. ADAMSON

LETTER NUMBER SIXTY-ONE

Scott County, Miss.
July 29th, 1863

Dear Sister,

I take pleasure this evening in dropping you a few lines, which leaves me well at present, hoping these few lines may reach and find you all enjoying the same blessing. I have nothing to write that will interest you in the least.

We have been here for about ten days. Our wagon train was sent away Sunday morning, it was said to Enterprise, and have been ever since expecting to leave for that place, but we may have to go somewhere else.

I guess we will take the cars when we leave here. Many believe that they are preparing to send us to Savannah, too. I have no such belief. It is useless to say we have not seen hard times, but we have made out remarkably well, considering everything.

General Walker issued an order to the troops under his command respecting their soldiers --------- bearing at Jackson. I sent a copy of the order to The Atlanta Intelligence for publication. You will see it if it is published. Our company held a meeting today to pay a tribute of respect to our deceased companions. The program will be published in the Atlanta paper, so watch out in those papers and you will see it.

I have written to you several times but it is doubtful whether you have received them or not.

Lt. -------- and J. W. Carnes and W. N. Lawrence are expecting to go home today or tomorrow if they get them furloughs. I will send this by Lt. Huie and shall expect to hear from you when he returns. I will be glad when we leave here, for I can't say I like this country. Enterprise is some twenty miles below Meridian and near the Alabama line.

We hear no news to encourage us. These are dark times, but I hope we may soon see ------- change. Corpl. -------- of our company was captured and paroled at Yazoo City. A good many of our company are absent, sick. I will have to close as my sheet is all written. Write to me if you can. Send by hand.

Your brother,

/s/ A. P. ADAMSON

James W. Carnes was later wounded at Chickamauga and placed on detail for the remainder of the War due to his wounds. William N. Lawrence died in a Newnan, Georgia, hospital in 1864.

LETTER NUMBER SIXTY-TWO

Camp near Morton, Miss.
August 10th, 1863

Miss A. A. Adamson

Dear Sister,

With pleasure I avail myself of the present time of writing you a few lines, which leaves me well and enjoying myself finely. I have nothing of any interest to write and consequently you may expect a very dull epistle.

It seems as if we are going to remain here some time from present indications, although we hear many reports to the contrary. It is the belief of a great many that we will go to Tennessee in a short time. Others think we will go to some other point.

I understand that General -------- Brigade has been ordered to Charleston and Evans to Savannah but I do not know whether there is anything of it or not. Many had hoped that our brigade would have been sent there. For my part, I had rather go to Tennessee.

It is very uncertain as regards the future movements of this army. It cannot be supposed that it will remain here. General Pemberton is much censored by both civilian and soldiering for his management of affairs previous to the fall of Vicksburg. It is no doubt true that General Pemberton basely sold Vicksburg, from all the facts. It cannot be proven to the contrary.

Jeff Davis is also much abused for his censure of General Johnson, or, at least, the Richmond Sentinel, his principal organ, attaches all the blame to Johnson and it is known that Pemberton is Jeff's favorite officer, and, in all probability, will be placed in command again, but, if he is, the Army of Vicksburg is doomed, is lost to the country entirely.

I fear that it will be a long time before this war will terminate. I think that it should be managed upon a different scale in the future. Let General Lee, upon his next entry into Lincolndom, apply the torch to every city and town he reaches and then by this doing we could conquer a peace in forty days and if we were not considered justifiable in doing so we could point to the ashes of Mississippi, towns and hamlets, and call upon the world to decide whether or not we were justifiable in so doing.

But probably Davis and Lee knows best how it should be managed, but Davis has not shown much wisdom in a great many respects. As for Lee, he can't be beat, notwithstanding his bloody defeat, as it is called, at Gettysburg, Penn. But if we had all such Generals as Lee, Beauregard, Price, Breckenridge and Johnston, and such as Pemberton and Holmes dismissed, we could yet expect to be successful.

As regards the girls, I have almost forgotten that there are such beings since I have come here. I presume I could guess some of those foolish girls to whom you alluded in your letter, which I received by Mr. Huie, and fully agree with you in that respect. There is a few who I would like very well to see but as for corresponding with them I have resolved not to do so.

I have written you several letters since I left home although you make no mention of receiving them. I wrote on the 1st, 6th, 9th,

20th, 25th, and 28th inst. and the 1st of August. But I will have to close. Write soon.

Your brother,

/s/ A. P. ADAMSON

North Carolina Maj. Gen. Theophilus Hunter Holmes served in both the Seminole and Mexican Wars with gallantry. He fought in the Seven Days' Battles on the Peninsula, was severely criticized for his actions at the Battle of Malvern Hill, then served in the Trans-Mississippi Department. He was subsequently replaced by Gen. Kirby Smith and sent to Arkansas. He was in Arkansas at the time of the siege of Vicksburg and in command at the Butternut loss of the Battle of Helena, Arkansas, on 4 July 1863. He did not perform well during the Vicksburg siege campaign. He was eventually placed in command of the North Carolina Reserves to serve out the remainder of the War.

SUGGESTED READING

Bearss, Edwin C., and Warren Grabau, THE BATTLE OF JACKSON MAY 14, 1863; THE SIEGE OF JACKSON JULY 10-17, 1863; THREE OTHER POST-VICKSBURG ACTIONS, *Publication Sponsored By* The Jackson Civil War Roundtable, Inc., Gateway Press, Baltimore (1981).

Bearss, Ed, THE VICKSBURG CAMPAIGN, Three Volumes, Morningside House, Inc, Dayton, Ohio (1991).

Cisco, Walter Brian, STATES RIGHTS GIST: A SOUTH CAROLINA GENERAL OF THE CIVIL WAR, White Mane Publishing Company, Inc., Shippensburg, Pennsylvania (1991).

Cunningham, Edward, THE PORT HUDSON CAMPAIGN, 1862-1863, Louisiana State University Press, Baton Rouge (1994).

Foote, Shelby, THE BELEAGUERED CITY: THE VICKSBURG CAMPAIGN, DECEMBER 1862-JULY 1863, The Modern Library, New York (1995).

Govan, Gilbert and James Livingwood, A DIFFERENT VALOR: JOSEPH E. JOHNSTON, Smithmark, New York (1993).

Hankinson, Alan, VICKSBURG 1863: GRANT CLEARS THE MISSISSIPPI, *Osprey Military Campaign Series*, Osprey Publishing Ltd., London (1993).

Hoehling, A.A., VICKSBURG: 47 DAYS OF SIEGE, MAY 18-JULY 4, 1863, The Fairfax Press, New York (1991).

Martin, David G., THE VICKSBURG CAMPAIGN, APRIL 1862- JULY 1863, Combined Books, Inc., Conshohocken, Pennsylvania (1990).

Raab, James W., W.W. LORING; FLORIDA'S FORGOTTEN GENERAL, Sunflower Publishing (1996).

Symonds, Craig L., JOSEPH E. JOHNSTON: A CIVIL WAR BIOGRAPHY, W.W. Norton & Company, New York (1992).

CHAPTER NINE

"The Red Badge of Courage at Chickamauga."

The unequal contest of four brigades against such overwhelming odds is unparalleld in this revolution, and the troops deserve immortal honor for the part borne in the action. Only soldiers fighting for all that is dear to free men could attack, be driven, rally and attack again such superior forces.

William Henry Talbot Walker,
Major General, C.S.A.

The monument on the field of Chickamauga to the gallant charge of the
30th Georgia at 8:30 a.m., 19 September 1863.

Union Maj. Gen. William Starke Rosecrans and his Army of the Cumberland had maneuvered Confederate Gen. Braxton Bragg and his Army of Tennessee out of Kentucky and through middle and eastern Tennessee from October 1862 until September 1863. The bloody Battle of Murfreesboro, also known as Stone's River, was fought 31 December 1862 to 2 January 1863 between these protagonists. Bragg clearly prevailed during the first day of that battle, but then retired his frustrated forces from the field two days later after the Union forces withstood his further attacks. After the Secessionist defeat at Vicksburg, Rosecrans' Yankees pushed the Rebels first into southeastern Tennessee, during as the Tullahoma Campaign, and then out of Chattanooga and into northwestern Georgia. Rosecrans misjudged his opponent in thinking that he was on a demoralized retreat and permitted his forces to be spread out and vulnerable to attack in detail in the folds of the wild mountainous terrain in northwestern Georgia. Bragg understood these sought-after military opportunities, yet he missed several. Finally his subordinates pounced on Rosecrans initiating the Battle of Chickamauga. Indubitably the greatest Confederate victory in the west, it was not properly followed with sufficient pugnacity and expedition. Unfortunately, it could be equitably stated of General Bragg after his performance at Chickamauga, *vincere scit, victoriam uti nescit* (he knows how to win a victory, but not how to exploit it). If Bragg had been as persistent and relentless as many of his subordinates were demanding, he may have caused the Federal forces to capitulate or flee pell-mell to the Ohio River.

In late summer 1863, Bragg wished to consolidate his divisions, borrow several from other theatres, and advance on the foreign invader. To this end, Walker's Division was sent from Mississippi by rail on 24 August 1863 traveling through Montgomery, Atlanta, and Rome, Georgia, with some units arriving on 27 August, and the last on 31 August. The 30th Georgia arrived in Atlanta on 28 August at 2:00 a.m., leaving at 5:00 a.m. on the Western & Atantic Railroad, and reaching Chickamauga Station that evening. Straggling was a problem, particularly in the Atlanta area where many of the men of the 30th took "French leave." This is alluded to in A.P's correspondence dated 30 August. However, most of the men who had taken unauthorized leave to visit their families returned to their units before the battle. From Chickamauga Station the 30th was sent to Tyner's Station, Tennessee, where it remained until 7 September when the unit returned to Chickamauga Station. On the 8th they went to Ringgold, and on the 9th made a hard march to Lafayette. The division camped at Chickamauga Creek as part of Maj. Gen. Daniel Harvey Hill's Corps.

Meanwhile, on 4 September Walker was alerted to be prepared to move to assist in repelling Federal forces threatening Rome. This move did not take place since Union General Rosecrans moved his troops not east and upstream of Chattanooga as had been predicted by Bragg, but rather downstream on the Tennessee River advancing into north Alabama and north Georgia. On 5 September Walker was temporarily placed in charge of the Reserve Corps. He retained his brigades as part of the Reserve Corps, but Brig. Gen. States Rights Gist was placed in command of Walker's Division for the Battle of Chickamauga itself, under temporary Corps Commander Walker. The Reserve Corps was to serve as a "troubleshooting" backup to any unit or area that required the assistance.

LETTER NUMBER SIXTY-THREE

Atlanta, Ga.
Aug. 28, 1863

Mr. N. C. Adamson

Dear Father,

I avail myself of the present opportunity of dropping you a few lines to let you know how I am getting along. We left Morton on Monday evening and have just got here. It is now three o'clock in the morning. We leave this morning, reports say at five o'clock. Our company have all gone home, nearly. I believe there was 54 of them went.

Those that are here now are: Sergt. Buchanan, Anthony, Dickson, Privates J. R. Adamson, J. W. Carnes, Dickson Gallman, Hamilton, Toney, M. T. Boynton, Langston, G. B. Stephens, Touchstone, and myself, besides four or five of the men who were assigned to the company. I should not be surprised if we do not have hot times at Chattanooga. We will get there today, I suppose.

Tell Ma to try and send me something to eat when J. T. Sanders comes back. We have only about 150 men left in the regiment out of 450. I could have easily went, but thought it best to stay.

I don't know whether I will see Cousin Billy or any of Uncle Weldon's folks or not. I would be very glad to see some of them. I will send this letter by Lt. E. Huie or J. T. Haines. I will have to close. I will write soon. I am not to say well, but am doing tolerably well. As well as could be expected. Nothing more.

Your son, etc.

/s/ A. P. ADAMSON

LETTER NUMBER SIXTY-FOUR

Hamilton County, Tenn.
Aug. 30th, 1863

Miss A. A. Adamson

Dear Sister,

With pleasure I avail myself of the opportunity of writing you a few lines, which leave me well at the time and well satisfied. I received your letter by Hightower yesterday and was very glad to hear from you and especially to hear that you are getting along so well at school.

We left Morton, Mississippi, last Monday and arrived here on Friday evening. We are encamped near Chickamauga Station, about thirteen miles from Chattanooga, on the Western and Atlantic Railroad. I am well pleased with our transfer to this Army; also with the country, although it is the hilliest country I ever saw, the hills being almost like mountains.

We passed through a very beautiful country between Atlanta and this place and in many places very fertile, especially in Gordon, Catoosa, and a portion of Whitfield Counties. We also passed through some thriving towns on the way. Ringgold, Dalton, Marietta, and Reseca are, indeed, beautiful places.

It is very probable that a hard battle will take place somewhere on the Tennessee River in a few days. The enemy have at last taken ---------- and will soon advance in this direction, but I am confident that we will be able to drive them back with the army we now have. A. P. Hill's Corps is here from Virginia, I understand, and also Longstreet. Our division belongs to D. H. Hill's Corps, who is known as a great General.

I am very sorry now that our regiment acted as they did in going home. Out of about 450 men, more than half are absent without leave. Our company has 66 absent without leave. We have only 19 men here, four of whom are men who were assigned to the company. The boys will have to pay dearly for their trip; they will not come off as easy as many of them think. I hear it is their intention to stay till Monday week, but, from what I heard an officer say yesterday, they will be apt to come sooner. Tomorrow is muster day, when the troops will all be mustered for payment, and I understand it is the intention of Colonel Mangham to stop their wages and punish them besides. I believe he is the maddest man I ever saw. He considers his regiment disgraced, it being the only regiment that done so, but probably his passion will cool down before the boys get back.

You are right in thinking our county is spoken of as a Lincoln county. Wherever I go among the Georgia troops I hear something about it, but I am gratified to find but very few of them who will encourage such. I hope all those Croakers will read the letters of Colonel J. M. Smith to A. G. Murray.

I see Colonel Smith is a candidate for Congress in the 7th District and I trust he will be elected. I should like to see the name of all who are candidates for Congress. I have seen the names of Hugh Buchanan and Glenn in the 8th, Bell and McMillian in the 9th, Hartridge and King in the 1st, and I do hope that Buchanan, McMillian and King will be successful.

I fear that Hill will run Brown a close race, but I do not think that he will beat him. I think that Providence would interpose first.

When such a low, sneaking politician and a man of as little ability as Joshua Hill gets to be Governor of Georgia, then I for one will be ashamed to own that I am a Georgian. He is undoubtedly the poorest chance for a Governor that could be found among all the -------- men in Georgia, but his supporters care nothing for that. They want a man who is willing to bow his neck to the yoke of the tyrant at Washington, and Josh Hill is the man that will suit them for that purpose.

As for McBride, I don't think he will get a single vote in our company, provided anybody runs against him. I think he had better stay where he is. If it was known, I have no doubt but he has been calculating to run for a long time. But let the election go as it may for Representative. I feel more interest in the election of Colonel Smith and Joe Brown and I humbly trust that Georgia will never be disgraced by such a Governor as ---------, but nothing more upon that subject.

Tell Ma, if convenient, to send me something to eat by Jesse Sanders when he returns. I also want Pa to send me some money, as it may be some time before we draw.

We are getting plenty of crackers and bacon to eat, but I am getting very tired of such diet. We have excellent water here. The spring where we use water is the largest I ever saw. It is about forty yards in circumference. I will have to close as nothing more.

Your brother,

/s/ A. P. ADAMSON

Direct to Chickamauga Tenn.

There is a melancholy irony in noting that A.P. was admiring the towns of Ringgold, Dalton, Marietta, and Resaca. They would each bear witness to the cudgels of conflict within mere months.

Virginia Confederate Lt. Gen. Ambrose Powell Hill led the famous "Light Division" before becoming an Army of Northern Virginia Corps commander under General Lee. His service at the Battle of Williamsburg was distinguished. The next month, June 1862, he fought valiantly at First Cold Harbor, also known as Gaine's Mill, and Frayser's Farm. In conjunction with "Stonewall" Jackson, he fought his men well at the Battles of Cedar Mountain, Second Manassas, Sharpsburg, Fredericksburg, and Chancellorsville. He was famed for wearing a red "battle shirt" when going into combat. His performance at Gettysburg was good, mediocre at Bristoe Station, and on tenterhooks at Wilderness. He was then ill much of the time with an old malady acquired during his West Point days. He was killed on 2 April 1865, at the breach of the lines at Petersburg, one week before General Lee was compelled to submit at Appomattox.

Like many other officers in the armies of both belligerents, South Carolina Maj. Gen. Daniel Harvey Hill honed his military skills during the Mexican War. He was pugnacious, aggressive, popular with his troops, courageous, and a fervent Christian. His brother-in-law was the redoubtable "Stonewall" Jackson. He was also caustic and did not control his tongue well. Although he eventually became a corps commander, he irritated both General Lee and President Davis. His military skills at Chickamauga were sharply criticized and he became a scapegoat for General Bragg. Nonetheless, he stood resolutely with the fledgling Confederate nation until the end.

Georgia Lt. Gen. James Longstreet was considered as Lee's "old war-horse." A wounded Mexican War hero, he admirably led his men at First Manassas. He eventually served as a corps commander in the Army of Northern Virginia fighting with distinction on the Peninsula and the Seven Days' Battles, Second Manassas, Fredericksburg, Gettysburg, Wilderness (where he was seriously wounded), and serving through the siege of Petersburg up to the end at Appomattox. While his performances at Suffolk and Knoxville were not up to par, his leadership at Chickamauga was nothing less than spectacular. He preferred a defensive offensive strategy. He thought little of Gen. Braxton Bragg, and expressed himself accordingly. Longsdtreet had been a close friend of Union Gen. Ulysses S. Grant since their days at West Point. The cigar-smoking Longstreet was Grant's best man at his wedding!

Providence only listened to A.P.'s election preferences with half an ear. In 1863, Georgia sent to the Confederate Congress Julian Hartridge from the 1st District, W.E. Smith from the 2nd, M.H. Blanford from the 3rd, Clifford Anderson from the 4th, J.T. Shewmake from the 5th, H. Echols from the 6th, Colonel James M. Smith from the 7th, George N. Lester from the 8th, H.P. Bell from the 9th, and Warren Akin from the 10th. Although Buchanan, McMillian and King did not prevail in the elections, former Georgia governor Colonel Smith was elected. A.P.'s trepidations regarding Joshua Hill were fears without consequences. Governor Brown was re-elected handsomely. The New York *Herald* predicted that Joshua Hill would win!

LETTER NUMBER SIXTY-FIVE

Camp, 30th Ga. Reg.
Near Harrison, Tenn.
Sept. 1st, 1863

Dear Father,

I write you a few lines this morning while I have an opportunity, which leaves me well at this time. I wrote to Augusta on the 30th but she may not receive the letter. I then wrote from Chickamauga but we left there yesterday morning and marched about ten miles to this place.

We are now about five miles from Harrison, a place on the river above here where it is expected the Yankees will attempt to cross the river. I do not suppose we are nearer than four or five miles of the enemy. I don't know how long we will stay here. We may leave today. We are very well situated here, have very good water, and get plenty to eat. We are on the railroad running from Dalton to Knoxville.

It is currently reported that Bragg's whole army will soon make an invasion into Kentucky and there may be some truth in the report. Since I began this letter we have received orders to have three days' rations and be ready to march at a moment's notice. Some think the Kentucky trip is about to begin. I expect our boys will have some trouble in finding us. You had best not send me anything by J. T. Sanders. He may not get to us in some time.

The report of the fall of Knoxville turns out to be false. Hill's Corps is in that direction and, as our division is attached to that Corps, it is very likely we will go that way also. I will have to close. You need not write till you hear from me again. Nothing more.

Your son,

/s/ A. P. ADAMSON

P. S. Gallman and Hamilton have just been elected in the place of ----
-----, who went home, and Hurdle, who was captured.

A.P.'s letter is dated 1 September 1863. Knoxville was taken by Union General Burnside on 2 September, thereby blocking the most direct rail communication from Lee's Army in Virginia. This became important inasmuch as the decision had been taken to send Lt. Gen. James Longstreet and 12,000 of his troops from the Army of Northern Virginia to assist Bragg in the coming campaign. In order to complete this clandestine transfer, Longstreet's two divisions had to detour over a succession of railroads of differing gauge and not always inter-connected for a total of some 775 rail miles in an operation termed "Westward Ho." This was another of the many military "firsts" that derived from this tragic war. The movement of two divisions from one active combat theatre to another by rail for almost a thousand rail miles in time for immediate entry into battle was a remarkable logistical masterpiece. History correctly gives Longstreet credit for this notable achievement. This troop transfer, however, caused a delay of one day in Bragg's assault at Chickamauga. Longstreet's Corps literally arrived at the battle site during the night of 19 September just in time for his history making charge of a column of brigades at the Brotherton Farmstead on 20 September. Of interest, Longstreet's antagonist was Maj. Gen. William Starke Rosecrans, his roommate at West Point!

LETTER NUMBER SIXTY-SIX

30th Ga. Regt.
Near Lafayette Walker County, Ga.
Sept. 9th, 1863

Mr. N. Adamson

Dear Father,

I drop you a few lines tonight so you may know something about where and how I am getting along. When I wrote last from Chickamauga, Tenn., we were expecting to take the cars and go to Rome but were disappointed. On the night of the 7th we worked all night loading commissaries at Chickamauga.

On yesterday morning, the 8th, we left there and marched till late in the evening to ---------- Ringgold, Ga. This morning we again started early and have marched all day and one of the hardest marches I ever saw. We have come 26 miles today and we are now within a mile of Lafayette, the county seat of Walker County. I suppose we will have to try it again tomorrow. We are probably on our way to ------------- or, likely, to Cherokee County, Alabama.

It is thought by a great many that we are ---------- but it is not known. The enemy have been severely whipped near that place twice, once yesterday and once the day before. They are within ---------- place. One hundred of them were captured above here this morning in a fight which took place.

I will have to close. I am very tired and sleepy. It is now about 9 o'clock and I have slept very little for two nights. I have stood the march finely. I am well, although very much fatigued. I will mail this letter at, I think, Lafayette. I will close and go to sleep ------------- tomorrow.

Your son,

/s/ A. P. ADAMSON

On 9 September, General Bragg ordered Gen. D.H. Hill to send a division, in conjunction with General Hindman's Division, to attack the exposed division of Union Maj. Gen. James Negley at McLemore's Cove. Rosecrans had erroneously been convinced that the Confederates were in retreat, and in his enthusiasm to catch Bragg's presumably demoralized army before it could escape, his divisions became strung out, uncoordinated, and potentially exposed to defeat in detail. This was a well planned Confederate trap, and Rosecrans was entering it with celerity. Negley was a full twelve hours ahead of his closest support element, Gen. Absalom Baird's Division. Negley was ordered to close on Lafayette, Georgia, by way of Dug Gap, crossing McLemore's Cove. Regretfully, D.H. Hill received his instuctions late and claimed that he could not participate, but General Hindman advanced to the cove. Hindman then became overcautious and equivocating. Meanwhile, Bragg sent re-inforcements to Hindman. Negley was out-numbered at least three to one yet Hindman hesitated. Negley then realized his critical exposure and rapidly withdrew. Baird came to assist Negley, and then replaced them in a defensive posture as Negley further retreated into Stevens Gap. Baird's Division followed, with only his rear guard briefly engaged by Hindman's timorous advance. This was a lost opportunity on a grand scale. Both Generals Hill and Hindman were severely criticized for this bungled godsend. Even A.P. repines in this next letter.

Two days later, Bragg suspected another offensive opportunity when Gen. Nathan Bedford Forrest reported Union troops crossing his front. Bragg then ordered Gen. Leonidas Polk to attack at dawn on 13 September. For whatever reason, Polk did not attack. Rosecrans' Army was still fragmented, but the possibility to destroy at least part of it had been seemingly lost twice.

The near disaster at McLemore's Cove caused Rosecrans to become aware of the Army of the Cumberland's dangerous predicament. He then ordered his spread out corps to concentrate just south of Chattanooga. On 17 September, the XIV and XX Corps united at McLemore's Cove, and then advanced to unite with the XXI Corps on Chickamauga Creek. Bragg waited for his Virginia reinforcements, but then ordered an offensive movement for 18 September on the Federal left flank north of Lee and Gordon's Mill. That day Confederate units had seized the crossings over Chickamauga Creek at Reed's Bridge, Alexander's Bridge, and a ford. At long last Bragg was poised to hurl his army

189

between Rosecrans and his base at Chattanooga and defeat the despised despoiler.

LETTER NUMBER SIXTY-SEVEN

Walker County, Geo.
Sept. 17th 1863

Dear Sister,

I write you a few lines this morning while I have an opportunity of doing so. We have been here and in this vicinity for a week. I wrote to Pa the night we got here. I then thought we were going westward. We have been very busy ever since we have been here.

The Yankees have twice attempted to flank us here but have been driven back both times. The first time, last Friday, which only resulted in some skirmishing with a small loss on both sides. Our brigade was then held in reserve again on Sunday, and Sunday night we lay all the time in line of battle some eight miles north of this place. At one time a general advance was ordered but it was found the enemy had fallen back. We returned to this place and have been cooking rations ever since. We have been heavily reinforced and a general advance was ordered last night, to begin at daybreak this morning, but we are still here.

General Bragg, in his orders, says we have twice thwarted their designs and the time has now come when we must force them to an issue, and victory, he says, must be ours. Some are of the opinion that he intends going towards Nashville and others think to Kentucky. The latter I think most likely of the two, but we may meet up with them somewhere near Chattanooga. I presume we will go back by Ringgold, as the wagons have gone that way.

It is very likely that the coming struggle is to be a bloody one and I need not say I do not dread it, but, trusting in all wise Providence, I feel confident that we will be successful. I have great confidence in General Bragg, and all the abuse that has been heaped

190

upon him was ill-timed and unwise. There is no doubt of his being the best disciplined General in the service. I saw the old General the other day. He is, indeed, a rough-looking old fellow.

I have also seen General Breckenridge and he is all that I believed him to be. General Hindman of Arkansas is here and is a great old fellow. I have also seen Lt. General D. H. Hill, and Polk. I hear that our reinforcement consists partly of Longstreet Corps from Virginia and -------- Division from -------.

I would be glad if I could give you a description of our ups and downs through the mountains, but time and space forbid. We are a half mile from the beautiful little village of Lafayette and are nearly surrounded by mountains which presents a beautiful scenery.

We came very near bagging 10,000 Yankees the other day. Had General Hindman arrived at the Gap a short time before he did, we would have succeeded in getting the whole of them. We have heard that Capt. Towles of Company A, a brave officer who was wounded at Jackson, is dead. Also, Lt. John Smith of Fayette County.

I guess it will be some time before you hear from me again. I don't know where we are going and what may turn up. As far as myself, I am anxious for the Kentucky try.

I see that T. M. Furlow has become a candidate for Governor. I don't think he will hurt Brown much. There are so many reconstructionists I fear will get a good vote. If Brown's beat, let it be by --------------.

I will send this to some by someone, but I don't know where. I will close. I regretted that I could not be at the association but at the time we were hearing the cannons booming. So, nothing more.

/s/ A. P. ADAMSON

Arkansas Maj. Gen. Thomas Hindman was passionate for Southern rights and independence. He was a distinguished Mexican War veteran, former member of the U.S. Congress from Arkansas, and a friend of Maj. Gen. Patrick Cleburne. Ruefully, his battlefield skills were left wanting. His performance at McLemore's Cove was questionable. He later served under Johnston in the north Georgia campaign.

North Carolina Lt. Gen. Leonidas Polk was unique for both belligerents. He was an ordained and practicing Episcopalian Bishop. He was also a friend of President Davis. He defeated Gen. Ulysses Grant at the Battle of Belmont in November 1861, personally led four charges at the "Hornets' Nest" at Shiloh, and performed credibly at Perryville. His performance at Murfreesboro was marginal. He was accused by General Bragg of inaction at Chickamauga. After serving under Bragg, whom he disliked, he served under Gen. Joseph E. Johnston in the north Georgia campaign. He was killed on 14 June 1864 atop Pine Mountain, Georgia, when he was struck by an artillery round. He performed the conjugal rights for Gen. John Hunt Morgan, and baptized Generals Joseph E. Johnston and John Bell Hood. Bishop Polk baptized Hood at 8:00 p.m., 11 May 1864, at his headquarters outside of Dalton, Georgia, by candlelight and using a horse bucket for a baptismal font!

A.P.'s analysis of the gubernatorial candidacy of the Hon. Timothy M. Furlow was sound. Buttressed by the Milledgeville *Recorder*, Furlow strongly supported President Davis. Whereas Joshua Hill was a representative of the conservative element and the rallying point for a growing Union fragment in North Georgia, Furlow was a secessionist and ardent supporter of the War. It was anticipated that he would draw his votes from Governor Brown's base. Therefore, the Hill party hoped for a split election, and that it would be forced into the legislature for resolution (Governor Brown had significant opposition in the legislature), and *voilà* Hill would be elected. Furlow was wealthy, devoted to the Southern cause, and popular. As posited heretofore, Brown won.

This was the last letter written home by A. P. Adamson before the Battle of Chickamauga. He was wounded at that battle during the first day's strife, and disabled for several months from active service. He spent his time recuperating at his home in Clayton County, Georgia.

From the official report of Lt. Col. James S. Boynton, the name of A. P. Adamson was listed among the casualties of the 30th Georgia Regiment in the Battle of Chickamauga, 19-20 September 1863.

The next letter in this collection of A. P. Adamson's War Between the States letters is dated 6 February 1864.

"The Red Badge of Courage at Chickamauga."

**Corporal Augustus Pitt Adamson in the color guard at the charge of the
30th Georgia at Chickamauga.**

Chickamauga

There were four crossings over the Chickamauga Creek. Bragg planned on using all four in his offensive as he advanced from the east towards the partially unsuspecting Federals to the west of Chickamauga Creek. Reed's Bridge was the first crossed at 7:00 a.m., 18 September, by Confederate Brig. Gen. Bushrod Johnson's troops on the far right of the Confederate advance. They were quickly followed by General Walker's Reserve Corps attempting a crossing at Alexander's Bridge. Cavalry commanders Forrest and Wheeler covered the army's respective northern and southern flanks. Both Reed's and Alexander's bridges were in General Forrest's area of operations.

Several miles south of Reed's bridge, Walker's Reserve Corps was confronted at Alexander's Bridge by elements of Yankee mounted infantry using repeating rifles, the Confederates took a number of casualties, but then outflanked the Federals by using another unguarded ford a mile downstream. Walker finally managed two divisions across the Chickamauga Creek. Wilson's Brigade bivouacked that night near Byrum's Ford.

The next morning, the 19th, the Federals had thought that only a single Southern brigade had crossed and they advanced anticipating the capture of an isolated Confederate infantry brigade. In the dashing to-and-fro, General Forrest formed some dismounted troopers into a defensive line. Union Gen. John Croxton's Brigade attacked the troopers about 7:30 a.m. near Jay's Mill, but hesitated to push inasmuch as he was unsure of Forrest's strength. The aggressive Forrest logically sought reinforcements, and meeting Generals Bragg and Walker near Alexander's Bridge, was provided Claudius C. Wilson's Brigade. Wilson's Brigade then counterattacked Croxton's Brigade northwesterly around 8:30 a.m., having formed to the east of Alexander's Bridge Road and from north of the area around Jay's Mill Road through the forest and across the Brotherton Road (where today there is a monument to the 30th Georgia's gallant charge and near the cairn of cannonballs marking Bragg's Headquarters) into the scrub and forest beyond. Wilson's Brigade, including the 30th Georgia, hit Croxton's flank and pushed him back. Meanwhile other units were engaging on both sides. In his afteraction report General Forrest stated,

...the first brigade of which, under *Colonel* Wilson, formed on my left, advanced in gallant style, driving the enemy back and capturing a battery of artillery, my dismounted cavalry advancing with them. The superior force of the enemy compelled us to give back until reinforced by *General* Ector's brigade, when the enemy was again driven back.

Col. Claudius C. Wilson stated in his offical afteraction report:

General Forrest...informed me...and he directed me to select a position and form line of battle on the left of the road. I formed my line on the ridge of the long hill, which from the northeast overlooks and commands the plain where our first encounter with the enemy took place, posting the artillery by sections on the most elevated positions and opposite to the intervals between regiments...the brigade moving off by the right flank, and, filing up the Alexander's Bridge road about three-eighths of a mile, was formed into line.... The order was given to move forward at once, and the line stepped off with the enthusiasm of high hope and patriotic determination, and the precision and accuracy which only disciplined and instructed troops can attain. The enemy's skirmishers were encountered at once and driven in on their first line, which opened upon us a terrific fire. Steadily the line moved forward and poured into the enemy's ranks a well-directed fire, which very soon caused his line to break and flee from the field in confusion.... The command still pressed forward on the retreating foe and soon encountered a second line of battle, which seemed to have been drawn up 300 or 400 yards in rear of the first. Then again the contest was renewed with great energy and the position disputed with stubborn resolve.

With Wilson's Brigade and his troopers, Forrest drove through the second Northern line, following which he encountered a third line behind well constructed defenses. Southern General Ector's Brigade now appeared, but likewise did Union reinforcements. A heavy Federal column then advanced beyond Wilson's flank enfilading his troops causing Wilson to retire his brigade.

The captured guns were retaken by the Bluebacks. As the men fell back, the Federals did not advance further than their original position. At this time, General Walker rode up and took personal command of his infantry. The fighting had lasted here from early morning to about 1:30 p.m. A little after noon, Cheatham's Division arrived to relieve Walker's men.

To back up to 8:00 a.m. on the 19th, Wilson's Brigade was formed up with the 25th Georgia on the right, then the 29th Georgia, the 30th Georgia, the 4th Louisiana Battalion, and on the left, the 1st Battalion Georgia Sharpshooters. According to A.P. in his later history:

> The line moved forward, and after going a short distance, wheeled into line by the right flank at double quick time and formed behind a fence with an open field in front, in which, among the weeds, the Yankee skirmishers were hidden. We advanced, preceded by Company E, commanded by Capt. Dollar, as skirmishers; the enemy's pickets were driven back into the woods to their line. Our column continued to advance in the face of heavy and destructive fire, but still they pressed forward until the terrible firing from both front and left flank tore their ranks to pieces and checked them for a while. The scene was dreadful to behold. Amid the roar of musketry could be heard the rebel yell and the shouts of the officers encouraging their men, and the shrieks of the dying and wounded. The intrepid Mangham was wounded in the hottest of the fight, while in front, gallantly leading his men. Almost at the same time the gallant Lieut. Huie, afterwards Captain of Company E, received three wounds.... The color guard consisted of ... **A.P. Adamson**, of Company E.... The three last were wounded and taken from the field ... the color bearer, came out unharmed. The odds against our lines were too great, and the regiment was compelled to fall back a short distance, but rallied and held their line until reinforcements arrived, and the enemy driven back. [Emphasis added.]

To recapitulate, the battle would flow north to south this day as each side fed in divisions and brigades. Confederate Brig. Gen. Matthew Ector's Brigade, Walker's Division, engaged against Federal Col. Ferdinand Van Derveer's Brigade to the right of Wilson's Brigade. Forrest then stabilized the Confederate line. Union General Thomas drove back Wilson's and Ector's Brigades with elements of Federal Generals Brannan's and Baird's Divisions. Both Wilson's and Ector's Brigades suffered severely and were steadily forced back toward Jay's Mill by Baird's and Brannan's Yankee Divisions until 11:00 a.m.

Although with fewer men at this point than his opponent, Union Maj. Gen. George Thomas, Forrest maintained the initiative. After Walker arrived on the field, he sent Southern Brig. Gen. St. John Liddell to the attack at 11:00 a.m. The Union regiments of Col. Benjamin Scribner disintegrated, followed by those of Starkweather's Brigade and King's Brigade. Although this advance had penetrated two Federal lines, they could not force the third line, and withdrew a mile and a half. Northern General Van Derveer managed to contain this Confederate assault by 3:00 p.m. forcing Liddell's Division and other units back towards Jay's Mill where they remained during the afternoon. Losses were severe on both sides. For four hours, this slender force of four Rebel infantry brigades and some dismounted cavalry held back the advance of an entire Yankee corps.

Southern Maj. Gen. Benjamin Cheatham's Division advanced to the left of Walker's Division, subsequently relieving it by 12:30 p.m. and gained the crest of a ridge pushing Croxton's Northern brigade, who were then reinforced by several other Union brigades. Cheatham withdrew after his antagonists were assisted with more units. To Cheatham's left, the Federal lines were penetrated by Confederate General Stewart's Division to the front of the Brotherton Farm. Stewart's advance was halted when he did not receive further support. Several more Butternut assaults took place but without conclusion, stabilizing the lines. At twilight, Secesh Gen. Patrick Cleburne launched an attack that rolled over part of the Federal line and continued for a mile before darkness prevented further penetration. As the fighting closed for the day, Chickamauga Creek and its invaluable water was completely within the Southern lines. This lack of water for the Federals would bring untoward hardship and effect the course of battle on the morrow.

After the sanguinary successes of Saturday, 19 September, came the breakthroughs of Sunday, 20 September 1863. During that intervening night, the Federals had pulled back to a defensive position roughly aligned along the north-south axis of the Lafayette Road. The Butternut assaults began late due to the dilatoriness of Gen. Leonidas Polk - he had not yet concluded breakfasting! There were some tactical successes with General Breckinridge's advance, but by 11:00 a.m. only Stewart's Division of Longstreet's wing was engaged.

And then at precisely 11:10 a.m., the dogs of war were unleashed on the anti-secessionists with one of the grandest charges in American military history. Union General Rosecrans committed an error of ineffable magnitude. He moved a division out of line to fill in a non-existent gap. This created an existent gap. It was this quarter-mile breach in the center of Rosecrans' line at the Brotherton Farm that only moments later was hit by the Gen. James Longstreet's 23,000 screaming Rebels formed in a column of seventeen brigades. The Yankee line was split asunder. Half the Blueback army was swept away in a panic-stricken horde. Most of five Federal divisions vanished in pandemonium. It is difficult to convey to the reader what an indescribable surrealistic Hell occurred - the roar and flash of cannon and rifle, over-turned caissons, jumbled wagons, the glint of the cold steel of bayonets, panicked riderless frothing horses, and all with the Yankees screaming, praying, swearing, running, bleeding, and dying. The aroma of death and defeat pervaded. Included in this *sauve qui peut* rout was the commander of the Union army, Gen. William S. Rosecrans, who was swept up and did not halt until he had reached Chattanooga!

The unflappable Virginia Unionist Gen. George Thomas rallied several of the fleeing Federal units about his own troops on Snodgrass Hill to make a determined stand against the advancing Southern waves. Forever after he would carry the sobriquet of "Rock of Chickamauga" for his actions this day. Assailed many times by intrepid Southern rushes, Thomas and his brave band held firm. He put up a stout defense until after dark when he at last withdrew his units from the Chickamauga battlefield towards Chattanooga and their commander Rosecrans. From end-to-end of this field of glory resonated a spontaneous cheer from thousands of Southern throats in recognition of their achievement.

With such field commanders as Longstreet and Forrest, the intrepid officers and yeomanry of this newly born American Republic had executed a pre-eminent victory for Southern arms, while its titular commander, Bragg, sat disconsolate on a log not comprehending what his men had accomplished!

The butcher's bill for these two days of holocaust was 33,000 Americans. One of these was Augustus Pitt Adamson.

SUGGESTED READING

Arnold, James R., CHICKAMAUGA 1863: THE RIVER OF DEATH, *Osprey Military Campaign Series*, Osprey Publishing Ltd., London (1992).

Bowers, John, CHICKAMAUGA AND CHATTANOOGA: THE BATTLES THAT DOOMED THE CONFEDERACY, Avon Books, New York (1994).

Bridges, Hal, LEE'S MAVERICK GENERAL: DANIEL HARVEY HILL, University of Nebraska Press, Lincoln (1961).

Cozzens, Peter, THE SHIPWRECK OF THEIR HOPES: THE BATTLES FOR CHATTANOOGA, University of Illinois Press, Champaign, Illinois (1994).

Cozzens, Peter, THIS TERRIBLE SOUND: THE BATTLE OF CHICKAMAUGA, University of Illinois Press, Champaign, Illinois (1992).

Davis, William C., BRECKINRIDGE: STATESMAN, SOLDIER, SYMBOL, Louisiana State University Press, Baton Rouge (1974).

Eckenrode, H.J. and Bryan Conrad, JAMES LONGSTREET: LEE'S WAR HORSE, University of North Carolina Press, Chapel Hill (1986).

Freeman, Douglas Southall, R.E. LEE, Four Volumes, Charles Scribner's Sons, New York (1935); *Abridged version* by Richard Harwell, Macmillan Publishing Company, New York (1961).

Hassler, William Woods, A.P. HILL: LEE'S FORGOTTEN GENERAL, University of North Carolina Press, Chapel Hill (1962).

Henry, Robert Selph, "FIRST WITH THE MOST" FORREST, Smithmark Publishers, New York (1987).

Hurst, Jack, NATHAN BEDFORD FORREST: A BIOGRAPHY, Alfred A. Knopf, New York (1993).

Lytle, Andrew Nelson, BEDFORD FORREST AND HIS CRITTER COMPANY, J.S. Sanders & Co., Nashville (1992).

Parks, Joseph H., GENERAL LEONIDAS POLK, C.S.A.: THE FIGHTING BISHOP, Louisiana State University Press, Baton Rouge (1992).

Robertson, James I., GENERAL A.P. HILL; THE STORY OF A CONFEDERATE WARRIOR, Vintage (1992).

Robertson, William G., THE BATTLE OF CHICKAMAUGA: CIVIL WAR SERIES, *National Park Civil War Series*, Eastern National Park and Monument Association (1995).

Spruill, Matt, GUIDE TO THE BATTLE OF CHICKAMAUGA, *The U.S. Army War College Guides to Civil War Battles*, University Press of Kansas, Lawrence, Kansas (1993).

Tucker, Glenn, CHICKAMAUGA: BLOODY BATTLE IN THE WEST, Konecky & Konecky, Publishers, New York (1961).

Wert, Jeffry D., GENERAL JAMES LONGSTREET: THE CONFEDERACY'S MOST CONTROVERSIAL SOLDIER, Simon & Schuster, New York (1993).

Wills, Brian Steel, A BATTLE FROM THE START: THE LIFE OF NATHAN BEDFORD FORREST, Harper Collins publishers, New York (1992).

Wyeth, John Allan, THAT DEVIL FORREST: A LIFE OF GENERAL NATHAN BEDFORD FORREST, Louisiana State University Press, Baton Rouge (1989).

CHAPTER TEN

"Defending the Hearth; Johnston and Sherman - Fortify and Flank."

Since Atlanta I have felt as if all were dead within me, forever.... We are going to be wiped off the earth.

Mary Boykin Chesnut.

Sojourns of a Patriot

After A.P. was seriously wounded on 19 September 1863, he would have been sent first to a field hospital (called an infirmary in the South), then to one of the military hospitals in Atlanta, and finally on home furlough to recuperate. Of course, he would return to his unit when well enough. Although we do not know the exact day of his return, it would appear from his correspondence that it was in the first days of February 1864. He was still bothered by his wounds, and continued to be plagued by them until his capture near Calhoun, Georgia on 17 May 1864.

A.P. had taken a ball in the hip. The War statistics disclose that 94% of all War Between the States battlefield wounds were caused by bullets. These low velocity round or cone shaped lead balls weighed about an ounce. They usually created a large wound, frequently fractured the bones, and produced infections. Amputation by contract surgeons was the normal course for wounded limbs. Often the wounded would wait for hours or even days on the battlefield for the stretcher bearers and likewise for any attention in the infirmary. Hospital organization was woefully lacking; improvisation was the rule. Antibiotics were unknown and general hygiene was crude at best. Such pain suppressants as morphine were only available when captured from the enemy. Surgical instruments were not washed after each use. Surprisingly, a wounded soldier generally had a seven-to-one chance for survival. During A.P.'s care at the Medical College Hospital in Atlanta, his Co. E friend, Dr. Nicholas Drewry, was one of those who attended him.

After Chickamauga, the 30th Georgia was present, but not engaged, in the disaster at Missionary Ridge on 24-25 November 1863. However, the regiment did lose many men captured. This caused the Army of Tennessee to retreat into north Georgia to the Dalton area and go into winter quarters until army movements resumed in the spring. The Federals did the same outside Chattanooga. The winter of 1863-1864 was a severe one. The soldiers built crude log cabins along carefully laid out company and regimental streets. Generally a cabin would provide shelter for four or more soldiers. The architecture routinely called for a rectangular hole to be excavated a foot deep the length and breadth of the future cabin, often 6 by 12 feet. The log walls would be about four feet high chinked with mud and wood chips. The roof would be planks, thatch, or canvas. Straw or pine needles went on the floor. Fireplaces would be constructed of stone or mud-coated logs. Boredom was the worst problem for troops in winter quarters.

After the November 1863 debacle at Missionary Ridge, Gen. Braxton Bragg was at last replaced by Gen. Joseph E. Johnston. Through good management and care he restored the lost morale and the fighting spirit of this army. Meanwhile, Gen. Ulysses S. Grant, who had managed the Northern victories of Lookout Mountain and Missionary Ridge at Chattanooga, was promoted to command all Federal armies. He moved his headquarters to the Army of the Potomac, and left his friend and associate, Gen. William Tecumseh Sherman, to command the Union forces at Chattanooga. They planned a joint spring offensive against both principal Confederate armies - that of Lee in Virginia, and that of Johnston in Georgia. Sherman had almost 100,000 men constituting the Army of the Cumberland, the Army of the Ohio, and the Army of the Tennessee to Johnston's 45,000 men constituting the Confederate Army of Tennessee. During much of the month of February Sherman was raiding in Mississippi and General Thomas was in charge of the Yankees before Dalton.

Johnston's Confederates had dug themselves into a series of formidable fortifications at 1500 feet high elevation Rocky Face Ridge running in a north-south direction just north of Dalton. Southern military engineering had created an exceedingly strong defensive position. Sherman advanced with his armies in early May 1864. From 7 to 12 May there occurred a series of skirmishes, probes, and attacks at Rocky Face Ridge. During these actions, Walker's Division was on nearby Hamilton Mountain to the east of Rocky Face Ridge. The Yankee assaults were all to their north and west; they saw little fighting. After realizing that he could not frontally take the Rebel position at Rocky Face Ridge, Sherman opted for a feigned attack to hold the Secessionists in place, and then a rapid flanking maneuver - on this first occasion towards Resaca. This pattern of attack, hold in place, and flank would repeat itself time and again in Sherman's advance towards Atlanta. Likewise, Johnston understood what Sherman was trying to accomplish, and would parry with strong impregnable fortifications and entrenchments. Johnston's plan was to cast a wary eye to the flank, and at the first suspicion of being flanked, make a rapid retrograde movement to a new set of impregnable positions further south to protect Atlanta. The continued interposition of his army between the advancing Yankees and Atlanta was paramount. It was the prudent Fabian strategy under the circumstances. Johnston's strategy was one of waiting until his opponent committed an error, and then pouncing on the unwary foe, and defeating him in detail.

On 22 March, the famous Dalton snowball fight took place wherein Cheatham's Division of Tennessee troops attacked Walker's Division of Georgia troops with snowballs after a late winter storm had dumped five inches of snow. These same miscreants also went through the quarters of the 30th Georgia, but most of the men were out on picket at the time (presumably including A.P.). This snowball fight involved five to six thousand men complete with flags, "officers to lead them," and regimental organization! Eventually, Walker's Georgians were routed through their camps and into the woods. One of Walker's colonels cried foul, claiming that half of the men in his regiment had never before seen snow! There were reported casualties. History also records similar occurences in the Army of Northern Virginia.

LETTER NUMBER SIXTY-EIGHT

Camp, 30th Ga. Regt.
Near Dalton
Feb. 6th, 1864

Miss A. A. Adamson

Dear Sister,

I take this present opportunity of writing you a few lines to let you know ------------------------. Our camps are some four or five miles from Dalton. The troops have all got very comfortable houses and are faring better than I expected to find them.

A grand review of the Army took place yesterday. Nearly all the Army were present. I never saw so many men together before. Our brigade is now composed of the 25th, 29th and 30th, 66th Georgia, 1st Battalion, and 26th Georgia Battalion. The brigade is now commanded by Colonel Nisbet of the 66th Georgia.

There is no indication of a fight here soon, as I can see, but we may look out when the bad weather breaks. It has been raining here all day and it is very cold this evening and the cold is increasing. The water here is tolerably good. The worst difficulty is the scarcity of wood.

I do not think that the ---------- manifest much disposition to re-inlist. But few have done so thus far and the chance is bad. I understand that I will draw 33-1/3 cts. per day for the time that I stayed at home. Also, some 70 or 80 dollars clothing money, which I can get in a short time. This leaves me about as well as when I left home. I think I am doing very well.

As I have nothing to write, so I will close. Write to me soon and a long letter. Write everything that has transpired since I left. Direct to Dalton, Georgia, 30th Georgia Regiment, Wilson's Brig. Walker Div.

Your brother,

/s/ A. P. ADAMSON

Walker's Division was temporarily under the command of Brig. Gen. States Rights Gist at the Battle of Chickamauga, 19-20 September 1863 (General Walker was temporarily in command of the Reserve Corps), again under his command 12-28 November 1863 (Walker was on leave during this period), and a third time, 12 January-10 February 1864 (Walker was on a leave of absence). Wilson's Brigade was under the temporary command of Col. James C. Nisbet of the 66th Georgia Infantry after Brig. Gen. Claudius C. Wilson died on 27 November 1863. Wilson died of "camp fever," otherwise known as typhoid fever. South Carolina Brig. Gen. Clement H. Stevens was then placed in command of the brigade. Thereafter it became known as Stevens' Brigade, Walker's Division.

LETTER NUMBER SIXTY-NINE

Dalton, Georgia
Feb. 28th, 1864

Miss Augusta A. Adamson

"Defending the Hearth; Johnston and Sherman - Fortify and Flank."

Dear Sister,

    I embrace the present opportunity of writing you a few lines, which I -------- reach and find you well. I have nothing to ----------can be of much interest to you.

    The past ----------- been a busy week ---------- the active movements going on in the West, the departure of troops for the theatre of action there, together with the late advance of General Thomas' Army upon our front here have all had a tendency to produce stirring times with us.

    You are already aware of our anticipated trip to Mississippi, which we confidently believed we would take. We left camp last Tuesday evening, not knowing where we were going, but the general opinion was that we would take the cars and go West, but instead of taking the cars we were marched through town to the upper part of the place, where we remained, expecting a powerful time the next day.

    The next day we ---------- with slight skirmishing, and artillery firing began at an early hour and continued nearly all day. Stevenson's Division had gone to the front on the Tunnel Hill Road and, together with Stewart and a portion of Breckenridge's old division, met them and repulsed them with considerable loss in the evening. Our loss was said to be some eight or ten killed and 450 wounded among the latter.

    Colonel Curtis of the 41st Georgia -----------. This was the only general engagement which took place. The fighting was to be desperate along a portion of the lines, the enemy making several desperate charges upon Pettus' Brigade of Stevenson's Division, being each time repulsed. This brigade is comprised chiefly of Alabamians, I think.

    Being driven back in their advance upon the ---------- Road, it was reported they would next endeavor to ---------- by the Cleveland Road upon which our Division --------- other troops were posted, but instead of doing so, back beyond Ringgold, and instead·of gaining ground ----------. We remained out on the Cleveland Road until yesterday morning, when -------- to town to --------- and are now

207

quartered in the court house. Have plenty of -------- to do, but the boys all are anxious to remain as we have excellent quarters, and living in town besides. The troops have mostly left the front since the retreat of the enemy and returned to their old camps. Our regiment may have to remain here for some time yet.

I saw three of Uncle Jim's boys last Wednesday. They were Greenberry, James, and John. Cousin John W. Adamson is in the 26th Georgia Battalion of our Brigade, and I saw him the other night. Lt. Huie, W. P. Conine, T. G. L. Cook, and several others have got back to us again.

Today is Sunday. I went to meeting today out at the church in this place and it reminded me of old times, as it was unlike the meetings we generally have. Probably I will go again tonight. I would like to be at Tanner's next Sunday and see all the girls again, especially a few of those first in my estimation, but you know how that is.

I want you to write to me soon and write longer letters than your last. You certainly must have been somewhat bewildered, or probably it was something else, but I can look over it, but do better the next time. You have a better opportunity to write than I do and consequently you can write to me oftener than you do.

I have been very unwell for the past ten days and if I do not get better in a few days I shall try to get to the hospital or somewhere else. Let me know if you know anything of -------- Sanders. We have not heard since he left. So, nothing more.

Your brother,

/s/ A. P. ADAMSON

As indicated, the Mississippi expedition never occurred. The need became moot. Meridian, Mississippi, was a major Confederate supply depot containing an arsenal, repair shops and a rail center. Sherman wanted to burn and destroy all this. Essentially he managed a massive raid with 26,000 troops. At the onset of this destructive expedition beginning from Jackson on 5 February 1863, Confederate Gen. Leonidas Polk was uncertain of Sherman's goal. Initially he thought that it was to be Mobile. Polk's soldiers were spread out over part of Mississippi, and there were characteristically far fewer of them than the men available to Sherman. Polk requested re-inforcements to meet the threat. President Davis instructed General Johnston in Georgia to send three divisions of Hardee's Corps, those of: Cheatham, Cleburne, and Walker. Cheatham's Division was entrained and sent first on 20 February, quickly followed by Cleburne's Division on 22 February. Walker's Division was then prepared for departure. However, on this same date of 22 February, Sherman's army initiated a return to Vicksburg after having spent some 5 days in and around Meridian eliminating every vestige of its being with ax, crowbar, sledge, and fire - cutting "a swath of desolation 50 miles broad across the State of Mississippi." Union Cavalry Gen. William Sooy Smith rode to assist Sherman. Unfortunately for Sooy Smith, Confederate Gen. Nathan Bedford Forrest was pursuing him with one-third the force of Smith. On 22 February, Forrest caught up with Smith at Okolona, Mississippi, and achieved one of his great victories. With Sherman's return to Vicksburg, the *en route* troops from Hardee's Corps returned to Georgia, and Walker's Division was not sent.

From 24 to 26 February 1864, the troops of Union Gen. George Thomas skirmished along Rocky Face Ridge. During these actions, Thomas realized that Buzzard Roost Gap, through which runs the railroad, is almost impregnable to attack from the north. He also began to perceive that the Rebels might be vulnerable to a flanking maneuver. On 25 February there was some fighting at Dug Gap, south of Buzzard's Roost. It must be these engagements that are referenced in A.P.'s letter.

A.P.'s uncle, James Jefferson Adamson, had several sons in the military at this time. Joseph Greenberry Adamson and James Greenberry Adamson both served in Co. K, 56th Georgia Infantry. Joseph was captured and paroled at Vicksburg, and fought subsequently at Chattanooga, New Hope Church, Atlanta, Jonesboro, Nashville, and Bentonville. He was with Johnston's army when it submitted at Greensboro, N.C., 26 April 1865. James enlisted in May 1862, was elected a corporal, and captured and paroled at Vicksburg. He fought at Chattanooga, New Hope Church, Atlanta, Jonesboro, Nashville, and Bentonville. He was captured in April 1865, days before the end. Their brother John is an enigma to the editors, as explained previously. His other first cousin,

John Whitfield Adamson, was the son of William Coates Adamson. He enlisted 12 August 1863 in Newnan, Georgia, in Co. C, 26th Georgia Infantry Battalion. He was elected a sergeant. He saw action at Chattanooga and in the Atlanta campaign. He was sick in hospital, and became a hospital steward. His uncle, Nathaniel Coates Adamson, the father of A.P., performed his nuptials.

LETTER NUMBER SEVENTY

Dalton, Georgia
March 2nd 1864

W. F. Adamson

Dear Brother,

I write you a few lines this evening as I am idle and seldom have such an opportunity in consequence of the duty we have to perform. We are stationed here in the court house, doing police duty. It is very heavy but I am willing to remain here. I have been very unwell for some time but am nearly right again. The first three days we stayed here I was almost past travelling but we are so well quartered a man can't stay sick long.

All danger of a fight is over for the time, but I presume active operations will soon commence, when we may again expect to hear the owl hollow. We have got a splendid army, better than I expected, and one of the best Generals in the Confederacy, and if General Thomas does come he will meet with a bloody reception, but I much rather he would stay the other side of Chickamauga.

I have seen Moses Shields today. He is doing very well. I am getting very anxious to hear from home. I have got ------- little short letters since I left --------. I think all must have forgot how to write. Write me a long letter and, by the way, write about all the girls, especially Miss ----------. I would like very much to see her. Also, I want to hear how all the -------- gets along a courting. I hear they are quite ---------- of late. I admire their but think, like myself, -------, they ----------.

"Defending the Hearth; Johnston and Sherman - Fortify and Flank."

Write to me and tell me all you know, and a little more, if you will. How many parties you have been to, and was there anybody there that I would have like to have seen. Tell Augusta to do the same. I guess you may postage on this. So ----------.

/s/ A. P. ADAMSON

Virginia Union Maj. Gen. George Henry Thomas was probably the best Union general in the Federal western armies. A Seminole and Mexican War Veteran and slave-owner who remained loyal to the Union, he won the first important Union victory in the West at Somerset against General Crittenden (this was the battle wherein General Zollicoffer was killed). He fought at Shiloh, Perryville, Murfreesboro, and Chickamauga. He was unflappable, quiet, meticulous, steadfast, courageous, and regarded affectionately by his men. He became known as the "Rock of Chickamauga" for his heroic stand on Snodgrass Hill.

LETTER NUMBER SEVENTY-ONE

Dalton, Georgia
March 5th 1864

Miss Augusta Adamson

Dear Sister,

I embrace the present opportunity of writing you a few lines which I will send by Lieutenant Huie, who will start home tonight on furlough. I have nothing new or interesting to write. We are still here on Provost Guard and may remain some time. Everything is quiet along the front. No present indication, as we hear of, of army movements being made by either army, but this quiet, I fear, will not continue long. In all probability ---------- for a general advance ---------- but has eyes open, and they ---------- with a handsome reception when they do ----------.

211

Our duty here is very heavy but, notwithstanding, I believe the most of our boys are very well satisfied. I suppose we fare as well, if not better, here than in camps. We about enough to eat and have excellent quarters, and I think we ought to be satisfied with this much, although the men are on guard about every alternate day.

An election took place yesterday in Company B for a Lieutenant, which resulted in the election of John N. Wilson. His opponent was -----------.

We have the privilege of going to church every night, when not on duty, at the Methodist Church. I went last night. Several ministers of different denominations -----------. Thirteen joined the church, with certificate to join any church they like.

I would like very much if I could get me ----------- and obtain a furlough for forty days. I have written to -------------- about the matter. If I were at home I think I could get -----------. Tell Pa to try Allen, and if he will come, make arrangement to come back with Lt. Huie who will return about the 19th inst., but he must pass ---------- under eighteen. I would be willing to pay anybody liberally, if I could get them by doing so, and I believe such is becoming very common with soldiers.

I would like the best kind to see all the girls, especially the one you mentioned in your letter the other day. Nothing could give me more pleasure than to see her. I understand our friends, as they are generally called, --------- around like the very mischief here of late. I would like to be at home today and tomorrow to go to church at Tanner 's. I know you have been this very day.

I hear ---------- has made his way home, just as I expected. I guess Miss Susan is very glad of it. But, by the way, how is she getting along with -----------? But enough of that. I received your letter of the 29th inst. after a long time. You must write again soon. This leaves me about as well as I have been since I got back. Nothing more.

Your brother,

/s/ A. P. ADAMSON

212

"Defending the Hearth; Johnston and Sherman - Fortify and Flank."

The Provost Guard were the equivalent of today's Military Police. They policed areas under martial law and the rear lines, exerted crime control measures, prevented desertion behind the battlefield, placed soldiers under arrest when apropos, guarded prisoners, and in general regulated and maintained control in the military area of operation.

John N. Wilson died of smallpox in 1864.

LETTER NUMBER SEVENTY-TWO

Camp, 30th Ga. Regt.
Near Dalton, Ga.
March 20th, 1864

Miss A. A. Adamson

Dear Sister,

 I embrace the present opportunity of writing you a few lines, which leaves me in tolerable health. I have nothing interesting to write at this time. Things at present wear a dull appearance. I received yours of the 15th inst. in due time and was truly glad to hear from you. I intended to have written to you by Mr. Huie, who went back on the 18th, but failed to do so.
 I also wanted to have sent some clothing by him but, owing to the drill on that day, was prevented from doing so. I shall probably send by express on Tuesday morning, if not prevented. I have a shirt, two pairs of drawers, pants, two coats, overcoat, and likely some other little things to send. There will be others who will send with me but the things will be marked so they can be known. I think that we will start it about Tuesday, so Pa may look out.
 There is no indication of any active movements being made by the enemy on our front at the present time. All is quiet, but I fear will not continue so long. We have to drill now nearly every day, division drill at that, which is not an easy job. Old General Stevens is strict but I think is a reasonable old fellow but he will have

discipline. Hendrick is in command of the regiment and has been nearly all the time and I don't care if he continues to command.

The weather at present is rather blustering and cold, which is not very agreeable. We get about enough to eat, such as it is, and I think are doing finely. We have been getting plenty of clothing of late. I have drawn two coats, two pairs drawers, one shirt, and a pair of pants, the most of which I shall send home.

Today is my twentieth birthday. I will celebrate it by going on guard this evening. A poor celebration, I think.

I was pleased with ---------- message, which I think the best I have read yet. I reckon I might as well close. Excuse this hurriedly written letter. I am really ashamed to send it. Write soon.

Your brother,

/s/ A. P. ADAMSON

Brig. Gen. Clement H. Stevens, formerly colonel of the 24th South Carolina Infantry, and wounded at Chickamauga, replaced Brig. Gen. Claudius Wilson as brigade commander when he died of typhoid on 27 November 1863. The promotion had been delayed, so that Col. James C. Nisbet of the 66th Georgia had been interim commander. Stevens had been senior colonel of Walker's Division. He was mortally wounded at the Battle of Peachtree Creek near Atlanta on 20 July 1864. His horse was shot out from under him, and as he stepped off the fallen animal, he received a ball in the head just behind the left ear. He died on 25 July. Command of the brigade devolved temporarily upon Col. George A. Smith of the 1st Georgia Confederate Infantry. Colonel Smith was wounded at the Battle of Atlanta on 22 July (it was also in this battle that divisional commander Gen. William H.T. Walker was killed), and command then passed again to Colonel Nisbet of the 66th Georgia who was promptly captured that same day. Command then passed to Col. William D. Mitchell of the 29th Georgia. In the aftermath, Georgia Brig. Gen. Henry Rootes Jackson was brought from Savannah to head the brigade, now known as Jackson's Brigade until the cessation of hostilities.

Maj. Henry Hendricks had been captain of Co. A until January 1863 when he was promoted to major of the regiment. He was in temporary command at the time of the composition of this letter. He was wounded at the Battle of Jonesboro in August 1864. He was captured at Nashville 16 December 1864, and sent to POW Camp Johnson's Island on Lake Erie until October 1865, long after the War had concluded.

LETTER NUMBER SEVENTY-THREE

Camp, 30th Ga. Reg.
March 29th, 1864
Miss A. A. Adamson

Dear Sister,

I write you a few lines this morning which I will send by Captain Dollar who is expecting to start back this evening. I have nothing to write that is of any importance. Everything seems to wear a dull appearance here at the present time. Nothing transpires which is calculated to arouse the feelings of the army from the dull monotony which seems to control a large portion of it.

We have had some very bad weather for several days. We had another snow last Thursday night and, with the exception of Sunday, we have not had a pretty day in nearly two weeks. Last night we had a very hard rain. I just come off guard last night and missed it.

Our company went out on picket on the river yesterday evening. They will return this evening. Division and brigade drill are becoming very common now, more so than I like. Several of our company have returned this week. Y. M. Barton, J. Dailey, G. B. Stephens, and J. W. Conine have got in in the last two days. ---------- went before the board this morning. I do not know what will be the result.

Captain Dollar's resignation has been accepted. Mann will be our Captain. I cannot say that I will be entirely satisfied with the change, although I will be as much so as any of them.

I would be glad to be at home on Sunday to go to church, but that is impossible. I am not very well now, nor have not been for some time. I will close for I have nothing else to write. Write soon.

Your brother,

/s/ A. P. ADAMSON

P. S. I think that as for the prospect for us to get a good 3rd Lieut., it is very bad.

Pvt. Yancey M. Barton enlisted 1 May 1862, was captured at the Battle of Jonesboro 1 September 1864, exchanged, and survived the War. James W. Conine enlisted 1 August 1862, captured near Nashville on 16 December 1864, sent to POW Camp Chase, Ohio, and died from an abscess there on 22 March 1865. He is interred in grave No. 1733. The other men have been previously commented upon.

LETTER NUMBER SEVENTY-FOUR

Camp, 30th Ga. Regt.
April 17th, 1864
Miss A. A. Adamson

Dear Sister,

I take the present opportunity of writing you a few lines in answer to yours of the 10th inst. You must excuse me for not writing to you sooner but I have not had a suitable opportunity of doing so. I have been very unwell for some time and am so at this time. I had the jaundice last week, which served me rather bad, but I returned to duty on Wednesday feeling tolerably well that day but I again had to try the sick list this morning. I hope I will be alright in a few days.
I do not hear of any movements that indicate hot work in this quarter. We can hear the firing of cannon nearly every day, but I suppose they are only practicing. I would be very glad if our regiment

could be transferred elsewhere. I think it would suit me better. I would try and get a transfer but I fear it would avail nothing. Probably I can make an exchange with someone. Anyhow, I think I shall make such an effort. It is not from dissatisfaction of officers that makes me anxious to get out of the company.

The Rev. Jesse H. Campbell preaches to our brigade today. I would like to hear him but do not feel like going out today. We get a plenty to eat now. We hardly ever see any beef, bacon being issued to the troops at present, but I don't know how long it will continue.

Lieut. Mann has been examined and I suppose will soon be promoted to Captain.

I did not get any April fools. I think I could guess who sent yours. I reckon you guessed right about it. I sent my comfort home by Joe Buchanan. I reckon you got it. I would like very much to be at home a while, at least till I could get alright, but there is no probability of such.

Nothing further remains of this letter.

According to DORLAND'S ILLUSTRATED MEDICAL DICTIONARY, 27th Edition, "Jaundice is a syndrome characterized by hyperbilirubinemia and deposition of bile pigment in the skin, mucous membranes and sclera with resulting yellow appearance of the patient." There are numerous sub-categories and etiological explanations. Without further descriptive detail, we cannot say at this point with which variety A.P. was afflicted.

First Lieutenant John F. Mann was never promoted.

LETTER NUMBER SEVENTY-FIVE

Dalton, Ga.
April 24th, 1864

Miss A. A. Adamson

Dear Sister,

I write you a few lines although I am at a loss to know what to write. I received yours of the 18th inst. and was glad to hear from you. I am getting along very well now compared with how it was one week ago. I would be glad to be at home now. I think it would suit me finely. I want to get where I can get something to eat besides our usual diet. Something in the way of vegetables would take so well with me now.

I want you to write to me where Ben Stevens command is at. I have a motive for wanting to know. If in your power, let me know the easiest opportunity.

I suppose Lieut. Huie will be our Captain, although we don't know yet, but I think that he stands a good chance for it.

I would like to be at Tanner's the first Sunday in next month. I know the pretty girls will be thick there then. You want to know how your sweetheart is getting along, and don't tell me who it is, but I can make a very good guess, believing it is one of the two young men.

I hope we will not have to stay here all through the Summer. I am really tired of upper Georgia and would prefer a great many places to this. Capt. Walthall is now senior Captain of our regiment, as good a one we could get.

I will have to close, having nothing else to write. Write to me soon and let me know where B. H. Stevens' regiment is.

Your brother,

/s/ A. P. ADAMSON

Letters Number 71 and 72 were written on the same piece of paper.

Capt. Felix Leonard Walthall of Co. I served from 1861. He was elected first lieutenant in 1861, and captain in May 1862. He was wounded at Chickamauga and again at Decatur, Georgia. He was commissioned as a major in 1864, and then after the Battle of Franklin promoted to lieutenant colonel.

He was captured at Nashville and sent to POW Camp Johnson's Island from which he was paroled.

A.P.'s first cousin, Benjamin Hardy Stephens, is known to have served in Co. F, 4th Georgia Infantry Battalion in 1863. He may have served in another unit in 1864.

LETTER NUMBER SEVENTY-SIX

Camp, 30th Ga. Regt.
April 24th, 1864

W. F. Adamson

Dear Brother,

I take the present opportunity of writing you a few lines. I have nothing at all important to write at this time. I am getting along tolerably well now, although I am not to say well. Notwithstanding, I am doing duty.
We expect to have to go to Dalton, or near there, today to work on the fortifications. Our regiment went one day. I did not go then. The order was countermanded about going today. We have heard some talk of the Yankees being on the move in front but we don't know the truth of such reports.
I have had some hopes we would be transferred to North Carolina, but I fear we will have to remain here. I think most any other place would agree with me better than this. I intend to try and make an exchange with someone, provided I can hear of anyone willing to make such exchange. Furloughs of all kinds are stopped here now. No chance for a fellow to get off on furlough without he's sick enough to be furloughed by the board.
Our regiment has recruited a great deal of late. It begins to have its old appearance again in point of numbers. We have not drawn any money yet, although we have been expecting to draw some time. I would be very glad if we would draw, for all are out of

219

money here. I would be very glad to get to stay at home a short time. I let you know I am tired of cornbread and bacon and would be glad of something else, but will have to put up with what we get.

It is thought by a great many that there will be hard fighting here soon, but I hope for the better. I will have to close as I am about out, have nothing else to write. Write to me soon.

Your brother,

/s/ A. P. ADAMSON

LETTER NUMBER SEVENTY-SEVEN

Camp, 30th Ga. Regt.
Near Dalton
April 29th, 1864

Miss A. A. Adamson
Dear Sister,

With pleasure I avail myself of the present time of dropping you a few lines, although I have nothing to write that can possibly be interesting to you. And, consequently, you may expect a dull and uninteresting letter.

I received yours of the 24th and 21st inst. yesterday and was exceedingly gratified at receiving it and glad to hear that you was all well, but I cannot say that I am, by any means, in the enjoyment of that inestimable blessing. I am again on the sick list, not feeling able to perform the usual routine of duties which we are subject to.

Our regiment has gone to work in the fortifications today near Dalton. Our regiment goes out of the brigade every day. I myself have been able but once. The regiment has to go every four days. We are also expecting fortifications out some three miles from here on the Spring Face Road on the Conestauga River, if I am not mistaken in the name.

It is probable that a battle will take place here in a short time, judging from the present movement of our army. Hood's Corps, composed of Stevenson's, Hindman's and Stewart's Divisions has already gone to the front, and likely some of Hardee's also. Our division received orders two or three days ago to send off all surplus baggage and be in readiness to go at a moment's notice. There is no telling whether we will have to go or not. I hope they will let the fighting alone.

I hear it reported that one column of the enemy has fallen back from Red Clay to Cleveland. They were reported to be coming forward from three directions, namely, Cleveland, Ringgold, and Lafayette. Nearly all day yesterday heavy artillery firing could be distinctly heard in the direction of Tunnel Hill. It also can be heard this morning. I do not know whether they are shelling each other or whether they are only practicing.

The weather has been good for some time. The roads are getting in good order. Active movements will not be delayed any longer. I do not think General Grant is reported in Chattanooga. It was generally believed he was on the Potomac, and likely is.

I shall not be able to perform any marches if we leave here soon unless I improve very fast. We get plenty of bread rations. Our meat rations are a little short and now consists of beef. We drew bacon until a few days ago. I myself make out with a very little.

Tom Cook left yesterday for Atlanta, having been recommended by the Medical Board for a detail in the Medical Department.

Since the dry weather commenced, the water has dried away a great deal and water will soon be hard to get here unless we dig wells or move.

Company K, which has been at Savannah for a long time, come in yesterday morning.

You are certainly becoming very intimate with Miss Hillard, as you and her are together a great deal.

We have drawn no money yet, nor no probability of getting any soon. I will close. You must excuse the badly written letter. I feel but little like writing and have written in a hurry. If I can get a postage in the whole company, which is doubtful, I will pay postage on this. Write soon.

Your brother,

/s/ A. P. ADAMSON

[P.S.] Orders have come to move at any time. The troops are cooking rations. The Regiment has not yet returned. I have been to the surgeon today. He says he will send me to the rear with the wagon train. I guess the regiment will leave tonight.

Georgia Lt. Gen. William Joseph Hardee served in both the Seminole and Mexican Wars. In 1855, he wrote the standard textbook, RIFLE AND LIGHT INFANTRY TACTICS, which was ultimately used by both Confederate and Union forces. In the War Between the States, he performed reputably at the Battles of Shiloh, Perryville, Murfreesboro, Chickamauga, and Chattanooga, and in Johnston's north Georgia campaign. He did not concur with much of General Bragg's strategy. He obstructed General Sherman's infamous March to the Sea with little success, but this is not to his discredit considering what little he had to work with at this point in the War. He performed well at the Battle of Bentonville (where his 16 year old son was killed) submitting to Union authority with General Johnston in North Carolina on 26 April 1865.

The mention of the artillery firing near Tunnel Hill probably refers to the skirmishing there on the morning of 28 April. Tunnel Hill is a railroad passage south of Ringgold and north of Buzzard's Roost Gap. There was a Federal cavalry probe which was aggressively counterattacked by troopers of Gen. Joseph Wheeler's Confederate cavalry. The Yankees had seized the village of Tunnel Hill. Members of the 10th Ohio Cavalry burned down the few buildings there and killed thirteen Confederate captives. They were driven back by Wheeler's cavalry.

The 50 men of Co. K had been serving on the Savannah River Batteries under Col. Edward C. Anderson, along with two companies of their sister regiment, the 29th Georgia.

LETTER NUMBER SEVENTY-EIGHT

Camp, 30th Ga. Regt.
In the woods near Calhoun Gordon County, Geo.
May 13th, 1864

Mr. N. C. Adamson

Dear Father,

    I write you a few lines this morning, as I will probably have a chance of mailing. I wrote to you yesterday and mailed my letter at Resaca. We left the place we were at, above Resaca, yesterday evening, marched by way of Resaca to this place. We have to march very fast. I could not help and did not come up with the regiment till this morning. I do not feel very well today.

    The wagon train is now moving towards Calhoun. I presume we will also start in that direction even though we may go back towards Resaca. They are now fighting to the left of Resaca. The enemy are trying very hard to flank our army. Heavy firing continued yesterday to the left of Dalton. It has been a continual skirmish, fighting for more than a week. Probably we will have to try them soon. It is their intention to reach the railroad and cut off communication, if possible.

    I hear this morning that Jesse Sanders is dead ----------- as all the company have to hear.

    This company is a great deal better than Whitfield. The ------- is very good. I took supper last night at a house on the road. Paid one dollar. Was very glad I got an old-fashioned meal that cheap. I cannot keep up with the command if we have to march ---------. I will make out. The regiment came about eight or nine miles in three hours.

I have written in a hurry, as I don't know what moment we will leave. I haven't heard from home in about two weeks. I will close.

Your son,

/s/ A. P. ADAMSON

[P.S.] We're now in about a mile of Calhoun.

The Battle of Resaca occurred 14-15 May 1864. Union General Sherman had found General Johnston's Rocky Face Ridge lines near Dalton to be virtually impregnable. His forces totaled about 104,000 men. He decided to send McPherson's Army to the southwest through Snake Creek Gap to outflank Johnston while Generals Thomas and Schofield feigned an attack on Rocky Face Ridge. McPherson's movement caused Johnston to pull back his roughly 66,000 men from Rocky Face Ridge to Resaca. When Sherman's soldiers approached the town of Resaca from the west on 13 May, they found that the Rebels had entrenched themselves in a four-mile position between the Oostanaula River and the Conasauga River. Johnston had precisely surmised Sherman's intent. Walker's Division was just across the Oostanaula River in plain view. Although some of the time his division's rifle pits were under fire, the division did not participate in the battle. The Federals made a frontal assault on 14 May and were slaughtered. General Johnston saw this as an opportunity and counter-attacked with two divisions of Gen. John Bell Hood. The counter-attack was partially successful, but Union reinforcements prevented Hood from accomplishing more. Again, on 15 May, Sherman sent his men into a charnelhouse. However, in a separate action, they managed to make a river crossing below Resaca that threatened the Confederate rear - in the face of Walker's Division. Realizing the threat this posed to his rail communications, Johnston had to abandon Resaca to prevent his being outflanked. On the 16th, when the Unionists prepared for an assault, the Confederate army had vanished from its strong lines. Yankee losses were about 3,500, and Rebel losses about

2,600. The Confederate army would now move further south towards Calhoun, and A.P.'s rendezvous with captivity.

Walker's Division had moved to Lay's Ferry Crossing on the Oostanaula River and fought there on 15 May against Sweeny's Second Division, Dodge's XVI Corps. Elements of Walker's Division had dug rifle pits on the southern side. Under a heavy artillery and small arms covering fire, and using an abandoned flat-boat, Northern forces then drove off the Confederates from their rifle pits and gained a bridgehead. Within an hour an entire Union brigade had been ferried across the river. It was in part this forced bridgehead crossing that had required Johnston to move his army out of its Resaca positions.

The next day, 16 May, the Confederate divisions of Cleburne, Bate, and Walker of Hardee's Corps engaged the Federals at Rome Crossroads in a surprise delaying attack. Hardee's artillery opened up on the wagon trains following Sweeney's Division. His spirited assault kept the Unionists at bay. In this engagement the 30th Georgia participated, at one point forcing back a strong line of the enemy for some distance, but they also sustained a loss in killed and wounded. The regiment was commanded by Maj. Henry Hendricks at this battle. Hardee's divisions held this position until 1:00 a.m. on the 17th so as to allow the Southern trains following Johnston's retreat to pass Calhoun and make clean their escape south to Adairsville. There then followed the retreat of Stevens' Brigade, Walker's Division, Hardee's Corps from the Rome Crossroads and through Calhoun towards Adairsville. It is during this retreat that A.P. was captured.

After the Battle of Rome Crossroads, the 30th Georgia suffered hard fought Georgia battles at Peachtree Creek on 20 July, Atlanta on 22 July, and Jonesboro on 31 August-1 September. Later, after Gen. John Bell Hood had replaced Gen. Joseph Eggleston Johnston, A.P.'s regiment went on to further carnage in Tennessee at the Battles of Franklin on 30 November, and Nashville on 15-16 December 1864. One last battle was to be persevered - Bentonville in North Carolina on 19-21 March 1865. When the regiment submitted at Greensboro on 26 April 1865, there were only about forty men on the roll.

SUGGESTED READING

Bearss, Margie Riddle, SHERMAN'S FORGOTTEN CAMPAIGN: THE MERIDIAN EXPEDITION, Gateway Press, Inc., Baltimore (1987).

Bradley, Mark L., LAST STAND IN THE CAROLINAS: THE BATTLE OF BENTONVILLE, Savas Woodbury Publishers, Campbell, California (1996).

Cannan, John, THE ATLANTA CAMPAIGN MAY-NOVEMBER 1864, Combined Books, Inc., Conshohocken, Pennsylvania (1991).

Castel, Albert, DECISION IN THE WEST: THE ATLANTA CAMPAIGN OF 1864, University Press of Kansas, Lawrence, Kansas (1992).

Davis, Burke, SHERMAN'S MARCH, Vintage Books, New York (1988).

Horn, Stanley F., THE DECISIVE BATTLE OF NASHVILLE, Louisiana State University Press, Baton Rouge (1991).

Hughes, Nathaniel Cheairs, Jr., GENERAL WILLIAM J. HARDEE, OLD RELIABLE, Louisiana State University Press, Baton Rouge (1965).

Kennett, Lee, MARCHING THROUGH GEORGIA, Harper Collins, New York (1995).

McDonugh, James Lee and Thomas L. Connelly, FIVE TRAGIC HOURS: THE BATTLE OF FRANKLIN, The University of Tennessee Press, Knoxville (1983).

Scaife, William R., THE CAMPAIGN FOR ATLANTA, William R. Scaife, Atlanta (1993).

Sword, Wiley, THE CONFEDERACY'S LAST HURRAH: SPRING HILL, FRANKLIN, & NASHVILLE, University Press of Kansas/Harper Row, New York (1992).

PART III

LETTERS AND DIARY

"Captivity."

Raven Days, dark Raven Days of sorrow.

Sidney Lanier.

Sojourns of a Patriot

"Captivity."

The reader must realize that A.P. would have been most aware of the probability that his correspondence would be censored by prison authorities, and that if he were to write anything offensive about them or prison conditions, that this could jeopardize both his sending and receipt of highly valued mail.

LETTER NUMBER SEVENTY-NINE

Rock Island Barracks
Rock Island, Illinois
May 31st, 1864

Mr. N. P. Adamson

Dear Father,

I this evening take the opportunity of writing you a few lines in order that you may know where I am and how I am getting along, as you have, no doubt, heard ere this that I was missing.

I was captured on the 17th of this month five miles below Calhoun, Geo. Was very unwell at that time. I was brought here a Prisoner of War. Arrived here on the 27th inst. and am getting along finely. Get good treatment and plenty to eat and am in better health, by a great deal, than I was in when I was captured. You and Ma need give yourselves no uneasiness on my account.

W. P. Conine and Matthew H. Huie of Company E are with me and are getting along finely. We are on Rock Island, Illinois, on the Mississippi River, and near the Iowa line.

Captain Huie will, I suppose, settle with you as regard my wages. I am owing J.E. Lites and T.G.L. Cook. If you see them personally, settle with them. Also, let Captain Huie -------- Isaac -------- -- Co. G. Robinson, A. Minor Co. G, J. P. Hall of Co. C. --------- too there. I hope the war will soon be over and that I can see you all again. In the meantime, rest easy on my account, for I will do the best I can.

You can write to me. Direct your letter to A. P. Adamson, Rock Island Barracks No. 79, Rock Island Illinois. Write to me as soon as possible. Nothing more.

Your son,

/s/ A. P. ADAMSON

To N. C. Adamson, Jonesborough, Clayton County, Geo.

LETTER NUMBER EIGHTY

Rock Island, Illinois
June 25th, 1864

Miss A. Adamson

Dear Sister,

 With pleasure I again take the opportunity of writing you a few lines. I wrote to Pa once since I have been a prisoner, the 31st inst. I am getting along very well, with the exception of a severe cold. We are very comfortably situated and do as well as could be expected. I was captured the 17th of May and have been here since the 27th. W. P. Conine is with me and is well. Also, Mr. Huie.
 I want you to write to me as often as you can. You have a good opportunity of writing. You can use those postage stamps I left at home. You will also have to put a CS stamp on. I would be glad if you would send me two or three confederate stamps. I have but one more.
 I enjoy myself here much better than I first expected. We have meeting here every night. Mr. Roan of our regiment is here and preaches occasionally. But, oh, how I would like to go to church at old Tanner's again and hear Mr. Tribble preach once more. Nothing would please me more. I pass off the time here very well reading the Testament and Yellow Back Novels, which is all I have to read.

"Captivity."

I find here several Coates and one man by the name of Adamson, who is from Texas, but his grandfather is from North Carolina. I also have heard of several others. I also find men here from Anderson District, South Carolina. One of Banister Bray's sons is here with me. John Smith of Clayton County is also here.

We are on the Mississippi River, just opposite Davenport, Iowa. I send you a list of the counties which we passed so you can see the route we came after leaving Georgia. I would write more if I could, but when I see you I will tell you all. God grant that this may be soon.

I will close. Write to me soon. Direct your letters to Rock Island Barracks No. 25, care Provost Marshall. Our barracks have been changed from 79 to 25 since I wrote to Pa.

Farewell. If we never meet again on earth, let us try to meet in Heaven.

Your brother,

/s/ A. P. ADAMSON

It is to be noted that A.P. is clearly ascertaining his family tree with those ɔrisoners of familar surnames to his own family. As the reader is aware, his ;rand-mother was a Coates.

THE WAR BETWEEN THE STATES DIARY

OF

A. P. ADAMSON

PRISONER OF WAR

ROCK ISLAND, ILLINOIS 1864-1865

DESCRIPTION OF THE DIARY

The cover of the diary which A. P. Adamson kept while he was a Prisoner of War at Rock Island, Illinois, in 1864-1865 is light brown leather and has lined pages. The diary measures three and one-half inches by five and three-quarters inches and contains forty lined pages. The writing was done by pencil.

Written on the inside of the diary is: Augustus P. Adamson, Company E, 30th Geo. Regiment. The words were written very closely together and there were no paragraphs as such. In copying the diary, paragraphs have been made for easier reading. The first few pages of the diary begin with: Details and incidents connected with my capture and imprisonment. After that, the first entry is 9 June 1864, ending with the day he arrived home to Clayton County, Georgia, on 17 March 1865.

TRANSCRIPTION OF THE DIARY

Details and incidents connected with my capture and imprisonment.

I was captured in the rear of General Johnston's Army early in the morning of the 17th of May 1864, together with two of my comrades, William P. Conine and Matthew H. Huie.

For several days previous to that time I had been very unwell and unable to keep up with the command while marching. The surgeon in charge of the group, like a great many others of his rank, not seeming to care what became of the sick, neglected to make any arrangements to prevent their being captured while the army was retreating, which arrangements he could easily have made, as ample time was given him to do so. But it was neglected and this and like neglect upon the part of medical officers resulted in the capture of a great many of General Johnston's Army.

We were captured several miles below Calhoun, Geo., by the 5th Kentucky Cavalry and taken by them to Major General John A. Logan of Illinois, who placed us in charge of a guard from the 111th Illinois Regiment, which regiment we remained with during the day, marching immediately in their rear.

On the 18th we were taken with their army to Adairsville, and on the 19th to a point near Kingston. On this day we were placed under a different guard, who were from a Missouri brigade and from whom we received the best of treatment we could expect, but no better than our previous treatment by the Illinois guard.

On the evening of the 20th our crowd, which by this time numbered about fifty men from various commands, was taken to Kingston and put upon the cars and sent to Resaca, where we stayed until the next day when we again took the cars for Chattanooga and bid farewell to Georgia.

All along the route from Resaca to Chattanooga the ravages and destruction of property, which always follow the presence of a large army, are plainly visible. But this only reminded me of the prediction which I made, and heard others make several months ago, that the people of Georgia would soon feel the effects of the war in a manner which many of them little expected.

It is useless for me to attempt to portray my feelings and the many thoughts which crowded my mind upon leaving my native state, especially at such a crisis as this, believing as I did that the two armies would soon reach and devastate my own section of the country.

I was about leaving my native state on my journey to a strange and distant land; was about being separated, perhaps forever, from father, mother, brothers, sisters and friends; the land I have so often *trod with delight, indulging in many reflections of the dear and cherished memories of the past and fondly anticipated hopes of the future.*

I was about leaving what was dearer than all besides the soil beneath which reposes the last remains of an infant brother and a dearly beloved sister. Ah, well do I remember the last visit I paid to their graves. Yes, it's only a few short months ago since last I stood beside my sister's grave and there indulged in the fervent hope that I might, in a coming day, be buried beside her. God grant that it may yet be so.

But the past is only the past, the Eternal Past, and brings to memory the joys of days departed, never to return; of buried hopes beneath the power of earthly resurrection; of objects dearer than life itself; of love with its purity, its transports and its graces; of hate with its withering rays of madness and despair; and of affections hallowed by the tender smiles of Heaven. But now! Alas, many of the joys and anticipated hopes of the future are destined to be blighted forever.

We arrived at Chattanooga on the night of the 21st and remained till the evening of the 22nd, when we took the cars for Nashville, which place we reached the evening of the 23rd. We were placed in the enclosure around the State Penitentiary and remained till the morning of the 24th, when we started for Louisville, Kentucky, where we arrived late that evening, passing through the most beautiful section of the country I ever beheld.

At Louisville we stayed one night and the next morning crossed the Ohio out of Dixie into Indiana at Jeffersonville, which place we did not leave until late in the evening of the 25th, and arrived at Indianapolis the next morning, where we remained nearly all day. We reached Michigan City - which place is situated on Lake Michigan - early the next morning. Here we were not detained but a short time but proceeded on our way to Rock Island, where we arrived on the evening of the 27th and were confined in the prison barracks situated on the Mississippi River just opposite Davenport, Iowa.

The prisoners now numbered about three hundred and were divided into companies consisting of one hundred men each and assigned to quarters, each company occupying a house about one hundred and twenty feet long by twenty-five wide, containing three rows of bunks in each side and a room at one end for cooking.

The houses were all surrounded by a high plank enclosure and a strong guard placed around it. Our quarters were much more comfortable than I had expected and our rations amounted to nearly as much as we obtained in the Southern Army, but the narrow space and the strict orders to which we were confined made me fully realize the nature of a prison life.

For the first few days the time seemed to pass off very slowly. The hours seemed like days and I, of course, was very despondent and low-spirited and did not think I could long endure such confinement but am now becoming somewhat habituated to it; but, oh, how I will know to appreciate liberty if I ever again obtain it.

JUNE 9th, 1864

It is now the ninth day of June. We have been here nearly two weeks and I am becoming more accustomed to my prison life. When I first came here I was very unwell and continued so for several days but am now, by the blessing of God, about to regain my former state of health.

The time seems to pass off much more agreeable but I cannot enjoy these bright and merry days of June in the way I did twelve months ago when I was at home, surrounded with everything I desired. And I need not here be told that the atmosphere around me is soft, that the clime is pleasant, that the gales are filled with balm, and that the flowers are springing from the green earth; for I know that the softest air to my heart is the air which hangs over my native land. It would be more grateful than all the gentle gales, it would breathe the low whispers of anxious affections, and would be far more pleasant to my eyes than the bloom and verdure which only more forcibly remind me how far I am from that one spot which is dearer to me than the world besides.

JUNE 27th, 1864

It is very cold and cloudy today, almost like Winter. Well do I remember this day twelve months ago as being the day I left home and started to Mississippi. But, oh, how different it was with me then.

Prison life is very unpleasant to me. Were it not for my Testament and other books that I get to read, I don't know how I could stand it. Oh, how it makes me long for liberty to think of the past and anticipate the future. When I gaze upon the beautiful green shores of Iowa just across the river it only increases that anxiety and reminds me of my own dear cherished land.

God grant that I may soon tread that cherished soil again and be united to those who occupy my thoughts the greater part of the time.

JULY 3rd, 1864

This is the Sabbath Day and I am convinced it is better observed by the prisoners here than by the Army of the Confederate States. Oh, how I long to be at home today and have the pleasure of once more going to church in my own neighborhood. Yes, it would indeed be a pleasure to me to hear my favorite minister preach once more. But, how long? Oh, how long will it be ere I have that blessed privilege? Perhaps never.

But I will not despair of all hope of again being restored to home and friends and to the enjoyments of former days, but will commit myself to the guardian care of the Great Ruler of the Universe, believing that in the end all things will work out for the best.

JULY 9th, 1864

The following letter was written to A.P. during his imprisonment from Robert Lloyd Adamson. This Adamson was a second cousin descended from the brother of Greenberry Adamson, John, through his son John Lloyd Adamson, to his son, the correspondent Robert Lloyd Adamson. Obviously

A.P. had researched his genealogy in order to localize this Northern cousin. The eldest daughter of John Adamson married William Prather. They had two sons, one of whom was the Henry Prather of Decatur, Illinois, who corresponds at least twice with A.P. It is perhaps somewhat ironic that Henry Prather was, through his wife, the brother-in-law of the radical Republican Governor Richard Oglesby. Politics aside, Brig. Gen. Richard Oglesby is an intriguing character. He was born in Kentucky, orphaned, and became a lawyer by profession. He was a Mexican War veteran, and a personal friend of Abraham Lincoln. He was grievously wounded at the Battle of Corinth in October 1862, and was expected to die. He did not. He went on to serve two terms as governor of Illinois, and then was sent to the U.S. Senate.

Mr. A.P. Adamson

Dear Sir:

> *I am a nephew of John Adamson. He is dead. He de'cd [died] in Arkansas six or seven years ago. I have sent your letter to Henry Prather who lives in Decatur, Illinois. He likewise is nephew of John Adamson and is able to help you. You had better write to him. If you ever get out of prison write again.*

Yours,

Robert Lloyd Adamson

JULY 13th, 1864

> *Nothing worthy of note hardly ever transpires. A great many rumors are afloat in regard to the present state of affairs; but none on which we can rely. Time passes swiftly along, notwithstanding my present confinement and all the suspense and anxiety I have to endure. I can while away the hours in a much more agreeable mood than I first expected.*
> *My thoughts are often returned to the past, to the bright scenes of younger and happier days when all seemed to be a continual ray of*

sunshine and of pleasure. The remembrance of these days will last as long as life itself. No time, no change can obscure the vivid images of our young days or efface the deep impressions of primeval joys. But more anon.

SUNDAY, JULY 31st, 1864

The past few days have been extremely warm. Today there has been a slight fall of rain, which seems to revive everything. Until today there has been no rain here for some time, and very little today.

During the past week a great many rumors have been afloat among the prisoners, many of which no doubt originated in the prison and contain no veracity.

All here seem to be anxious to be at liberty and again return to their native South. No one who has not experienced it knows anything of life in prison. Although, if treated well and surrounded with a great many things which are deficient in most prisons, there are other things which deeply concern them. They are separated from their homes and their fiends and seldom get any inclination of them, which causes a great deal of anxiety and suspense. But it will not do to give away to such things, but hope for a better and happier time.

AUGUST 4th, 1864

This has been a very disagreeable day. It has been raining all day and the clouds are dark and lowering and portend more rain.

Time is speeding swiftly by. The days pass off much more agreeable than could be expected. Some while away the hours all through the day with different kinds of games to amuse themselves; some are engaged at work of some kind, while others occupy the most of their time reading and refreshing their minds with useful knowledge.

Our rations at this time consist of the usual quantity of loaf bread, pickled and fresh beef, and a small quantity of rice. Previous to this we had either hominy or beans, and, at first, Irish potatoes instead of rice. We occasionally get some bacon and salt pork, which

238

is much relished by all. Vegetables cannot be had, only by those who are fortunate enough to have the Yankee greenback.

SUNDAY EVENING, AUGUST 14th, 1864

I have just returned from preaching, where we heard an excellent sermon. Rev. Mr. Roane from Henry County, Georgia, preached. His text was the 21st verse, 18th Chapter of First Kings. There is preaching here once or twice every day, so everyone has ample opportunities of hearing the Gospel preached.

The Biblical text that was the subject of this sermon reads as follows: "And Elijah came unto all the people, and said, 'How long halt ye between two opinions? If the Lord be God, follow Him; but if Baal, then follow him.' And the people answered him not a word." I Kings 18:21 (King James Version.)

AUGUST 22, 1864

The following letter was written to A.P. during his imprisonment from Henry Prather of Decatur, Illinois. Prather and his relationship to A.P. is mentioned in the commentary for 9 July.

Mr. A.P. Adamson

Sir:

It has been entirely out of my power to give earlier attention to your letter of the 16th inst. being from home most of the time since. I now enclose you care of Provost Marshall twenty dollars hoping it will relieve your present necessities. I will try to fix you up a box of nic-nacs as soon as I can find time but my business at present calls me from home most of the time.

Would it not be better for you to take the oath and quit this terrible war? Should you do so call this way and see me.

Respt yours,

H. Prather

*[P.S.] Should you still remain a prisoner let me hear from you again.
Also acknowledge the rect [receipt] of this.*

SEPTEMBER 7th, 1864

*The weather now is very disagreeable, being cool and rainy.
I do not expect to see many more pretty days here this year, for
Winter will soon set in and then we may expect a terrible time.*

*My health has been bad for the past three weeks. I have suffered
considerable in consequence of it, but, by the kindness of Providence,
I am once more on the mend.*

*A great many here are anxious to be exchanged, and entertain
strong hopes that some measures will be effected whereby a general
exchange will take place.*

*It would, indeed, be a great pleasure to be permitted to return
to our native South and again meet with old comrades. But, in all
probability, many would return only in time to encounter new
sorrows. To such it would be but little pleasure.*

SEPTEMBER 19th, 1864

*The past two days have been very cold, almost like Winter days
at the South.*

*There has been considerable excitement among the prisoners
here during the past week on account of the proposition of the
commander of the post proposing to receive them in the military
service of the United States, to serve against the Indians on the
western frontiers of the United States. A great many have agreed to
enlist but no disposition has as yet been made of them.*

*Although the hardship of the prisoners will doubtless be severe
during the coming Winter, I cannot enlist in the service of a
government which my state has renounced all allegiance to in order*

240

that I might thereby avoid the suffering which is inevitable, nor do I believe I would better my condition by so doing.

I shall endeavor, by the help of Providence, to endure all hardships and remain true to my native South until the termination of my imprisonment.

It seems that the usages of Christian warfare are entirely laid aside by the Northern Government, who positively refuse to exchange prisoners unless the Confederate Government agrees to exchange their own slaves (who have been incited to take up arms against their lawful owners) as Prisoners of War. This would be one step further than the Confederate authorities ought to take and it is to be hoped that they will not, by any means, agree to do so and thus relinquish the right to their own property for which so many lives have been sacrificed since the commencement of the present war.

SEPTEMBER 20th, 1864

Today I received two letters from home, which were welcome visitors indeed, being the first I had received since I have been here.

I hope the time is not far distant when I will again be permitted to return home and enjoy the society of loved ones there. But, alas, the beautiful green fields of my native state are now being laid waste by two powerful armies.

Already, great battles have been fought on ground which I have trod time and again. From the accounts which we receive, I infer that the Southern Army is now on the defensive in Clayton County, Georgia, and that my immediate vicinity has been marked with scenes of bloodshed, havoc and desolation.

The above reference is no doubt to the Battle of Jonesboro, fought 31 August to 1 September 1864 between Confederate Gen. John Bell Hood and Union Gen. William Tecumseh Sherman. The tactical commanders *in situ* were Confederate Generals Patrick Cleburne (Hardee's Corps) and Stephen Dill Lee (Lee's Corps), and Union Generals John A. Logan (XV Corps), Jefferson C. Davis (XIV Corps), David Stanley (IV Corps), and Francis P. Blair (XVII

Corps). Hood had erroneously believed that he faced one Yankee corps, not the four corps of O.O. Howard's entire Army of the Tennessee.

Jonesboro was the county seat for Clayton County and an important rail center to Atlanta. At this time it controlled the only remaining rail entry into that city for the introduction of military supplies and food items. If Jonesboro were to be cut off from Atlanta, then Atlanta would become militarily untenable and would fall. This is precisely what happened. The boys of the 30th Georgia, having been largely recruited in Clayton County, were literally fighting on their doorsteps. Their homes were being destroyed, their livestock killed, their families and friends threatened, and their cause diminished. They, like A.P., were to return to the apocalyptic devastation of all that they cherished. The two day sanguinary battle was the conclusion to Sherman's campaign to take Atlanta. The city was abandoned by Hood on 2 September.

Atlanta's stubborn defense had frustrated Sherman, so he clandestinely removed six corps, about 60,000 men, from the trenches around Atlanta and flanked the city to the west to seize and control the Macon & Western Railroad, Atlanta's last lifeline. Hood understood what was happening too late and sent two corps, about 24,000 men, on an all-night march to confront them. He then attacked the Yankees in their newly constructed breastworks bristling with artillery. His attacks were disjointed and un-coordinated. On the first day of fighting the Army of Tennessee lost 1,725 men; the Union forces only 170.

Although the Rebel forces held Sherman's army at bay during the second day, when Sherman counter-attacked, they could not prevent the inevitable with such a disparity of forces. Their defeat was a foregone conclusion. The historical novel, THE FAR SIDE OF HOME, relates to the Battle of Jonesboro.

It was at this point in time, and with regretful clairvoyance, that the famed South Carolina diarist Mary Boykin Chesnut wrote, "Since Atlanta I have felt as if all were dead within me, forever....We are going to be wiped off the earth."

OCTOBER 13th, 1864

The weather for the past week has been very beautiful. Although the nights are rather cool, the days are very pleasant.
Those who enlisted in the frontier service of the United States have been taken out. Upwards of fifteen hundred enlisted.

242

There is now strong hope entertained by the prisoners here that they will shortly be exchanged, and reports are current that an exchange has been effected after so long a time, and I trust such are not without foundation. But, in the meanwhile, I will try and be contented, hoping that by the help of Providence, all things will terminate for the best.

NOVEMBER 12th, 1864

Cold weather is now fairly began. The Ground is covered with snow. Everything wears a full and cheerless appearance. The hills on the Iowa shore, which I so admired last Summer, seem to have lost all their beauty. They now look white and naked, so unlike the green and blooming appearance they were last Summer. It really seems that everything now tends to depress one's spirits.

There seems to be no prospect of an exchange of prisoners, which was so anxiously looked for some time ago. The Presidential election, which took place a few days ago, has not yet been heard from. If the final result elects McClelland, we have some bright hopes ahead, but if Lincoln is re-elected, there is nothing but a dark and gloomy future before us.

Union Democrat Gen. George Brinton McClellan ran against incumbent Republican Pres. Abraham Lincoln in the 1864 presidential election. McClellan essentially ran on a peace platform. It was the contemporaneous prevalent belief that if he had been elected there would have been an armistice declared between the two warring nations. But the fall of Atlanta, Sherman's march to the sea, and the Federal victories at Third Winchester and Cedar Creek re-invigorated the faltering Northern civilian morale giving new impetus to the Republican war faction. Lincoln received 212 electoral votes to McClellan's 21. The popular vote was closer, giving McClellan 45% of the total.

DECEMBER 13th, 1864

The past week has been cold and stormy weather. The ground is all the time covered with snow. The Winter bids fair to be a hard one and it is likely that we will have to spend it here in prison.

DECEMBER 25th, 1864

By the goodness of God I have been spared to see another Christmas - which reminds me forcibly of the rapid flight of time. It seems but a short time since last Christmas, although the greater part of that time has been spent in trouble and wretchedness.

The return of this day recalls to my mind many vivid recollections of the past and of the manner in which I spent the time one year ago at home with my parents, brothers and sisters, from whom I am now far away from, separated perhaps forever. But I trust that I may be preserved to meet those dear ones again. But if the Almighty wills to the contrary, I hope to meet them in a better world where there will be no more wars, no separations, no imprisonment, but where eternal happiness reigns, the wicked cease to trouble, and the weary are at rest.

JANUARY 1st, 1865

The old year has gone and the new begins, with no cheering prospect before us. But I trust that ere long we shall see better times, and before many months of the year pass I hope again to tread the soil of my native land.

JANUARY 23, 1865

Following is the second letter received by A.P. during his imprisonment from Henry Prather of Decatur, Illinois. Of note, the correspondence between A.P. and his cousin, Henry Prather, continued after the War until Prather's death.

"Captivity."

Mr. A.P. Adamson

Sir:

> *I wrote about two weeks ago in reply to a letter of yours which I learned you had not got the articles of clothing I sent you by express from this place on 12th Decr.*
>
> *I then applied to the express office who said they would look them up but I am informed by the agent he has not yet heard of them. Please let me hear from you at once so that I can proceed against the express company if the articles are lost.*
>
> *I stated in my letter that I could find no way of obtaining your release on your taking the oath -- nor have I yet found any way and suppose you will have to weather it out.*

Respt Yours,

H. Prather

[P.S.] Are any geting released on taking the oath from your prison?

Ruefully, we never know what became of the package. It was not uncommon for the prisoners to never receive them. And, as we know, A.P., as a manifestation of true grit and moral courage, would never furnish the pressured Oath of Allegiance. His principles were otherwise.

FEBRUARY 3rd, 1865

> *Twelve months have now elapsed since I left home. The time has seemed long, although the return of this day reminds me most forcibly of the rapidity of time.*
>
> *On the 1st inst. I received another letter from home, which gave me a great deal of satisfaction, it being the first time I had heard from there since the departure of the armies from that section. I anxiously look forward to an exchange of prisoners and to the time when I can again return home to those loved ones who I know have*

245

experienced many of the hardships which invariably result from the presence of armies wherever they go.

FEBRUARY 14th, 1865

We are still in prison but the prospect is good for an exchange. We learn a general exchange has been adopted after so much discussion upon the subject. I now look forward to a speedy termination and to reunion of friends and relatives, and I know nothing would be more congenial with my wishes.

FEBRUARY 15th, 1865

A detachment of five hundred left today on exchange. The probability is that I will leave in a few days. I have already signed the rolls and will go with the next squad.

FEBRUARY 28th, 1865

ALTOONA, BLAIR COUNTY, PENNSYLVANIA

We are now on our way to be exchanged. We left Rock Island on the 25th inst. We go via of Harrisburg to Baltimore or Philadelphia, the former place most likely.

We are getting along finely and in a few days will reach Dixie. God speed that happy day.

MARCH 6th, 1865

RICHMOND, VIRGINIA

We have at last reached this place. We arrived here last night and are now at Camp Winder. There is a strong probability of receiving furloughs in a short time.

MARCH 17th, 1865

ARRIVED AT HOME TODAY.

Rock Island POW Camp was located on a swampy island in the Mississippi River between Rock Island, Illinois, and Davenport, Iowa. According to the builder, the prison consisted of 84 barracks more analogous to shanties than properly constructed buildings. Each barracks was 100 feet long, 22 feet wide, and 12 feet high. They all faced east. Also, each had twelve windows, two doors, and two roof ventilators, four feet long and two feet wide. Each housed about 120 inmates. The men slept in bunkbeds. There were six rows with fourteen barracks in each row. The buildings were thirty feet apart and all but one faced onto streets 100 feet wide. These barracks were enclosed by a stockade fence 1,300 feet long, 900 feet wide, and 12 feet high with a board-walk constructed on the outside of the fence four feet from the top for the ever observant guards. Every 100 feet there was a sentry box.

In December 1863 when the temperature read -32° Fahrenheit, and before the prison was completed, over 5,593 captured Confederate soldiers arrived. Within the first three months, thousands sickened and over 600 men expired due to smallpox. At this time there were no hospital wards or adequate medicines. At one point the War Department, after having the conditions explained, had to order the Commissary General of Prisoners, Col. William Hoffman, to complete the construction of a hospital that he had suspended from construction. Eventually six pest houses (contagious disease units) were also constructed. These horrid conditions received considerable negative publicity in the press causing some degree of alleviation of the worst excesses of mal-attendant care. Nevertheless, the Northern press was categorizing Rock Island in late 1864 as another Andersonville!

Commissary General Hoffman was considered an able administrator and prison chief throughout the War. But it has been suggested that his orders killed more Confederate soldiers behind the lines than the orders of most Union generals engaged in legitimate warfare. His frugality was so misprioritized that its very insensitivity caused starvation, pestilence, and death ·by freezing. He rationalized his parsimoniousness as "retaliation for innumerable outrages which have been committed on our people." But the Confederate government lacked the provisions to provide to its Union prisoners whereas Colonel Hoffman had resources readily available. Union prisoners in Confederate POW camps were subject to the same shortages of rations, matériel and care as suffered by the Confederate army; Confederate prisoners in Union POW camps were intentionally provided inadequate rations, matériel, and care, dissimilar from that of the soldiers of the Union army. It was purposeful maltreatment. This is a woeful and telling indictment of the Union government.

Pursuant to directions from President Lincoln's Secretary of War Edwin M. Stanton, Union Quartermaster General Montgomery Meigs intoned that POW Camps "should be put up in the roughest and cheapest manner, mere shanties, with no fine work about them." Resultantly, Commissary General Hoffman then directed that "so long as a prisoner has clothing upon him, however much torn, you must issue nothing to him."

Hoffman refused to utilize available funds to purchase fresh vegetables that would have cured many stricken Southern prisoners at other camps. At the conclusion of the War, he actually returned to the Federal treasury almost two million dollars from his accounts - monies that had been accumulated by the non-expenditure of funds to relieve the inhuman conditions at his prisons. Hoffman was rewarded for his stewardship of the prison fisc at the end of the War with a promotion to a brevet major generalship.

During Rock Island's 19 month operating existence there were some 12,409 men incarcerated therein with some 1,960 inmates dying from disease. Epidemics were a continual problem. This reflects a mortality rate of about 16%. There were drainage and potable water supply problems. An open sewer ran down the center of the main avenue. Prisoners were used as laborers with pay of five to ten cents per day which allowed them to purchase some food. Packages from home were permitted which supplemented their clothing allotment.

Rock Island Camp Commandant Col. Adolphus J. Johnson was considered by many of those incarcerated as "inhuman a brute as ever disgraced the uniform of any country." In 1864, while A.P. was there, Colonel Johnson reduced the already niggardly rations in order to save money for a "prisoners' fund" to be used for other matters. This caused an inflationary spiral in the value of rat meat. There is one anecdotal tale of the mal-nourished Rebels consuming a sutler's pet dog which had followed his master's wagon into the prison grounds to sell goods to the famished men; the dog's hide was found nailed to a tree the next day with a note attached "Send in another dog." Hunger precipitated feuds, bad tempers, and quarrels amongst the prisoners.

During that summer of 1864, a portion of the prison was set aside and the inmates were informed that any man who would take the oath and be recruited into the Yankee forces would be moved into this area and given "good clothing, bountiful rations, paid one hundred dollars bounty," and sent away to fight on the frontier. Confederates in many Northern POW Camps could escape the harsh barbarous conditions by taking the loyalty oath to the Yankee government. A.P. obviously forswore such behavior as perfidious. Those with more fealty to the South called such oath-swearing "swallowing the yellow dog," and disdained those who took the oath.

Federal authorities devised a plan to recruit Rebel prisoners to serve in the Union Army in exchange for leaving the conditions in the camp. However, they were not required to fight against their family, kith and kin - they would be utilized on the Western frontier fighting Indians. Perhaps 4,000 prisoners took advantage of Lincoln's oath and amnesty plan to swear allegiance and assume Federal military service. Patriotic Southern inmates were so concerned with this untoward pressure on the Southern prisoners that they initiated a Rebel re-enlistment drive within the prison! Over 1,300 men apparently indicated their willingness to re-enlist for Confederate service in a letter that was written to President Davis. An article in the New York *Daily News* for 3 January 1865 revealed that some 5,000 of the confined prisoners had resolved to die rather than submit to Federal recruitment. The article stated in conclusion, "Although they are wrong, is there not a sublime heroism in the adherence of these men, amid such trials, to a cause which they believe to be right."

For those caught in "rebellious ways," various punishments were devised such as "riding the rail," "hanging by the thumbs," and "wearing a ball and chain."

There is still great controversy regarding the mortality figures, actual numbers of those incarcerated, and prisoner statistics in general for both warring nations. The sequelae of the War have not abated. What is certain is that over 50,000 Americans from both sides died in inhuman and unnecessary conditions. There was ample inhumanity manifested by all those in authority both Union and Confederate.

Rock Island POW Camp has an associated cemetery presently located 1,000 yards southeast of what had been the stockade. The stockade and prison barracks area is now part of the Rock Island Arsenal Golf Course and officer's quarters.

The first government-sanctioned prisoner exchanges occurred in February 1862. Nonetheless, it was not until July that the formal Dix-Hill Cartel for the exchange of war prisoners was agreed upon by both governments. This system was fragile and quickly became bureaucratized. It also frequently broke down for political reasons. It broke down in May 1863 over the issue of Union utilization of former Southern bondsmen as troops and how they should be categorized when captured by Southern forces. The Cartel was not re-activated until January 1865. Of interest, prisoners were exchanged on the basis of: 1 general = 46 privates, 1 major general = 40 privates, 1 brigadier general = 20 privates, 1 colonel = 15 privates, 1 lieutenant colonel = 10 privates, 1 major = 8 privates, 1 captain = 6 privates, 1 lieutenant = 4 privates, 1 non-commissioned officer (sergeant) = 2 privates.

A.P. leaves us no written record of the actual exchange or his brief incarceration at Point Lookout POW Camp. Nonetheless the existent microfilm records at the National Archives list him as being at Point Lookout, albeit briefly.

Point Lookout was established in August of 1863 on a barren peninsula at the confluence of the Potomac River and the Chesapeake Bay in Maryland. It was the largest of the Northern POW camps. Originally designed for 10,000 men, at times it easily exceeded twice that number. It was made up of two enclosures of flat sand devoid of any trees or shrubs, one covering about thirty acres and the other some ten acres. Each enclosure was surrounded by a fifteen foot high fence. It was established as an enlisted man's prison where virtually all the inmates were living in over-crowded tents; there were no barracks to protect them from the heat and coastal storms. The camp was only a few inches above high-tide. Many deaths were attributed to the dampness and winter weather. Potable water was scarce.

There was never enough food or firewood. In fact, many Confederate internees supplemented their meager diet with the protein source of rat meat. Chasing and catching the rats became a favorite sport. Extant anecdotal literature indicates that there was considerable animosity between those incarcerated and their guards, many of whom were accused of abuse at best, murder at worst. It was easy to die at Point Lookout as some 4,000 men did.

"Captivity."

They died from disease, starvation, inadequate clothes and shelter, and the uncontrolled violent behavior of their guards.

REFERENCE READING

Beitzell, Edwin W., POINT LOOKOUT PRISON CAMP FOR CONFEDERATES, St. Mary's County Historical Society, Leonardtown, Maryland (1972).

Brown, Dee, GALVANIZED YANKEES, University of Nebraska Press, Lincoln, Nebraska (1986).

England, Otis Bryan, A SHORT HISTORY OF THE ROCK ISLAND PRISON BARRACKS, *Revised Edition*, Historical Office, US Army Armament, Munitions, and Chemical Command, Rock Island, Illinois (1985).

Hesseltine, William B., CIVIL WAR PRISONS, Kent State University Press, Kent, Ohio (1972).

Segars, J.H., ANDERSONVILLE: THE SOUTHERN PERSPECTIVE, Southern Heritage Press, Atlanta (1995).

POSTSCRIPT

Paradoxically, out of this phantasmagoria of war and devastation arose the regeneration and rejuvenation of the human spirit. The lesson learned, our indomitable Southern mettle, grounded in Christian faith, can never be extinguished by mere fallen man. Northern occupation imposed obdurate post-bellum circumstances on the South. This required the South to draw upon the patience of Job, the steadfast faith of Daniel, and the innate humility of John the Baptist. In his own fashion, A.P. Adamson symbolizes these immutable virtues. He gave his all as a patriotic young man for a nation that lost its struggle for independence. No doubt his participation in this war was the defining experience of his life. He saw all that he cherished despoiled. As Esau embraced Jacob in forgiveness for having stolen his birthright, A.P. accepted the new America. He learned by his harrowing experiences, accomodated to the new circumstances without loss of principle, and optimistically fashioned a new life and future. Like his beloved Southland, he arose as a Phoenix from the ashes.

When the cause was lost, what cause was it? Not that of the South only, but the cause of constitutional government, of the supremecy of law, of the natural rights of man.

Jefferson Finis Davis
President

The Letters of Augustus Pitt Adamson

BIOGRAPHIES OF THE AUTHORS

RICHARD BENDER ABELL

Born in Philadelphia, Pennsylvania, in 1943, Richard was reared in Chester County, Pennsylvania. He received both his undergraduate and law degrees at The George Washington University in Washington, D.C. In 1967 he volunteered for the Peace Corps serving in Colombia, South America, where he met his wife Lucía. Subsequently he volunteered for the military, serving with the 7th Cavalry of the 1st Air Cavalry Division. He is a decorated Viet-Nam veteran retired for wounds received in action. He has taught law, served as both a deputy sheriff and as an assistant district attorney, and served on the U.S. Senate staff. Richard was appointed by President Ronald Reagan to four governmental positions, ultimately appointed by the President and approved by Senate confirmation as an Assistant Attorney General of the United States. Currently he is a member of the federal judiciary. He is listed in WHO'S WHO IN AMERICA and in WHO'S WHO IN AMERICAN LAW. For the past seventeen years Richard has lived in Fairfax County, Virginia, from whence came many of his progenitors, with his wife, children, and four felines. He is also a member of the Society of the Cincinnati and the Sons of Confederate Veterans.

MARY FAY ADAMSON GECIK

Born in Ellenwood, Georgia in 1923, Fay was reared in the Clayton County, Georgia environs. She graduated from the Middle Georgia College in Cochran, Georgia, and the Draughan School of Commerce in Atlanta, Georgia. For many years she served as a legal secretary. However, her life has centered most on her retirement interests as a family historian and genealogist. She was married to Lt. Col. Michael George Gecik of Wilkes-Barre, Pennsylvania, in 1951 in a military wedding. They had duty posts in Maryland, Illinois, Alabama, Georgia, Japan, and Taipei, Taiwan. Her husband is interred in the Adamson Cemetery in Jonesboro, Georgia.